Drowning by Numbers

by
Adam Dickson

Castra publishing

Drowning by Numbers
Copyright ©2014 Adam Dickson

ISBN 978-0-9934776-4-5

A special thanks to the following:

Christine Poundford from Hobsons International, Rita Campbell, Dave Ball & Andy Baker for their valuable insight into the music business. Paul & Garry Pollak from Firebird Records, Portobello Market for additional music information.

Annabel Sampson for editing & proofreading, and for ongoing support and encouragement.

My colleagues at Wessex Writers for their critical appraisal, and Dunford Writers for continuing support and great barbecues.

Alex Dickson for the superb cover design and illustration and insisting I'm wrong when I know I'm right!

Liz Gordon from Brilliant Fish PR & Marketing for editing, proofreading and tireless promotion.

www.adamdickson.co.uk

1

I come to in a strange room. Things drift into focus. The crumpled duvet I'm under. The pale green shirt hanging over the back of a chair. I try to sit up and instantly feel nauseous. Cutlery crashes downstairs. The sound of a radio. I lay back down again, cocooned from the outside world, the legions of hell pounding in my head.

The pair of black leather boots under the window look ominous, the tips honed and pointed – right at me. The longer I stare at them, the worse it gets. Confusion. Fear. The beginnings of a nightmare that won't go away.

A woman walks in. She has a narrow, pitted face and no make-up. Her eyes gleam with a malicious kind of humour she doesn't try to hide. In a sudden move, she strides across the bare boards and yanks open the curtains. Bright sunlight spills over the duvet and hurts my eyes. For the moment I'm safe, wrapped in the pastel shades and varnished wood of the room, a child emerging from sickness.

She stands by the bed, arms folded, looking down at me.

'Good morning, Joe.'

'Where am I?'

'You don't remember?'

'No.'

'You're in Islington, sweetheart.'

'Islington?'

She laughs scornfully. 'Where did you think you were – Bel Air?'

I lie there in shock. Missed appointments loom. Images of

Jake, standing outside the school gates, waiting for his dad.

'What day is it?'

'Saturday.'

'You're joking!'

I push back the covers and sit up, hiding my nakedness with a corner of the duvet. Beads of sweat break out on my forehead, the onset of a plague for which there is only one known cure. Searching my memory, I find only fragments, the odd glimmer. Obscure, dreamlike images fade in and out. Walking along a promenade in the early hours of the morning. Travelling in a car with strange people.

Islington!

This coarse-looking woman in front of me doesn't fit the picture. She shouldn't be here. I shouldn't be here. The whole thing's a terrible mistake, brought on by too much drinking and the little white pill someone gave me in the Portobello Gold.

But that was Thursday.

I throw back the duvet and put my feet on the bare boards. The view from the window offers no fresh clues. Rain-washed slate roofs and crumbling chimneys. A green tarpaulin flapping in someone's back garden. Bone-aching dizziness comes over me. If I can make it to the bathroom I might be alright. Splash cold water on my face and kick start my senses back to reality.

With a seductive roll of her hips, the woman moves to the door. I'm aware of great danger. Whoever she is, she's been sent to destroy me. Some grasping, middle-aged widow taking advantage of an innocent younger man. She's ravaged my bones in the night and my mind has blanked out the details.

Aware of her watching me, I make a move for my jeans and underwear strewn over the floor. Implications begin to dawn. Pockets of memory that open up through the dull ache in my head.

Brian Moorcroft, waiting in the Park Hotel with notebook and pen.

An invitation to work with Scott Levine.

The flight to New York that left on Friday.

'Fuck!'

'What's the matter?' she says coarsely.

'I've gotta go.'

What a way to blow what's left of your career. Missing the first date of the tour because you were stranded in Islington with some woman you've never met before. Moorcroft will write me up as a scumbag and slander my name in print. I'll end up playing weddings and bar mitzvahs for the rest of my life, banished from the inner circle.

'So. Where do you have to be that's so important?'

'Hammersmith,' I lie, without even thinking.

'Do you want to call anyone? … Your *wife* maybe?'

I look up, one foot caught in my jeans. She bares the same uneven teeth in the parody of a smile.

'You told me all about her last night. Remember? How she threw all your records out the bedroom window. Changed the lock on the front door.'

Ignoring her, I pull on my jeans and look around for my shoes. Her perfume fills the room. Toxic. Enough to make me want to gag. My mouth tastes like iron filings, brackish like the swamp I've crawled out from. The distillery. The one drink too many that sounded like a good idea at the time.

Her bathroom reminds me of home, a window ledge crammed with beauty products and exotic shampoos. Signs of tender femininity to tap into my burgeoning sense of guilt.

I study my face in the mirror. Glazed and bloodshot eyes. Hair a tangled mess. The bohemian look I've worked so hard to perfect that just isn't happening. Nothing's happening except the chaos that's attached to every single thing I do.

'I'm going,' I call from the stairs.

'Goodbye, Joe!' she calls back with cheery fatalism. 'Have a nice life, won't you!'

I leave quickly, a thief of the worse kind, full of remorse and getting sicker by the minute.

2

Bathed in a chemical sweat, and with a growing unease, I exit
the steps and pause beneath the Westway. An old Rastafarian
with long dreads and a greying beard shuffles by. His striped
jumper has a frayed hole in the side like a gunshot entry wound.
He gives me *the look*, part mistrust, part empathy, from his side
of the cultural divide. The video shop window reveals a glimpse
of my present state. The undernourished rock star fleeing the
scene of his latest misdemeanour. Funny how appearances can
mean so much, even at a time like this. The perverse need to
look cool, even when your insides are churning and your head's
been mashed, you're facing retribution on a biblical scale.

The perennially cheerful Don Warr waves to me from the
other side, on his way to open up the record store on Portobello
Road. 'How ya doing, Joe?' he shouts, with typical glee. I manage
a strangled response, full of bravado, and keep on walking.

Princess Diana gazes soulfully down at me from a poster in a
shop window. Perhaps she remembers me from the fundraising
gig we played in front of her and Prince Charles.We even share
the same birthday, but here the similarities end.She probably
remembers what she did yesterday – and the day before that.
She has commitments, responsibilities, the hopes and dreams of
an entire nation resting on her shoulders. I've got a new album
and a sixteen-date tour of the States resting on mine. If I don't
make the next flight out there somehow, my whole career could
be over.

Climbing the hill towards Holland Park, I'm hit with the
bleakness of the landscape. When the mind is consumed with

dread, even inanimate objects have the power to oppress. My thoughts and perceptions separate me from everything around me, but at the same time we're inextricably linked. This monstrous existence, ceaseless and inescapable. These awful things I've done, crowding in on my consciousness to remind me.

Home is a place I long to be, but I'm afraid of what I'll find when I get there. Justine, waiting with an injunction, a look of disgust on her face. Jake and Sadie lurking in the background, ashamed and despondent. And me, the instigator in the whole sordid drama, in no condition to fend off the accusations, the weeping and the wailing that's sure to greet me the minute I walk in the door.

How did my life come to this? Every day, the game getting harder to play. Struck down with amnesia, when I should be in New York. Whole chunks of time lost, as if it didn't exist. How do you reconcile yourself to that? And the moral dilemma. Waking up in someone else's bed and not having the decency to remember their name.

The truth is, I could use a drink. One small bottle of lager and ten milligrams of diazepam to level out the edges. But it's Saturday morning. I've been gone over forty-eight hours. I need to get back and find out what happened.

3

I creep in the back door like a ghost. Justine walks in from the hall and stops. She stares at me, open-mouthed. Now the backlash will start for real. The screaming and the shouting. Her voice like a lancet, driving me from the room. Instead, she slumps at the table, drained, and puts her head in her hands. No tears. No recriminations. Only these sharp, angry sighs from deep within.

I mumble a stricken apology. She looks up, icily calm.

'Get out of my sight.'

'Justine, I can – '

'I'm not interested. Just go.'

Sheepishly, I head upstairs out of the way.

The view from the bed isn't much better. Like being seasick on dry land, with everything spinning. And below me, Justine, her silence more ominous than any outburst would have been. No slamming cupboard doors and throwing crockery about. No stomping around in a show of aggression. But the accusation is there all the same. Consequences. Reminders. All the terrible things I've done that can never be forgiven.

Footsteps advance up the stairs.

She stands in the doorway, watching me.

'How long are you going to lay there like that?'

'I'm ill.'

'You want sympathy?'

My strangled plea makes no difference. She stiffens visibly, viewing me with distaste. 'I'm going to pick Jake up from Alice's. Don't be lying around the house like that when we get back.'

I look on, helplessly. With her hair up and fastened with a slide, she looks different – alluring and reserved in a poised, businesslike way. I feel like the smallest speck of dirt in her presence.

She turns to go and stops.

'Have you any idea how many people you've let down because of this?'

'I'll make a few phone calls later.'

'Oh, and that'll make it alright, will it? You breeze in after three days and expect everything to carry on as normal.'

'Justine – '

'I don't want to hear it. Clean yourself up. Have a bath or something. You look terrible.'

The front door snaps shut.

I'm alone.

The horror movie starts up in my head, the inevitable result of comedown. A freeze-frame of all the awful things there are in this world. Nicaraguan death squads. Terrorist attacks. The hellish jaws of a Great White. Intercut with these images, the trouble I've caused at home. Missing the flight to New York. Letting the band down. Everything falling apart spectacularly after that.

But there are other factors here. I didn't wake up in Islington by choice. I was kidnapped. Held to ransom by the dealers. The faceless, back-street chemists who put these mind bending concoctions together. Justine thinks I'm a liability – understandably so, in the light of my actions – but is it my fault completely? Even the experts haven't been able to find out what's wrong with me over the years. All the doctors, psychologists and counsellors who've analysed my warped psyche. Not one of them able to reach any satisfactory conclusions.

I need a little sympathy. A chink of sunlight on the dark horizon before I crack-up completely. The resurrection of my ailing career to remind everyone I'm still out there. Joe E Byron – Indie Guitarist of the Year, two years running. Self-styled fashion guru and cultural pioneer. Big in Japan, but forgotten in the home country.

I can't go under.

I'm immortal for Christ's sake.

*

The plague worsens. A search of all my favourite hiding places reveals nothing. No pills, no booze. Not even a stray paracetamol to take the edge off things. Water has to suffice.Flush out all the toxins and start the healing process all over again.

I sit in the music room and suffer quietly. My guitars hang around the walls like works of art, each with its own special place in my memory. The Gibson SG Classic, with me through the first tour of the States in '86. The Fender Blacktop I used in the studio on the second album. Seeing them hanging there collecting dust fills me with sadness. Bitterness, too. Sold out by the new management, an archaic record deal like a chain around my neck. Swallowed up by the machine, the big, fat corporate monolith that deals in bullshit and dollar bills. Sooner or later you start to feel the disillusion, the weight of your own compromise dragging you down. Is this really it? The sum total of my career? Delayed flights and vacant airport lounges. Hours and hours of waiting around with nothing to do. The face of some model I fucked in Budapest, staring back at me with bored indifference.

A list of priorities forms in my head.

Call Goldstein's London office and find out what's happening.

Start packing for the rest of the tour.

Get hold of Carla and score some pills for the flight over.

Maybe it's the touring that's getting me down. The only job I've ever had that meant anything. The only reason I bother to get out of bed in the afternoon. I've tried other things. Acting. Modelling. A brief stint in a takeaway when I was sixteen. Being in a band was supposed to be the dream job, the perfect occupation for those of us who've never grown up. But there is a downside. Sitting around waiting for phone calls. Forced into having a schedule, an itinerary. Every aspect of your life

9

controlled and implemented by other people.

The front door flies opens.

Jake's footsteps explode along the hall in a sudden dash for the biscuit tin. I'm filled with a new terror. Having to explain to a four-year old kid how his daddy ended up an MIA. I'm sinking, further and further down, lost to the horror movie playing in my head.

*

We watch *Space Jam* with the volume up. The invalid and the wilful child, one needing medical attention, the other entertainment at all times. Lying still in the foetal position, my head on a cushion, I can just about keep the devils at bay, but the sickness grows in me unabated. Jake lies sprawled on the floor, gazing up at the onscreen monsters, filling the room with unbearable noises.

'Have you missed me, Jake?'

'Uh?'

'I said have you ...'

Jake's not listening, spellbound by his favourite movie. The sense of separation hits me. The impact of where I've been and what I've done. What's the point in trying to reach out to him? I've been gone three days and he's not even aware of it. Even the cartoon villains are more important in the scheme of things.

Justine hands me a letter.

'This came yesterday. Read it.'

The single sheet has the bank's iconic logo in the top right hand corner. I read it with one eye clamped shut, an intolerable pain in my head.

'Dear Mr and Mrs Byron, our records show that the agreed period of your overdraft has now expired. We note that no attempt has been made to reduce this sum and therefore have no option but to ask for full and complete repayment of ...'

My eyes begin to blur. The pounding in my head gets worse.

Justine hovers over me waiting.

'Well?'

'It's just a letter.'

'Read it again. It's a final demand for the overdraft *you* took out months ago.'

She sighs deeply, shaking her head.

'I had to ask mum for the money to pay for Sadie's dance lessons, while you were out squandering everything. How do you think that makes me feel?'

'Sorry.'

'No you're not. If you were you'd do something about it. We wouldn't have to go through this charade every time.'

Jake edges towards me on his hands and knees, pushing a shiny yellow car. *'Brmm! Brmm!'* Up the arm of the sofa and along the cushion, inches from my stricken face. For a moment my sins are forgotten. We share this unique father and son moment that doesn't need words. I'm comforted by his closeness, his fine blonde locks, the freshly laundered smell that emanates from his clothing.

'Brian Moorcroft phoned,' Justine says resentfully. I picture Moorcroft's bearded, wind-reddened face and a strange fear sets in.

'When?'

'Yesterday.'

'What did he want?'

'He was phoning to cancel his meeting with you. Quite convenient, under the circumstances, don't you think?'

Relief washes over me, the thought that my tarnished reputation might still be salvageable.

Jake parks the car on top of my head and stares at me candidly.

'Where do dinosaurs live?'

'Not now, Jake.'

'Do they eat people?'

'Probably.'

'Can we find one?'

'Jake. I'm really not up for dinosaurs at the moment, mate. Daddy just needs to lie here quietly and get plenty of rest.'

Jake doesn't understand hangovers. Hopefully he never will. He'll grow up to be a scientist or an explorer, too busy with research to bother with the dark underbelly I trawl through regularly. Ladbroke Grove's version of Dorian Gray, reeking of gin mills and unspeakable excess. My abominable portrait locked away in the attic so no one can see it.

Justine lingers in the doorway.

'Oh – in case you're wondering, I've contacted Hugh Hanley.'

'What did he say?'

'He thinks you need professional help.'

She turns to go.

'Justine!'

'What?'

Don't leave me like this. What about the tour?'

She pauses, making me wait.

'He's going to reschedule a flight so you can pick it up in Philadelphia.'

Now and then I get a glimpse of the woman she could have been, had she chosen to pursue her legal career instead of sticking around to look after me. The keen, analytical mind intent on justice, and recouping outstanding royalties from recalcitrant record companies. She used to like me. She used to laugh at my jokes. Now she's become the jailor, watching out for the next time I try to escape.

Baywatch starts. Pamela Anderson, running along a deserted beach in a lycra swimsuit. Shamefully, I'm too sick to respond. The Moorcroft incident still bothers me. Music journalists are all the same. Gourmet diners, picking apart the chef's special to find something they can moan about in print.Moorcroft's cynicism is almost as legendary as his beer-intake, but he does have influence.

Bodmin wanders in and jumps up onto the window sill. The charcoal-grey fur-ball with electric-blue eyes. My suffering eludes him. He'd climb over my corpse to get at the Whiskas.Bob Dylan said a man's a success if he gets up in the morning, goes to bed at night and in-between does whatever he wants. That must make cats the ultimate winners, living rent free and never paying taxes, refusing to do anything that would compromise their feline integrity.

Light footsteps tramp the staircase. Boards creak in the back bedroom, the heavy thud of a bag dumped on the floor. The footsteps return, minutes later, lighter and deliberate. I sense a presence in the doorway, eyes boring into my back.

'Sadie?'

Instinctively, I retreat further beneath my blanket, overcome by a strange and insidious fear. How can you be afraid of your own children? The concept doesn't make any sense. I'm the one who put a roof over their heads and paid for their school uniforms. They should be beholden to me.

'You *can* come in, Sadie.'

Silence.

'Sadie, I said you can – '

'Where have you been?'

The sharp, adult monotone might have been funny if I hadn't felt so ill.

'I stayed with friends for a few days, OK?'

Silence.

'Sadie, come over here where I can see you.'

'I don't want to.'

'Why not?'

'Because I don't.'

How am I going to survive the next few days, among these strange, alien creatures who can't stand the sight of me? Sadie, the eight-year old child prodigy, who regularly beats me at chess – whose maths teacher says she has the calculation and memorisation skills of a twelve-year old. Where does she get the moral superiority? The adult disapproval? You'd think she was the parent and I was the child. It's humiliating.

*

Justine comes to find me later when the kids are in bed. I'm lying, pale and sickly, in the glow of the TV.

She sits in the armchair, facing me, worryingly calm and

serene.

'I've cleared out all the drink in the house.'

'What?'

'I don't want you bringing it in anymore. And I don't want to find it hidden under the sink or in the wardrobe. OK?'

Silence.

'And another thing. You're going to the doctor, first thing Monday morning.'

'What for?'

'You're going and that's it.'

She watches me coldly.

'If you ever do this to me again. Leave me with two small children in the house and the phone ringing all day, while you're off running round God knows where. I swear, that's it between us.'

She gets up slowly.

'Think about it.'

I do think about it.

One more layer to add to the burden. The price you pay for being strung out on the frontline while everyone else is at home eating pizza.

4

I ring the bell. Nothing stirs inside. I keep ringing, looking up at the drab net curtains on the first floor. Carla says the place is under surveillance from the Drugs Squad, but that could be her paranoia. I feel sorry for her, stuck inside all day like a recluse. She should get out more, widen her social contacts like I do.

The window opens and a pale, spectral face peers down.

'Fuck do you want?'

'Come on, Carla, don't be like that. I've been stood out here for ten minutes!'

'What time is it?'

'Time you were up.'

She rubs the sleep from her eyes and scans the road, left and right.

'I'll open the door. Don't make a noise coming in.'

The front garden's a mess. A rusty old oven against the wall that's been there for months. Engine parts visible through the long grass, the remains of a motorbike left by a previous tenant. The one time elegance of the Victorian block has long since fallen into disrepair, turning out bedsits for junkies and the long term unemployed. The kind of place that attract rats, and not just the ones that go rooting through the garbage either.

Carla lets me in, snapping the lock down and sliding back the double bolt out of habit. Visitors have to be vetted, and even then you'd better have a good reason for turning up unannounced. She's like a vampire. Daylight hours are too much for her to bear. She prefers the darkness, when all the lost souls come crawling out of the woodwork desperate for something to happen.

She fills the kettle, nimble in her bare feet. Her long, silk dressing gown makes an odd contrast with the drabness of the kitchen, the sense of chaos that permeates the place.

'Seen Danny lately?' I say conversationally.

'Last I heard, he was moving his mum. Why?'

I laugh unintentionally, the image amusing me. The man who keeps a baseball bat under the bed for intruders has a soft spot for his dear old mum.

She stares at me quizzically, hand on hip.

'What's so funny?'

'Nothing.'

'Why does everyone associate me with Danny?'

'Er – because he's round here all the time?'

She shakes her head dismissively. 'He's like a leech. Just turns up whenever he wants and you can't get rid of him.'

The front room overlooks the terrace, an extended view of Ladbroke Grove from a pauper's armpit. I clear a pile of magazines from a chair and sit at the table. The room is small, claustrophobic, the nicotine veil palpable. Carla curls herself on the sofa and draws up her knees. Her silky gown parts to reveal pale ankles and the calloused soles of her bare feet. She looks good. The model bone structure and tall, willowy frame of a film star. Yet to all intents she's a prisoner. Stuck in this place with her roll-up cigarettes and daytime TV.

She lights-up and exhales gently with eyes closed. The smoke hangs around with the dust particles, the big old house like a tomb, a throwback to the Rachman era, full of stiff-backed chairs and heavy, dated furniture. She's always threatening to leave, always talking about moving on, but she never does. This summer she'll have been here two years and the landlord still hasn't fixed the heating.

I sip coffee from a cracked mug and think about my lost weekend. Three days technically absent from the planet.

'Ever woken up in someone else's bed without a clue how you got there?'

'Several times, why?'

The details come back to me in fragments. The strange

room. The woman striding in and throwing open the curtains. The realisation of where I was and where I should have been. Carla listens to the details blank-faced. The conundrum of being me. The nightmare of being stranded in Islington with a couple of quid in your pocket, when you should be in Manhattan, warming up for the opening gig at the Bottom Line.

'What did Justine say?'

'She went ballistic. She's been making phone calls, trying to reschedule the flight. In the meantime, I'm grounded. I had to sign an affidavit just to get out the house for a couple of hours.'

Implications. The mystery of my disappearance that started with one drink in the Portobello Gold. Fragments, is all I can recall. Being with Danny on the Green. Drinking sambuca with Kamikaze Bob in Finch's. The rest is blank, a cinema screen after the credits have rolled.

The blackouts bother me more than I care to admit. Losing chunks of time when you're pissed is an occupational hazard for a seasoned boozer like me. But waking up in a strange bed, the previous forty-eight hours erased from your mind is a different proposition altogether.

'Was I with you at any time?'

'You don't remember?'

'Well, it's hazy to say the least.'

'You came back with Danny, Thursday night. The pair of you were irritating the shit out of me, shooting cars with an air rifle through the window.'

'Doing what!'

'Danny said he bought it from some bloke in the Warwick. You were both so out of it I told you to piss off back there before you got us all arrested.'

She uncoils her legs and stretches. Her dressing gown parts and reveals a glimpse of bare thigh she hastily covers up again.

Her scornful gaze comes back to me.

'So, what are you gonna do?'

'Start packing, I suppose. Justine spoke to Hugh Hanley yesterday. He's rescheduled the flight so I can pick up the tour in Philadelphia.'

'And what did that paragon of virtue have to say about it all?'

'He made some sarky comment about me needing professional help. Pretty much what you'd expect coming from him.'

She inspects her outstretched feet. Magenta nail varnish chipped and worn. A silver toe-ring glinting in the light. She probably detests Hugh Hanley more than I do after the way he treated her. Spreading rumours about her heroin addiction. Freezing her contract with Goldstein so she couldn't get work with anyone else. One of the best backing singers in the business consigned to the ranks of the unemployed. You can understand her bitterness at the way things have turned out. That whole period surrounding her downfall. The drugs. The eventual loss of her career. All that lurid speculation in the tabloids. But that's what happens when you lose control. Especially under the bright lights in front of thousands of people.

Carla's experience highlights my current situation. I can't help sinking further into despondency.

'I know what it is,' I say morosely. 'I've been working too hard lately. I need a break from it all.'

'Oh, you poor boy.'

'Seriously. People hassling me all the time. It gets on my tits. Why can't they all leave me alone?'

'Then what would you do?'

'Work on my own stuff. Move into production.'

'What – and live without James T? The greatest songwriting partnership since Lennon and McCartney?'

I'm loathe to even talk about James T. We argued about style and musical direction almost constantly. He saw us a cross between Bauhaus and The Velvet Underground – with a touch of brash commercialism thrown in. I leaned towards a more progressive, west coast sound, in the tradition of early Santana and Steely Dan. Somehow our differing tastes seemed to gel when put together. Out of these awkward, sometimes turbulent sessions came what was to be known as our trademark sound.

She stubs out her cigarette and stands, the hem of her gown falling softly at her ankles.

'I'll get dressed. Make another coffee if you like.'

'Got anything stronger?'

'What like – filter?'

She wanders off, smirking, her model derriere encased in silk.

I mooch around in the kitchen. The washing up water has a film of scum over the surface, the thought of physical contact making me gag. I dip my fingers in gingerly and fish out a teaspoon. In the bedroom across the hall, I hear Carla moving around, and imagine her disrobed, standing naked in front of the mirror. Vague, lustful thoughts assail me. The fact that we've never exchanged more than a platonic kiss in over ten years makes any sudden liaison unlikely to happen. We're like siblings. We bicker and argue constantly, and yet we connect on a level I've yet to understand.

'There's no milk!'

'Use powdered!'

The cupboards are bare. One tin of baked beans, a tin of peas and a packet of tomato soup. The tin of Marvel sits at the back, a scant measure of powder at the bottom. The sparseness of the small kitchen reflects my inner state, the feeling of emptiness gnawing away inside. Somewhere, deep in the recesses of my mind, is the notion that I'm out of control, unhinged even. Shooting cars with an air-rifle isn't the worse crime on record, but it does have a juvenile lunacy. The kind of thing you might do when you're still at school. And, hanging round with Danny! What was I thinking?

*

Carla needs a lift. Now I'm a taxi service to take her from A to B. She mentions the name of someone I know vaguely, as an incentive, but it fails to move me. We have a small dispute in her front room, like a couple arguing over the weekly shopping. I'm under house arrest, I remind her. My marriage is about to be kicked into touch. But she's not interested. The only thing that matters to Carla is getting her own way. She has that singleness of purpose common to all selfish people.

'I can't hang around long,' I say bluntly.

She gets her coat.

No thanks. Nothing.

Sickness dogs me on the drive over. Carla's oblivious, smoking a cigarette, elbow on the window, gazing out at the street life with clear disdain. Danny reckons she's agoraphobic. She rarely leaves the house in the daytime, unless it's an emergency. Today must be one of those occasions, forcing her out to get whatever she needs to pacify the cruel world.

'So where am I taking you?'

'Edgware Road.'

'Can you be more specific, the meter's running?'

'Keep driving. I'll tell you when we get there.'

She flicks her cigarette stub at a shop front in a show of contempt, her taciturn silence somehow binding us together. It feels good to be with her, in spite of her demands and my ongoing sickness. Like riding with an empress, the queen of some strange underclass on the fringes of society.

'You scoring weed?' I say.

'No, solid.'

'Can you get me some pills?'

'What kind?'

'Diazepam. Codeine. Anything.'

'You feel that bad?'

'I've felt better.'

Her fur-trimmed coat lies open at the waist. White tee-shirt and denim skirt, trainers scuffed and dirty. She's relaxed, self-absorbed. No sudden urge for conversation. But she knows what it's like to take a dive. Touring the festival circuit with big name acts – to this. Virtual recluse, living in squats with steel bars on the door. She should, at least, feel some kind of empathy.

'Five minutes,' she says. 'Can you wait?'

'Sure. Bring me back a goody-bag.'

I park opposite a bakery and turn off the ignition. My stomach churns at the thought of food, only a bag of crisps and a Mars Bar since yesterday. Nothing unusual given the hammering my body's taken in the last forty-eight hours.

A crisp bag loiters in the wind. Church bells peel in a far-off place. The man standing at the cashpoint could be a decoy for the Drug Squad. He looks innocent enough, but you never can tell. Maybe it's the greasy hair and the worn leather jacket, the furtive glance as he takes his money and strolls hurriedly away. A fat teenage girl in khaki trousers takes his place and jabs at the panel with stubby fingers. She looks hostile, belligerent, staking her claim like everyone else.

Sweat spots break out on my forehead. My aversion extends to everyone. The dog-walkers and the pedestrians, the unemployed. Mixed with this is a degree of envy. What it must be to be normal. To get up in the morning and go to work in a job that demands nothing more of you than the hours you're required to fill in. To have your family waiting around the dinner table when you get home at night, ready to share the stresses of your busy day. There must be something to it. There really must. But I can't, for the life of me, think what it is.

Carla appears, ambling along with her head held high. The glamour queen from Neasden, fur-trimmed coat and scuffed trainers a fashion statement in reverse.

'Sorry I took so long,' she says. 'I got held up talking.'

I start the engine. She gives me an awkward glance.

'I would have invited you in, but they're paranoid about everyone at the moment. You know how it is.'

'Did you get any pills?'

'There's nothing about at the moment. Sorry.'

We settle in for the return journey. She tells me about the exotic plant life growing in someone's attic, careful not to reveal the occupant by name. Outside the circle of paying customers, the dealers like to keep their identities unknown.Inevitably word gets round and everyone finds out, but that doesn't stop them from trying.

'You should see the stuff he's got growing in there,' she says admiringly. 'It's Incredible. One joint and you can't get out the chair.'

I focus on the road ahead, feeling like death. What I'm going through is nothing, a self-induced drop in the ocean, compared to the suffering that's already out there. How do cancer patients get by when the morphine stops working? How does anyone cope with terminal disease, the ageing process? Hangovers are grim reminders. Postcards from a place you've been before but never want to visit again.

I slip in the tape Cribbs gave me. Music has the ability to heal – maybe not with the same potency as 10 milligrams of Valium but it comes a close second.

'Listen to this.'

'Who is it?'

'Just listen. She's gonna be massive.'

A haunting female vocal fills the space, the minor chords of an acoustic guitar. In spite of my sickness, I feel a tingling excitement. We're on the verge of discovery, hearing something of commercial and artistic appeal that might one day be heard by millions.

'What do you think?'

Carla shrugs vaguely. 'Sounds alright.'

'And?'

She stares ahead, expressionless.

'Come on, Carla! Just tell me what you think. Do you like it or not?'

She pops a strip of gum in her mouth and chews vigorously.

'Who is she?'

'Naomi Seaton-Smith.'

'That's her real name?'

'Forget the name. Listen to the voice. She's got class. She's going places.'

'So what's your angle?'

'I'm going to produce her first album.'

'*You're* going to produce it?'

'Sure. What's wrong with that?'

I hear the cogs of doubt and cynicism grinding away.My enthusiasm begins to wane. Naomi's good, but she's just another side project, waiting to slip from my grasp.The business is filled with stories of takeover bids, future stars snapped up by wealthy producers because the guy who discovered them originally didn't have the clout to make it happen. I need to contact Cribbs and arrange a meeting. Get Naomi in the studio before some millionaire svengali comes along and she's wrenched from my grasp forever.

We pull up outside Carla's. She pauses, one hand on the door, and gives me a curious frown. 'You really don't look too good, you know.'

'Thanks.'

'Go home and go to bed.'

'Have you met my family?'

She smiles in a parody of sympathy and gets out.

'Wait here, I'll see what I can find for you.'

She climbs the steps and pauses, searching her bag for the key. A furtive glance at the neighbourhood reveals nothing. No obvious signs of surveillance. No suspicious-looking vehicles parked at the kerb.

Minutes later, she's back, striding down the path, glancing left and right. Leaning on the window, she palms me a small plastic medicine bottle.

'All I could find. Don't say I don't give you anything.'

I stare at the bottle transfixed.

'Thanks, Carla. I owe you one.'

'You don't owe me anything. Just don't tell Danny. I don't want him round here accusing me of giving all his merchandise away.'

I slip the bottle into my jacket pocket. Already the world looks a better place.

'So what's the game plan?' she says.

I pat the tablets deviously. 'Drop a couple of these little babies and chill out, I suppose. Try and get my head round Philadelphia.'

She claps the roof of the car and stands back with a smirk. 'Good luck with that! Let me know if you need any help with Naomi.'

She climbs the steps, rifling her bag for the key. You have to feel for her, living in that lonely flat on her own. Junkies on the top floor hassling her for money and cigarettes when she's only been clean herself less than twelve months. At least she only smokes a bit of hash now and then. It's a start.

I head home.

First stop is a newsagent. I buy a bottle of water and sit in the car, staring at the little white pills in the plastic container.Eight in all. I cup two in the palm of my hand and wash them down with a slug of water. In ten minutes I should feel better – a wave of chemically induced bliss to take the edge off my sickness.

Priorities.

I need to go home and play the game, make up for my previous misdemeanours. Like leading a double life, where you're constantly changing course to divert the hassle you're getting from everyone else. The family man, trying to find time for the kids and the missus. Then my other persona. The restless spirit, chasing dreams down a one-way street. Never in one place long enough to put down roots.

5

Bodmin's caught a rat. Its obscene brown body hangs from his jaws like a corpse from a gallows. We stand by the backdoor and watch the spectacle, Jake peering cautiously out from behind my legs. My sense of revulsion is overcome by a profound admiration. Bodmin – the natural-born killer, justifiably proud of his expertise.

'Is it dead?' Jake says nervously.

'I hope so.'

'Is Bodmin going to eat it?'

'No.' I look at his anxious, upturned face. 'but we can chop it up and put it in the stew, later. What d'you reckon?'

Bodmin does one more lap of honour and drops the body on the concrete in front of us. Even in death, the rat has a sinister power. Thousands more out there, lurking in sewers and disused buildings. An army of vermin, waiting for a nuclear holocaust to wipe out the human race so they can take over the planet.

Justine joins us and freezes, staring at the spectacle transfixed.

'Please! Get rid of it!'

'Me? What am I supposed to do with it?'

'Bury it! Throw it in the bin! Just get rid of it!'

Bodmin slinks away to watch from a distance. We're left with the crime scene, the murder victim laid out on the slab, staring out from its sightless black eye.

The burial ceremony begins. A few minutes exertion with a spade and we have a decent sized hole. In goes the rat, ready for interment in his plastic body bag.

'What now?' Jake says.

'We say a few words to honour the dead. Here lies Rattus Norvegicus, brought down at the height of his career by Bodmin the Cat.'

After the finishing touches, compacting the dirt with the flat of the spade, we stand back and observe the rat's final resting place. Jake looks up at me quizzically, his low boredom threshold ever present.

'Can you take me to the park?'

'Not now, Jake.'

'Why not?'

'I'm waiting for an important phone call.'

'When then?'

'Later, OK?'

He wanders off dejectedly, his solemn little face reflecting his disappointment. I'm left behind, with the green rubber gloves and misplaced sense of duty, the insidious guilt trip that kicks in whenever he's around.

Justine starts as soon as I walk in the door.

'Did you get rid of that, *thing*?'

'We buried it down the garden with full military honours.'

'Don't joke about it. It's disgusting. I want that back door shut at all times from now on.'

Searching the fridge for orange juice, I'm acutely aware of palpitations in my heart, the strain on my internal organs brought on by all that digging. But there are other, more serious things to worry about.

'Has he called yet?' I say.

'Who?'

'Hugh Hanley.'

'No, he hasn't.'

'This is ridiculous. I've been sat around twiddling my thumbs for two days. Ring him again.'

She flashes me a weary look. 'He said he'll call back. You'll just have to wait.'

Orange juice minus the vodka, the dullest proposition of all. But at least it looks good to an observer. My last health kick lasted less than two weeks, undermined by my natural aversion to exercise and Vitamin C. This is worse. Coming back from a binge without a crutch, doing my best to drink lots of fluid and get plenty of rest.

The last of the pills Carla gave me are gone. Nothing left to fall back on in the event of an emergency. Now I'll have to put Plan B into operation and contact Danny.

'I spoke to dad earlier,' Justine says, viewing me coldly from the doorway. 'He's going to lend us the money to pay off the overdraft.'

I stop pouring, in shock.

'Don't look so surprised,' she says irritably. 'This has been hanging over us for months now. You've made no attempt to get it sorted whatsoever.'

I can't believe her attitude. Eight years ago I put fifty grand down on the house. We went on honeymoon in St Lucia, serenaded by a twenty-piece band. And what about all the touring and recording? Putting up with jetlag and exhaustion so she can wear Dolce & Gabbana and douse herself in Chanel No. 5. She forgets all that.

'I want that credit card you've been using as well,' she says, looming.

'What credit card?'

'Don't play games with me. We had all this before when you came back from Hungary. I'm not having you running up more bills.'

Mumbling my compliance, I turn to walk away.

'And don't even think about sneaking out tonight.'

'What?'

'You know exactly what I mean.' She stares at me evenly. 'Just make sure you're around when Hugh Hanley rings.'

It's like being a kid again. Everything you do is measured against your previous record for screwing things up. I'm a musician, for Christ's sake. I don't work a regular nine-to-five. She knew that when she met me. Why's she hassling me about it now?

Jake's watching *The Simpsons*. Homer's going through a mid-life crisis, and to prove his worth decides to build a barbeque in the back garden. I can relate to the desperation, the loss of self-worth. Jake laughs raucously, missing the pathos, taking great delight in other people's misfortunes.

Sadie sits on the edge of the chair, idly swinging her feet. On her face, a look of quiet stoicism.

'What's up, Bunches?'

'I want you to take me tonight.'

'Sorry, I can't.'

'Why not?'

'Because your mum won't let me. And I'm waiting for a phone call.'

'It's not fair.'

'Life's not fair, honey. I'll take you next week, OK?'

What can I say? I've let her down so many times before it hurts to even think about it. I'll have to build up the trust again. Become a responsible adult like the ones in the textbooks. Earn back the right to parent my own children.

Justine calls her from the hallway. She gets up quietly and walks out.

I'm left with the void, the almost palpable sense of disappointment that seems to follow me wherever I go. A few years ago I was someone, a celebrated artist with five albums in the bag and a walk-on part in a movie that got reasonable reviews. Now I'm an extra, forced to sit it out while a bunch of people five hundred miles away decide what to do with me.

Something isn't right. Hanley should have contacted me by now to confirm the new travel arrangements. I'm in danger of being sidelined, overlooked completely.

*

The phone rings. I hear Justine's voice out in the hall, professional, businesslike. From the hushed tones and long silences I guess it's something serious.

She comes in with a strange, disconcerted look that doesn't bode well for me.

'Who was it?'

'Carl Morrison.'

'And?'

'You've been dropped from the tour.'

In moments of such magnitude, you should have a speech ready, a few pertinent words to offset the shock. This time there's nothing. A mild sense of embarrassment, perhaps, that I didn't see it coming.

She straightens up, in control again. 'I'll get hold of Hugh in the morning and find out what's going on. They can't just drop you like this. It doesn't make sense.'

Something in me hardens, switches off. Hanley didn't even have the balls to do it himself. Had to call in one of his sleazy lawyers to do the job for him.

Justine looks down at me with a mixture of pity and contempt. 'I'm going to bed. Don't sit down here brooding all night, get some sleep.'

'James T had something to do with this.'

'Can we talk about it the morning?'

'Why should I get dropped, because of that pompous, fucking ingrate? He's been planning this for months.'

'Joe – I'm not going into all that now. I'll deal with it in the morning.'

In some ways it's a relief. No more sitting around in airport departure lounges. No more tedious radio interviews and record store giveaways. This could be it – the get-out clause I need to branch out and work on my own stuff. One day, the spineless wankers at Goldstein will look back and wish they'd treated me with a bit more respect. By then it'll be too late. I'll be guesting on chat shows around the globe, telling Jay Leno how leaving the band was the best thing that could've happened to me. How relieved I am to have left all that corporate bullshit behind.

The cat yawns, stretching out a paw lazily. I think of the dead rat, hanging from his jaws. An omen of some kind. Maybe it's a sign I need a rest, enjoy a little downtime before the next phase of the operation.

6

Jake's swing sounds like a crow on a railway line, unravelling what's left of my poor, tormented mind. He chuckles outrageously with each forward lunge, a clop of blonde hair rising on the breeze.

'Yeeeeee! I wanna go higher!'

The woman next to us looks mean and unforgiving, the type who could hold her own in a pub brawl. She pushes a little girl who sits forlornly, unimpressed with the free ride.

'Always want more, don't they?' the woman says, grinning. 'Never satisfied, God love 'em.'

We push in unison, side by side, Jake's creaking swing keeping time. The woman lights a cigarette and cups it behind her back, pushing the little girl gently with one hand. Runners and dog walkers compete for the narrow path ahead. Normal people, doing normal things.

'Weeeeeeee!'

Jake leaps from the swing and lands on the soft tarmac, laughing raucously, minus one shoe. I think about Doctor Kahn, the inscrutable Indian gentleman with smooth brown skin and patent leather shoes. Justine's vengeful call to the surgery to keep me grounded.

Looks like it's gonna rain soon,' the woman says, drawing on the cigarette. 'Bloody weather. Now I'll have to get home and take all me washing in.'

What it must be to have problems like that. Your whole life narrowed down to clothes lines and washing powder, the ins and outs of an uneventful day. Jake fumbles with his shoe, oblivious.

'Time to make a move, Jake.'

'I want more.'

'You've had more. Come on, let's go.'

We enter the second phase of the process. Bargaining. If he puts on his shoe and agrees to be good, I'll buy him some sweets. The promise almost clinches the deal, but he senses a weakness worth exploiting. I am his father, after all, the one half of the partnership that gives in too easily and lets him do whatever he likes.

'Can we go to the canal?'

'Not now.'

'Why not?'

'Because you'll get covered in mud and I'll get lynched. Put your shoe on, we're going.'

We head for the car park across the green. Jake runs ahead in his red bobble hat and gloves, a mini tornado in overdrive. Is this how my life's going to be from now on? Trailing after my kids like a lackey, forking out for sweets and ice-cream? Strains of my own childhood, pestering my dad for treats, knowing he'd give in. The roving jazz musician, never at home, coming back with presents as a consolation. Now my own kids sense the same conflict in me, the guilt I feel for being away so much. It's only natural they'd want to exploit it for personal gain.

Jake unwraps a Milky Bar while I stand by watching.

'Happy now?'

'Mmmm.'

The first law of child-rearing – be fully conversant with the art of bribery. Once the money runs out it gets harder. You have to find more subtle ways to gain control.

We head for the car.

'Can we go to Alice's house?'

'Not now, Jake?'

'Why not?'

'Because I said so.'

'But I want to!'

'Well you'll have to keep wanting, kid, cause it ain't happening!'

Parenting doesn't suit me. Unemployment doesn't help much either. In twenty-four hours, I've gone from a fully paid-up member of the avant-garde to a bum. Something better change pretty quick, or I'll be signing-on like Carla, recycling fag-butts and saving two-pence pieces in a whisky bottle. I'm bereft. Disillusioned. Stitched-up by the men in suits who couldn't give a fuck about anyone.

*

Justine feeds M&M's into her mouth with robotic detachment. Every few minutes she laughs at some vacuous comment on the TV, a gesture that somehow excludes everyone else around her. *The News* comes on and we're jolted back to reality. Paedophile rings. Ethnic cleansing in Azerbaijan. Ten-car pile-ups on the M1. The good news gets slotted in as an afterthought to make us feel better. Princess Diana strolling purposefully into the Serpentine Gallery in a revealing black dress. Nelson Mandela campaigning in Transvaal, his dignity intact after twenty-five years on the rock-breaking detail. Not a spark of resentment at the regime that stole a third of his adult life.

'Alice wants us to go camping,' Justine says, popping another M&M into her mouth.

'When?'

'Half-term. I presumed you'd be away.'

'In other words, you don't want me to go with you.'

'Did I say that?'

'No, but that's what you were thinking.'

The last time we stayed anywhere together was Glastonbury, just after Jake was born. She hated it then. Three days in a muddy field, watching the band – my stoned Jimi Hendrix impersonations in front of eighty thousand people.

'Have you phoned Brian Moorcroft?' she says.

'Not yet.'

'Why not?'

'Gimme a break, Justine! I've just been dropped from the tour. What am I supposed to say to him?'

'Suit yourself. I thought this might have been a chance to salvage something from the mess you've got yourself into. But if you can't be bothered ...'

'I'll do it tomorrow.'

The intricacies of having a wife and business manager rolled into one. Sometimes it's hard to work out which angle she's coming from. You start feeling like a commodity, an asset floated on the stock exchange.

The newsreader announces the next item. Paramedics wheel out a stretcher from a hotel to a waiting ambulance. A still of Kurt Cobain's face fills the screen. 'My God,' Justine says quietly. The newsreader announces that after lapsing into a drug-induced coma, Cobain has been rushed into hospital in Rome. She talks about his phenomenal success from a rundown housing estate in Seattle. His role as spokesman for his generation, as well as being the writer of several platinum selling albums.

'There you are,' Justine says.

'Huh?'

'Don't you think it's trying to tell you something?'

The scenario does have an ominous familiarity, a weird kind of déjà vu. Substance abuse on long haul flights. Drug dealers and room service. The ease with which it's made available when you know the right people. Most of my memories are coloured by the same things. Bizarre incidents buried deep in the subconscious. LA in '86. Floating in a hotel swimming pool, fully clothed, completely out of my head on Quaaludes and red wine. The week I spent at Rimmer's apartment in San Diego, trawling the bars at night for his dealer. Coming-to on an empty stretch of beach at five in the morning, the sun coming up and a date with hell around the corner.

*

Justine lies with her back to me. I'm aware of her breathing, softly, as I turn another page. *Nausea* – the kind of book you should read under sedation in case it tips the balance of your mind. The narrator, Antoine Roquentin, wanders the streets, consumed by the sheer randomness of existence. The sun shines, leaves fall from the trees and people meet endlessly in cafes. Nothing much matters beyond the passing of time, the brief glimpse you see of yourself in a total stranger.

'Remember where we're going tomorrow,' she murmurs drowsily.

'Tomorrow?'

'The Doctor's. I made an appointment for you. Please don't forget.'

The smooth, brown nub of her shoulder sits obstinately between us. Even after years of marriage, my desire for her is intact. The tension and lack of communication between us makes it stronger. Strange nuances, twisted by my frequent absences and the warped excesses of a hangover. We used to be a proper couple. We did things together. We had sex three or four times a week. Now all we do is bicker about money and how totally irresponsible I've become. But still the attraction remains, a photograph buried in a drawer neither of us can bear to look at.

I turn out the light.

Glastonbury '89. Hard to believe so much has happened in the five years since. Justine's thigh-length leather boots, caked in mud outside the tent. A young convoy girl on horseback selling acid in the predawn light. That gig should have been the pinnacle of my career. The one good memory in a decade that ended in chaos and disillusion. But that's part of the problem. When you achieve success, you always want more. Nothing you do after that is ever quite good enough.

'D'you think he's gonna die?'

She sighs. 'What?'

'Kurt Cobain.'

'I've no idea. Can we talk about it in the morning?'

America nearly killed me. Its vastness and limitless potential opened up my mind to a new and extraordinary degree. The land of dreams to a wide-eyed English boy who'd never been further than Newcastle. Sixteen dates in a tour that crossed five states, from New York to Cleveland, playing to crowds of up to sixteen thousand.

The last tour was different. I went missing in New Mexico. The band played two gigs with a guitar tech standing in and cancelled the last one due to intractable problems within. Exhausted and burned out, I flew home on a red-eye, mourning the fact I'd just turned thirty.

Justine's thigh is soft and warm. She stiffens instinctively when I touch her.

'Don't!'

'What's the matter?'

'I'm tired. I want to go to sleep.'

Red digits glow in the dark. 1:15, 1:16, 1:17. Each minute adds more weight to the bind I'm in. This sinking down into blackness. Being swallowed up in something terrible that doesn't have a name. The sobering fact that my own wife can't bear to touch me.

At 2:15, I slip quietly from the covers and locate my jeans. The stairs creak on the way down, but the act itself is strangely cathartic. The twilight zone. A time for reflection and sudden bursts of creativity. The place where songs get written and new concepts are explored while the rest of the world is sleeping.

The urge isn't there. Instead, I feel empty and hollowed out.

Beaten.

7

Doctors surgeries are strange places – halfway houses for the funeral parlour. Even the décor should make you think twice. Colour posters for heart check-ups and flu jabs. Second-rate pastoral scenes in gilt-edged frames. The old bat opposite me stares grimly at the wall, the look on her face confirming what I know already. You don't come here to get cured of some nameless virus, but to buy time and ward off the undertaker.

The toddler in the buggy keeps straining to get out. With each frantic twist his face gets redder, his wailing louder.The harassed teenage mum waves a cuddly toy in his face, powerless to stop him. The rest of us try and pretend it isn't happening.

After a while, the pressure becomes unbearable.

'Where the fuck is he?'

Justine looks at me severely. 'What's the matter now?'

'The doctor. He's twenty minutes late.'

'You'll have to wait like everyone else. Read a magazine.'

Flicking through a worn copy of *Hello*, I'm reminded how shallow the whole thing is. Photo shoots in the Algarve.Vacuous celebrities with too much money. I'm hooked into the dream like everyone else, but what happens when the dream becomes a nightmare? You're forced into doing things you don't want to do just to please someone else.

'Mrs Jones?'

The old bat rises stiffly and lopes off towards the corridor. The female doctor in the doorway flashes a wintry smile and steps back to let her through. My stomach lurches. One step closer to my scheduled ordeal and I still haven't thought what

I'm going to say when it's my turn.

'Joe Byron?'

The deep voice resonates through the surgery. I stand reluctantly. Justine drops her magazine on the seat and stands with me.

Doctor Kahn smiles cordially and ushers us both past.

'Last door on the right, please, Joe.'

The corridor is softly lit, a faint smell of furniture polish lingering. I think of all the man hours spent behind closed doors, the endless prescriptions doled out to stricken customers.

Doctor Kahn shuts the door and bids us take a seat. He sits in his high-backed leather chair and crosses his legs, suave and relaxed. Twin cherubs beam down from the portrait above his desk. The same darkly empathic look as their father. The same warm and engaging smile to put patients at ease. Behind him, the computer screen, full of classified information all about me.

The good doctor observes me casually above manicured fingertips.

'So ... how are you today, Joe?'

'I'm fine, thanks.'

He nods his head slowly. I nod back, wishing I was somewhere else. This subdued greeting has a history of implications for both of us. All the times I've sat here over the years for depression, insomnia, drug-induced psychosis. The repeat prescription for sleeping tablets that Justine found out about and had stopped immediately.

She sits upright beside me, her face taut with anxiety.

'I made the appointment because I'm worried about Joe's health. He's not been right lately.'

'In what way?'

She pauses, fingering the straps of her bag.

'He's drinking too much. Staying out all night. We've had all this before but it's getting worse.'

Doctor Kahn raises an eyebrow and turns to me. I shift awkwardly in the seat. The room is dry and airless, the perfect environment for extracting a confession. I focus on the tranquil landscape on the opposite wall and think about heroin.

'How's your sleep been lately, Joe?'

'Not too good.'

'Anything troubling you?'

'Not that I can think of.'

Justine glares at me. 'He went missing for three days last week when he was supposed to be in New York. It's caused all sorts of financial implications for us. He might even lose his job.'

'Joe?'

'I met up with a few people I hadn't seen for a while and got sidetracked.'

'Sidetracked!' She stares at me in disbelief. 'You were off your head. The same thing happened when you came back from Hungary. Remember?'

The doctor notes the disparities, careful not to side with either one of us. From past experience I know it's always best to play dumb, never to antagonise or level blame. The more accusing and angry Justine becomes the better it'll look for me.

'What were you doing in Hungary, Joe?'

'I did a small tour with the band.'

'And were you drinking then?'

'Not much.'

'Oh, please!'

I can't tell the good doctor what really happened. The nunnery on the Russian border we stayed in during the final leg of the tour. Benedictine nuns serving us home made soups and pastries all day long. The bunch of Eastern European ravers I met in Budapest were more my idea of fun. What a night! Ending up at an acid house party fifty miles away, totally off my nut on MDMA.

'The problems really started when I came home.'

'Can you be more specific?'

'Well … I had a lot of time on my hands. The tour had finished. We weren't gigging or recording. I got bored sitting around doing nothing all day.'

'He was suffering from exhaustion,' Justine says irritably. 'He should never have gone in the first place.'

Doctor Kahn crosses his legs. I note the tiny perforations

in his shiny brogues, the seam lines in his crisp, black socks. He has an enviable composure, an inner calm I've spent years trying to affect without ever quite pulling it off.

'How's your mood been lately?'

'Er – not too bad.'

'The last time you came to see me you couldn't sleep. You were having panic attacks, I believe.'

'The stress of touring. It's improved since I've been at home, though.'

Justine tuts audibly. 'He stays up half the night smoking cannabis and listening to music. Then he wonders why I get so frustrated when he stays in bed all day.'

'I don't stay in bed all day.'

'Oh, come on! You rarely get up before midday, and when you do it's usually to go out drinking.' She looks at the doctor in appeal. 'This has been going on a long time now. He comes home from a tour, or wherever he's been, and uses the place like a hotel. We hardly ever see him.'

Doctor Kahn reflects.

'You say you get bored when you're at home, Joe. What do you do when you feel like this?'

'Write songs. Listen to music.'

'And smoking cannabis helps, does it?'

'Sometimes it does, yeah.'

'What about other drugs?'

'I have used things in the past. You know. Cope with the stresses of touring and that. Not anymore though.'

Justine sighs. 'I knew this would happen. What's the point in sitting here lying about everything? Why can't you just tell the truth?'

The silence goads me. I could be on trial in a courtroom, with Justine as chief witness for the prosecution and Doctor Kahn as the judge. Everything I say, or don't say, has a huge bearing on the outcome.

He turns a few degrees in his chair to study me, chin propped on his fingertips.

'How much are you drinking, Joe?'

'Not much. Just lager mainly. I do have the odd short occasionally, but not often.'

'Do you drink every day?'

'Couple of times a week, maybe. Some weeks I don't drink at all. I haven't had a drink now since … last Friday.'

Justine shakes her head. 'He can go weeks without a drink. Then something happens and he's off again. When he came back from America the last time, he said he was going to stop for good, he was so ill. But he forgets how bad it was and it all starts up again. We can't go on like it financially either, with my parents bailing us out all the time.'

I focus on the good doctor's shoes and think about my abandoned health regimes. He once told me he plays squash and takes regular walking holidays in the Brecon Beacons. I've seen the new Beamer he drives with the personalised number plate and tinted windows. The man's a success and he knows how to handle it. What am I – a failure because I couldn't make it in the game?

He spins round to study the computer screen.

'OK, let's have a look here … You were due a blood test over a month ago. Are you still taking lithium?'

'Er – yeah. When I can remember.'

Justine shakes her head. 'Sorry, Doctor, but he isn't.The only thing he was taking were the sleeping tablets you prescribed. He was taking so many I rang the surgery and had them stopped.'

He shifts uncomfortably, his composure rocked for the first time. I share his discomfort, having deliberately abused his trust for my own ends. But needs must, and my needs were greater than his. My deepening love affair with the little yellow pills, to be indulged whenever possible. Temazepam, Diazepam, Trazadone. The perfect antidote to depression, the sweats and shakes of withdrawal. I mourn the loss of them like a good friend or recently departed lover.

Doctor Kahn glances at the screen.

'You went into treatment in October '92. What happened there?'

'He got thrown out for smoking cannabis,' Justine says

quickly. He nods solemnly.

'Would you consider going back, if you were referred again?'

How can I answer that without implicating myself further, with Justine sat alongside me, waiting to launch another vicious attack?

'I don't think treatment would help.'

'Why?'

'Because I don't have a problem. I mean, sure, I do have the odd drink now and then, but it's under control.'

Justine erupts. 'Under control! How can it be under control? Look at our wedding anniversary. My dad's birthday. The times you were meant to pick Jake up from school and forgot. How is that under control?'

'They were one-offs. I'm not like that all the time, am I.'

'Yes you are! You're so fucking selfish it's unbelievable!' She sits back, drained, and makes an embarrassed apology.Doctor Kahn reassures her gently and turns to consult the screen. I dread to think what's written up there. My entire life history edited down to highlights. Confidential information no one outside the room should see.

He turns back, observing me intensely.

'So – no changes in your mood lately?'

'Not really.'

'No strange thoughts? Feelings of grandeur?'

'No more than usual.'

Ignoring the comment, he turns to Justine. 'Have you noticed any changes in Joe's mood?'

She sits forward, eager to tell all. The nocturnal wanderings and the sleeping-in late. Countless promises made and broken. Then there's the bank loans and the overdrafts, threatening letters from credit-card companies and unpaid bills. All this and my volatile mental state, made worse by bouts of heavy drinking.

Doctor Kahn nods thoughtfully, his dark face passive, almost serene. His eyes have a strange hypnotic quality, compelling me towards the truth.

'Joe?'

I stare meaningfully at the floor and ponder.

'I'll be straight with you, Doctor. I do find it hard when I'm at home. And I do drink too much occasionally, I admit. But I'm working on it, I really am.'

'Until the next time!' Justine adds, glaring at me.

What else can I say? I've been turned over by scheming bandmates and corrupt lawyers. Pompous bank managers who can't grasp the fact that I'm still owed royalties for songs off the first album. Wouldn't anyone need a drink with problems like these?

The doctor thinks over the options, finally reaching a conclusion.

'I'd like you to see someone for me.'

'Who?'

'She's very good. Very knowledgeable.' He taps into his keypad, murmuring to himself. 'Ah, here we are.' He spins round like a game show host, to hit me with the punchline. 'Val Moody. She's a counsellor, specialising in addiction.'

'Addiction?'

'She can help you, Joe.'

'Yeah, but – '

'Just listen,' Justine says firmly, the two of them working as a team.

The good doctor's manner invites no argument. I can almost feel the escape hatches closing, one by one.

'I'll set up an appointment for you to see her. Is that OK?'

I shrug, browbeaten into submission. Justine sits up, vindicated.

'I'll make sure he keeps the appointment, Doctor Kahn.' She turns to me. 'He will if he wants to save his marriage.'

We don't speak on the way out. Justine fishes for the car-keys, eyeing me cautiously above the roof.

'Please don't make a big thing about this,' she says.

'About what?'

'The appointment with the counsellor. That's what you're so wound up about, isn't it?' She opens the door and pauses. 'Are you coming back with me or not?'

'I'll walk.'

I can't see an end to it. The straitjacket of ultimatums. Committees of doctors, psychiatrists and counsellors lining up to tell me what to do.

The passenger window opens and Justine leers up at me.

'Please don't go disappearing again.'

'I'm walking back, for fuck's sake! I need the air.'

'Don't take it out on me. All I'm trying to do is get you some help. You might thank me for it one day if it saves your precious career!'

Ten minutes later I'm cruising along Portobello, trying to put the whole thing out of my mind. A group of workmen sit outside a café drinking tea. One of them feeds titbits to a bull terrier perched at his feet. A toothless bag-lady comes along, muttering to herself in a strange tongue, causing me to almost rupture myself on a bollard trying to get out of her way.

Ladbroke Grove has a long history of subversives and cultural renegades who've all lived here at some point.Although it wasn't quite the same hotbed of revolutionary fervour when I moved in, it still had something. One of my first acts as resident was a drunken pilgrimage to Lansdowne Crescent where Hendrix died in 1970. This was followed shortly after by an equally hazy night on the town with Keith Allen, who I'd met and instantly bonded with in the Warwick.My past is littered with memories like these. Drunken escapades. Wonderful adventures.

The Duke of Wellington looms on the left. An old man sits in the window, drinking stout. He raises his pint and winks at me mischievously, but I keep moving. Too much at stake.My marriage, my children. My career. But the temptation eats away at me, a hand pulling me back. How does anyone stop drinking? Surely, you need something to get by? The odd toke on a joint now and then. A handful of pills to take the edge off things. Maybe I can strike a deal with the powers that be, and Justine will allow me the odd glass of sherry at her mum's on a Sunday afternoon, or a quick blast on the sacred weed.

Whatever happens, I'll need something to keep the demons at bay. Everybody needs something.

8

Carla has a strange way of entertaining visitors. She sits at the table rolling a joint, ignoring everything you say. The TV's on, volume muted. An incense stick burns in the corner, a thin coil of smoke rising to the ceiling. But somehow, you feel privileged to be there. There's a kind of ritual to it all, like watching royalty preparing for afternoon tea.

My traumatic visit to the doctor fails to impress her. Even my rants about Justine don't have the desired effect. 'Like a double act they were. The pair of 'em. Now he wants me to see this addiction counsellor – Val Moody. Can you believe that?'

'Why go if you don't want to?' she says casually, the joint poised beneath her tongue.

'What else can I do? Justine's set the whole thing up. If I don't go she'll divorce me and take the kids away. I'll end up on the embankment with all the other refugees.'

She moistens the paper's edge with her tongue and rolls the contents, sealing the end with a twist. A small firework, complete with mini fuse.

'Maybe it's what you need.'

'What?'

'Well. You know. Someone to listen to your problems and all that crap.'

'Yeah right.'

'Just a thought. Anyway, aren't you supposed to be in Philadelphia?'

'There's been a change of plan.'

'How?'

'I'm picking up the tour later.'

'Where?'

'I don't know yet. Justine's dealing with it.'

She lights the joint and inhales deeply. Late breakfast – the only form of sustenance she needs, along with the filter coffee she downs on the hour. I can't bring myself to tell her the truth. The shame of being dropped by Goldstein, the news relayed to me by one of Hugh Hanley's scheming lawyers.

After a record in-breath, she exhales blissfully and stares into space. 'I had a social worker once. We used to meet up in this café in Shoreditch. All she ever did was talk about babies.'

'Babies?'

'She'd just come back from maternity leave. Once you got her started on the subject she wouldn't stop. Kept her off my case, though. Silly bitch.'

The joint comes to me. Harsh smoke hits the back of my throat, the shared ritual bonding us in some way.

'So what you gonna do now?' she says.

'Play the game, I suppose. Keep out of Justine's way until it all blows over.'

The joint goes back and forth between us. My mind starts to expand. Flickers of unease skirt the boundaries. The room looks brighter. The worn furniture and ugly, tiled fireplace take on a sinister form. Nietzsche might have been right – that which doesn't destroy you makes you stronger – but smoke enough of this stuff and your brain gets scrambled, your thinking's never quite the same.

'What's happening with that girl?' she says.

'What girl?'

'The one you played me in the car the other day.'

'Naomi. I haven't spoken to her yet.'

'I thought you were meant to be producing her first album?'

'I was. I mean, I will be. Soon as Cribbs gets off his ass and arranges a meeting between us.'

She sniffs dismissively and stares out the window, the joint burning slowly between her fingers. Her silence goads me, reminiscent of all the petty quarrels we've had before. I know what she's thinking. A mixture of envy and disapproval from the old days. Resentment at the talent of another singer, especially a female. She was never this like this when she was on the circuit, working with big name acts all over the world. Now it's all sarcasm and acid put-downs. Nothing good to say about anyone.

The joint comes back to me, burning and crackling with a life of its own. Waves of paranoia circle, like sharks around a flimsy boat. I can't understand my reaction. There must be a major weakness in my personality, some underlying flaw that makes me feel this way. Carla smokes the stuff all day without any change in her outward demeanour. It has to be genetic.Some of us just aren't wired-up right.

'I ran into Ussef the other day,' she says, checking her nails. 'You wouldn't recognise him. He's shaved off all his hair.'

'What's he up to these days?'

'Living with a Thai woman in Hounslow, apparently.'

'Still clean?'

'Seems to be. He's into Yoga and health food now. Best I've seen him looking for ages.'

My memories of Ussef are tinged with sadness. One of the best sound engineers in West London, who gave it all up to repair potholes on the M1. The senselessness appals me.

'Good luck to him,' I say glibly. 'I'm gonna start a health regime too.'

She laughs. 'Doing what?'

'Seriously. I dug a hole in the back garden the other day and it nearly killed me. I need to get fit. Pump some iron in the gym.'

Fear of death, a subject so utterly compelling I can't get it out of my mind. Add to that the family history of early mortality and it's easy to see why. My jazz-obsessed father's untimely exit at forty-nine. Terry, the super-fit, football mad brother-in-law diagnosed with cancer less than a year later.These things shake your belief in everything. You start wondering when it's going to be your turn.

Carla eases the tip from her nail varnish bottle, applying the finish with a lazy sensuality. 'Ussef said he saw you in Subterranea one night and you ignored him completely.'

'When?'

She shrugs. 'I said you were probably off your head. Waste of time anyone trying to talk to you when you're like that.You're on another planet.'

'Thanks.'

'Well it's true, isn't it? What about that night in the Astoria? You and that little tart from the Finger Puppets doing coke all night. No wonder Hugh Hanley had to employ a minder to watch over you.'

Hanley – the ex-dance hall manager with a suite of offices in Tottenham Court Road. I picture him with his feet up on his desk, smoking a Marlboro, on the phone to some agent or promoter he was trying to impress. His customer relations were persuasive to say the least, a mixture of slick charm and toned-down aggression. Unwanted callers were dealt with swiftly.His secretary would enter at a prearranged signal and remind him of some fictitious appointment he was supposed to keep. Failing that, he might throw a chair across the room so you really got the message. But when it came to self-promotion, the man was in a class of his own. Even Carla would have to admit that.

The garish wallpaper blurs before my eyes. Smoking the joint hasn't helped. Like being seasick, you end up wanting to jump overboard to escape how bad you're feeling. I stand, focusing hard on staying afloat.

'What's the matter?' she says.

'I'm toasted.'

'Amateur!'

She finishes her nails, and gazes, mournfully, out the window. I wonder if she's secretly waiting for Danny to come back from his mother's in Lewisham, so they can resume whatever it was they were doing before he left. All that crap about her detesting him. I never believed it anyway.

'When was the last time you went out?' I say.

She looks up, frowning.

'Why?'

'Just wondered. I thought we could, you know, get over The Seven Aces one night and hang one on.'

She looks at me strangely. 'How does that work exactly?'

'Easy. You jump on the tube like everyone else.'

She shakes her head slowly. 'You've got a really short memory, haven't you.'

'Why?'

'What d'you think happens to me when I walk in a place like that?'

'You let your hair down and enjoy yourself, don't you? Isn't that what everyone does when they go to a club?'

She blanks me deliberately. Somewhere along the way she lost her sense of humour, but I suppose you can understand why. Coming off the gear is hard. The addict can always find a hundred and one reasons to go back. But it's staying off that's the problem. You think you can have a little taste now and then and that's it. By the time you've done the first bag it's too late. You're right back where you started.

'Look at this,' Carla says, aiming the remote at the TV. We watch as Tony Blair makes a speech outside Downing Street, his eyes shining with a missionary zeal. I can't resist an irreverent quip.

'Caligula!'

'What?'

'Check out a film called *The Robe*. The guy in it's a dead ringer for Blair. It's the voice, the look. Everything.'

Blair sums up his election as Leader of the Labour Party with a heartfelt pledge and a manic grin. *'I shall not rest until the destinies of our people and our party are joined together in victory.'*

'Tosser,' Carla says.

'Don't knock it. He's been sent to save us from the Tory nightmare.'

'And you believe that, do you?'

'No, but someone's got to. Skin another one up before my head caves in completely.'

The front door slams and foreign voices ring out in the hall. Heavy steps pound the creaking staircase. Carla's transient neighbours, the faceless tenants she never sees. Some of the stories are good though. Like the Iranian guy who flooded the place out and hid from the landlord in a wardrobe. Or the fight one of them had with a taxi driver on the front lawn.

'I need a favour,' Carla says casually.

'Here we go.'

'Seriously. I need a lift to Golborne Road.'

'What for?'

'I said I'd pick something up for Danny.'

The newsreader debates Blair's political future with a sour-faced correspondent. Carla switches channels. A man in chef's whites is busy chopping an aubergine, chatting to the camera with cool familiarity. Carla's request doesn't ring true. There's something missing but I can't work out what it is.

'Why can't Danny pick it up himself?'

'He's still in Lewisham … Can you take me or not?'

'Is this a reciprocal arrangement, or am I gonna be parked up scratching my nuts for half an hour?'

'If it's that big a deal, I'll get the bus.'

The chef prepares a duck for the camera, filling its gaping backside with sausagemeat and breadcrumb stuffing. I think of the rat Bodmin caught, laid out on the slab like an offering. Symbolic of my current malaise. My career hanging in the balance.

'Can you get me some pills?'

'What happened to the last lot I gave you?'

'They're gone.'

'What, all of them?'

'You only gave me eight!'

She must think I've got nothing better to do. Part time run-around for her and Danny. But there are some advantages to having links with criminals and drug dealers. You're first in the queue when the goods come in.

The sharks circle again. A sense of unreality that's hard to overcome. Even as a teenager, this weakness was there. I smoked a joint in the park one day and went dizzy in the noonday sun – like being strapped to a chair that measures G-force. Brought round by a bunch of old age pensioners who thought I'd had a seizure. What a dork. A lightweight in my own backyard.

*

'Five minutes,' Carla says, and gets out.

I park up in a loading bay and turn off the engine. I've been through this scenario before. It's not just the waiting, it's the assumption that I'll drop whatever I'm doing to ferry her around on some bogus mission.

Five minutes turns into ten, fifteen.

Then I see her, mingling with pedestrians by the post office. Head erect and shoulders back, an unwritten sign above her head that says, *Warning – I don't take shit from anyone!*

She gets in and slams the door.

'What's up?'

'He's not in!'

'Who?'

'Just drive, will you. Get me away from this fucking place.'

She says little the entire journey back, muttering about all the scumbags she knows, never in when they're supposed to be. I take it the deal, whatever it was, has fallen through.

I keep the engine running outside her place. She stares ahead, breathing heavily through her nose.

'Can I ask you something?' I say.

'What?'

'You don't have to answer if you don't want to.'

'Just, say it, please.'

'Back there. Were you looking for brown?'

She stares at me evenly. 'No. I was *not* looking for brown.'

'I just needed to know, that's all.'

She gets out and leans on the door, gazing in at me solemnly.

'You don't have to watch out for me all the time, you know. Like I'm fifteen or something. I can look after myself.'

She climbs the dirty steps and puts her key in the door without a backward glance. I can understand her frustration, her resentment. Everyone's actions tainted by things they've done in the past, things other people find hard to forget. We're the same

51

in that respect. Both looking for different ways to relieve the pressure. Maybe I shouldn't have questioned her about looking for gear, but it's only because I care. Who else is around to look out for her? I'm one of the few friends she's got.

Driving away, I think about Hugh Hanley. The nice little chat we had in his office one day about my future with the band. Tone it down, he said. All the drug taking and the running round with disreputable people. Start being more responsible. Turn up to meetings and soundchecks on time. Give interviews in a more positive state of mind. All this to the chime of the cash register playing in his head. The one thing he worships above all else.

I head back towards the Grove, wishing I had more pills. Justine's 'no booze' policy makes things even harder. I'm a few days away from the horrors of Islington but the fallout remains. The crushing sense of defeat at being dropped from the tour. An appointment with some sanctimonious drug counsellor looming on the calendar.

9

I drop Sadie at her dance class in Notting hill.

'Pick you up in an hour, Bunches. Have fun!'

I leave the car and stroll along the high street. The pubs looks inviting, music and laughter to lure the weary traveller inside. But not for me. I've made a promise to Justine and I intend to keep it. Somehow I find the willpower to walk on by.

A beggar steps out from the doorway of HMV, intimidating in green army surplus and a three day growth. He walks alongside me with a casual air.

'Got any spare cash so I can get home, mate?'

'No, sorry.'

He grins fiendishly. 'How 'bout a fag? Tide me over 'til I get back to the night shelter?'

These people don't give up easily. A semi-professional underclass, lurking in shop doorways and alleyways all over London. Resentfully, I offer the packet. He takes a cigarette with gnarled, bitten fingers and pops it in his mouth.

'Got a light too, mate?'

The lighter flares and, beneath a giant poster of Take That, we share a strange, fleeting connectedness.

I think of all the cash I've squandered over the years.Crazy, impulsive deals, like buying a half ounce of coke from a guy in a Manhattan nightclub, then losing it on the Subway somewhere between Madison Avenue and Times Square. Painful, sobering memories I'd rather forget. Dwell on them too long and you convince yourself that's all there was. The music was incidental, a colourful sideline between visits to the local medicine man seeking immunisation against the cruel world.

I call Cribbs from a phone box. We have this bizarre conversation about the stomach upset he's had recently, and the liquid consistency of his bowels. I broach the subject of Naomi with caution, knowing his excessive protectiveness towards her. His vagueness begins to irritate me.

'Cribbs, all I'm asking is you set up a meeting between us. What's the problem with that?'

'I can't.'

'What you talking about?'

'It's her dad.'

'What about him?'

'He's her manager. He vets all her contracts. You have to run everything by him.'

Beyond the scratched phone box window lies the cold, damp vista of West 11. I'm weary and disillusioned, anxious about the future. Nothing to fall back on. No booze. No chemicals. Justine at home, waiting for me to make a wrong move. Now this. Naomi's dad playing El Supremo.

'Does she know who I am? The kind of people I've worked with?'

'Yeah, I told her.'

'Well tell her to give me a call. Tell her, in twenty-four hours time she could be in L.A. laying down a demo with Scott Levine.'

I hang up and dig out the scrap of paper in my jacket pocket. Heart racing, I feed more coins in the slot and dial the number. A gruff-voiced woman answers.

'Is Danny there, please?'

'He's out. Who's calling?'

'Joe.'

'Try again in half an hour. He should be back by then.'

Frustrated, I move on. A grim looking newsvendor sits propped on a stool, rubbing his mittened-fingers against the cold. I grab a copy of *Melody Maker* and make a joke about the weather.

'Anyfin' else?' he says sullenly. I think of Jake with his

book of stickers, the pleasure he gets from collecting them and sticking them in.

'Two packs of Pokémon cards, please?'

'Don't do 'em.'

'Really?'

'S'what I said, wannit?'

Some people are naturally obnoxious. It's in their faces, their DNA. I feel like screaming across the counter at his cretinous face, *Don't you know who I am? I've toured the States with Aerosmith and Neil Young. I've played in front of Prince Charles and Lady Di. I'm a bona fide rock god, and you're treating me like a pleb, you backward fucking moron!*

*

I turn up at the dance class on the hour. A few bored mothers loiter in the hallway, waiting for the session to end. From behind the double doors, comes the up-tempo beat of Latin jazz and the sound of clicking feet. The strident voice of the lithe, female Instructor, calls out the timing.

'One and two and three and four!'

Sadie comes out red-faced and unsmiling. She looks strangely professional in her blue leotard and shiny black tights, as if she's just auditioned for the West End. I hand her the coat Justine insists she puts on after every session and watch her stroll out to the car.

'How'd it go, Bunches?'

'OK.'

'Happy with the production, or d'you suggest any changes?

Ignoring me, she climbs in and straps-up. I stick on a compilation tape and ease into the traffic. Music to soothe the troubled mind. Newcomers on the underground scene, plugging away in church halls and garages just like we were, hoping for a lucky break.

Sadie sits demurely beside me, hands crossed in her lap. She looks up at me expectantly.

'Can I stay at Rebecca's this weekend?'

'You'll have to ask your mum.'

'Why can't you say?'

'Because she's the boss. Don't you know that by now?'

I turn the music up as nostalgia creeps in. Cramped bedrooms and freezing bedsits. Ambitious teenagers lugging Marshall amps up three flights of stairs. The disappointments, the disillusion. Then the turnaround. Success when you're least expecting it. John Peel announcing us on his evening show in his gruff, Midlands tones. '... *And now, after some delay waiting for the tape to arrive, here's the band I saw in Brighton last week!*'

For someone who's had a guitar strapped around his neck for the best part of twenty years, I find myself increasingly estranged from my chosen instrument. Maybe it's the trauma of all that's happened recently. The uncertainty over my job, the cracks in my marriage. Or maybe it's a deeper, spiritual malaise, where I just can't find the inspiration. Whatever the reason, it's left a void, a part of me that's missing.

Sadie reaches for the glove compartment.

'What you looking for, Bunches?'

'The Happy Mondays.'

'What's wrong with this?'

'It's boring.'

Democracy loses out once again. But then I never was much good at controlling my own children. The Happy Mondays go on, and in a moment of pure surrealism, we join in the chorus on God's Cop, Sadie's black dancing shoes keeping time. I'm hit with a dilemma. What effect will the drug references and the regional slang have on an impressionable child, even one with such an advanced taste in music as Sadie?

I turn the music down a fraction and glance across at her.

'How's school, Bunches?'

'OK.'

'Mum said you got 98-percent in a maths exam, is that right?'

'That was ages ago.'

'So? You should be proud of yourself. That's amazing.Maybe you're gonna be a scientist or something when you're older.'

'I don't want to be a scientist, I want to be a vet.'

'Well that's good too, honey. You could have your own practise one day and reel in the dollar. Take us all on holiday, huh?'

A car cuts in front of us. I hit the horn and shout abuse at the driver. Sadie sits grinning up at me.

'You said the bad word!'

'No I didn't.'

'Yes you did. Twice!'

Beaming smugly, she sits back, my sudden loss of control increasing her future bargaining power.

I pull over at the kerb and turn off the engine.

'Listen – I've gotta make a phone call, honey. Five minutes, OK?'

The dialling tones ring on. Sadie peers at me, dejectedly, through the passenger window. I'm aware that what I'm doing isn't right, about as far from any concept of normality as you could get, but I can't stop myself. It's the only thing I can think of that'll keep me sane.

'Danny? … It's Joe.'

'Where d'you get this number from?'

'You gave it to me ages ago.'

Silence.

'Come on then, I'm busy. What d'you want?'

The arrangements are quick and simple. I give him a coded request, which he considers briefly, coming right back at me.

'Meet me on the Green, twelve o'clock tomorrow. And bring that forty quid you owe me.'

'What forty quid?'

'Don't fuck me about, Joe, I'm not in the mood. Just bring it, alright?'

You never know how Danny's going to be from one day to the next. One minute personable and charming, the next unhinged. If it wasn't for his sideline in certain 'goods' I'd have nothing to do with him.

Funny how the brain works at such moments, tapping into neurochemicals you'd almost forgotten. Fear of Danny on the one hand and a reckless craving for sedation on the other. Euphoric recall – the promise of something illicit that's stored in each cell, ready to burst into life the moment you evoke its memory. I can feel it already, working its way through my system, warm and relaxing, calming the stress factors down.

'Right, Bunches. Chips!'

I convince myself it's a one-off, a temporary measure until I get myself sorted. Then I'll back off and throw myself into work again. Rebuild my reputation. Win back some of the trust I've lost with Justine.

'Who were you talking to?' Sadie says.

'Oh, just an old friend I haven't seen for a while.'

'James T?'

'No, honey. Not James T.'

'What's his name?'

'Who?'

'Your friend.'

'Danny.'

She thinks.

'Is he in a band too?'

'No, he isn't. He's a sort of, freelancer.'

'What's that?'

I search painfully for an adequate description.

'He arranges things. You know. Like the monitors you have at school. He finds out what people want and he gets it for them.'

I hope Sadie never needs the services of someone like Danny. I hope she gets an education and a good job. Then I'll be happy. I'll be able to look back in years to come, safe in the knowledge I've achieved at least one worthwhile thing in life.

10

A lone figure comes striding up the path from the lower entrance. Sunlight glints on the chrome studs of his worn leather jacket, his unsmiling, angular face. He looks morose, preoccupied, a brooding James Dean, with dangling cigarette and wild shock of fringe.

He sits down, heavily, beside me and crosses his legs.There's a moment's awkward silence, before he looks up casually.

'How's it hanging, bud?'

'So so.'

He nods agreeably and relaxes, splaying his arms on the back of the bench. I'm wary of his casual manner, the significant change in him since we spoke on the phone.

'So where you been hiding lately?' he says.

I tell him about all the problems I've been having at home. Letters from the bank. Hassle from Justine. He draws on the cigarette, no outward sign he's even listening. When I've finished, he flicks the stub in the air, watching its lazy arc across the Green.

'Got the money?' he says.

'Not on me.'

'Why not?'

'I thought I'd – '

'I've gotta sit around waiting for you to find a cashpoint, have I?'

He stares at me intensely. I think of all the stories I've heard from Carla. Things I've witnessed personally from time to time.

His slow smile is unexpected, disarming.

'Real dark horse, incha, Joe.'

'Am I?'

'Yeah, you fucking are. Been on tour lately?'

'No, I'm taking a break.'

I resent the sarcasm, the lack of respect. Why should my job be so amusing to him, he's been unemployed most of his life. I've been on the road almost constantly for two years without a break. I've got a career. Talent. I'm going places.

Two young lovers sit on a bench further down. The classic impoverished student look, baggy jumpers and torn jeans, backpacks dotted with badges. He watches them, idly, before turning to me.

'What d'you want – a ten-bag?'

'That'd be good, Danny, yeah.'

'This won't be a regular thing, you know.'

'Yeah, sure. Whatever.'

The deal creates a strange, almost sexual tension, a reminder of similar transactions all over the world. The procedure is usually the same. You reel off your meagre shopping list to the dealer and wait for the go ahead, trusting his guile and expertise to come up with the goods. When it comes to tenacity, these people are always one step ahead of the game. Danny's no exception and prides himself on his ability to deliver. But he's only ever got me coke and E's before. This is new territory for both of us.

He sniffs abruptly. 'I'll have a word with a mate of mine, OK?'

'Thanks, Danny.'

'But you keep your mouth shut. I don't want Carla knowing about it.'

'No, course not.'

His pious look hardens into something mean and contemptuous. 'What you messing with that shit for anyway? I always thought you were more switched on than that.'

'I just use it occasionally to relax.'

'How many times d'you think I've heard that old one before? You're full of bullshit, son.'

He yawns and stretches his legs.

'Fuck they looking at?'

The young lovers across the way quickly avert their eyes. Danny stares at them, his lower jaw stuck out menacingly. He hawks up a mouthful of phlegm and launches it in their direction.

'Ever mention me, does she?' he says.

'Who?'

'Carla.'

'Sometimes.'

He thinks this over, tapping his fingers on the back of the bench.

'Who's she seeing now?'

'No idea.'

'What about that black cunt with the little round glasses?'

'Eugene? That was ages ago.'

'She must be seeing someone?' He looks at me slyly. 'How about you?'

'Me?' I laugh, mildly outraged. 'Why would I be seeing Carla, she's a friend of mine?'

'Oh, yeah? Bit of a shirt-lifter on the quiet, are ya?'

He watches me with lingering curiosity, chuckling away to himself as if I'm some kind of freak. If I had the balls I'd retaliate. Make some comment about his lack of education, the fact he's spent most of his life in prison. Instead, I just sit here and take it, envying his nonchalance, his brutish charm.

The student lovers depart, leaving behind a sandwich wrapper and a coke can. Danny watches them go, with a scowl. 'Who'd wanna look like that? I had a kid like that I'd shoot the fucker. Know anyone wants a Bosch angle grinder?'

'A what?'

'Diamond disc blade. Petrol runner. Fifty quid.'

'Er – I'll keep my ears open, Danny.'

He taps out a new rhythm right behind my shoulder, making me even more edgy. I can't help but pick up on the vibes he gives out. Nervous energy that could explode into violence at any moment. He's never threatened me, or given me any real reason to be afraid of him, but the potential's always there.

'Fancy a few in Finch's tomorrow night?' he says.

'I'd love to, Danny, but I can't. I'm, sort of, grounded at the moment.

'What for?'

'Justine gave me an ultimatum after the last time.'

'What happened the last time?'

'I woke up in Islington.'

He stares at me quizzically, a strange grin forming.

'How come I never met your missus before?'

'No idea.'

'What's she like? Bit of a looker is she?'

I shrug, reddening under his glare.

'Come on, son, you can tell your uncle Danny.'

His eyes drill into mine, forcing me to look away. He's like a limpet, gleaning information he can use against you at a later date. The same tactics he used in the school playground.

'I nearly got married once,' he says casually. 'We lived together for about six months. Drove me fucking nuts she did.'

'I sympathise entirely.'

He stares at me in horror. 'Do what!'

'I just meant, I know what it's like. You know. Living with a woman and all that.'

He looks out over the Green, quiet, brooding.

'You'd tell me if Carla was seeing anyone, wouldn't you?'

'Yeah. Course I would.'

He sniffs equably. 'Good lad. Get the fags out then.'

We smoke in silence. I'm baffled by the sudden change in direction. Danny, the surrogate doctor, using the hands-on method to assess his patients needs, while filling them full of bullshit at the same time. All his expertise gleaned from drunken conversations and clandestine exchanges in pub toilets. He doesn't have a clue what I've been through.All the years of hard work, the struggle to get known. The disappointment at having only one hit single in the UK in ten years. And yet, in a strange way, he's a part of my world. I've come to rely on him for all the little extras that make life more bearable.

Reggae music pulses hypnotically beneath the Westway.

Danny settles back, amiably, hands behind his head.

'How long you back for then, Joe?'

'Not long. Few weeks maybe.'

'So where's it to next – California?'

'Possibly.'

'What's the gear like out there?'

'Depends where you go.'

He nods intently, as if he's caught me out in some basic dishonesty. For a minute, I'm somewhere else. San Diego's endless beachfront, white sand baking in the sun. Rimmer's first floor apartment with its art deco walls and polished wooden floors. My gradual introduction to a whole new set of people. An alternative lifestyle from which there is no return.

'What's it like?' Danny says.

I'm confused.

'Heroin?'

'California – you fucking knob.'

I reel off a few innocuous details to shut him up. Sunshine and palm trees. Air-conditioned bars and beautiful women. His avaricious grin slips, replaced by a distinct look of envy.

'Just remember your debts, Joe. Don't go taking advantage 'cause I've laid you on a few times.'

California's soon forgotten, as we enter another tense round of negotiation. It's like being vetted. Your future employer making sure you're the right candidate for the job. I'm overcome with shame. Sat here with a known drug dealer, when I should be at home with my wife and kids. The possibility I could be arrested, or seen by someone I know. The stigma.

A skinny kid comes strolling up the path, hands in the pockets of a black duffel coat. He sees us and changes direction. Danny calls out to him.

'Oi – Slugnut!'

The kid keeps walking. Danny lurches forward aggressively.

'Oi! … What am I black or what? … Come over here!'

The kid turns, reluctantly, and makes his way over. We watch his leisurely approach with interest. The dirty whites of his Converse trainers. The sullenness of his expression.

Danny looks him, casually, up and down.

'What's on, Slugnut?'

'Nothing much.'

'What you ignoring me for?'

'I wasn't.'

'Got that twenty spot you owe me?'

The kid's mouth drops. Danny laughs abruptly.

'Only joking, son. How's your sister – still working in Gateway, is she?'

'Not anymore. She got a job with the council.'

Danny turns to me avidly. 'Right goer, his sister. Suck your brains out through a straw. Ain't that right, Slugnut?'

'Fuck off, Danny.'

The kid stands mutely, head bowed, his long fringe hanging over one eye. Danny sits back, stunned by his audacity.

'What you reckon I should do, Joe?'

I study the plaintiff objectively. 'I think you should make an example, Danny.'

Danny nods thoughtfully, the trace of a smile. 'How much cash you got on you, Slugnut?'

'Not much.'

'Empty your pockets out.'

'Honestly, Danny, I hav – '

'I said empty your pockets out – now!'

The kid sniffs miserably and turns out his pockets, collecting loose change in the palm of his hand as proof.

'Got any fags on you?'

'Only a bit of baccy.'

'Come on then, let's have it.'

Cash and tobacco change hands. Danny looks up, the feudal landowner extracting forfeits from a serf.

'Anything else?'

'No.'

'You sure?' Danny points a finger. 'I find out you're lying, son, you'll be walking home with no shoes on.'

The kid grins stupidly then thinks better of it. Danny looks him up and down.

'How much that coat worth?'

The kid glances at his coat as if noticing it for the first time.

'Not much. Me mum bought it for me from the market.'

'Take it off.'

'What?'

'The coat – take if off.'

'Danny, I can't – '

'Don't fucking argue, knob-end – just take it off!'

The kid looks at me in the vain hope I'll intervene, but it's too late. Danny's gone beyond reasoning. Slowly, begrudgingly, he unbuttons the coat and hands it over. Pale skinny arms hang limply at his side.

Danny assesses the coat and dumps it on the bench next to him. 'Right. Now fuck off outta my sight, and don't come back.'

'What am I going to tell me mum?'

'Tell her what you like. Tell her to come round and see me one night, I'll give her the same I give your sister!'

Head down, the kid shuffles off, his white t-shirt and skinny arms a symbol of defeat. Danny lets him get as far as the path and yells out.

The kid stops and turns back. Danny throws the coat in his direction.

'Think I wanna be seen lugging that piece of shit around all afternoon? Go on – take it!'

The kid scoops up his coat and slips it back on with quiet dignity. Danny watches him go, smiling affectionately.

'Little cunt … Used to nick fags off me while I was shagging his sister.'

The kid heads forlornly towards the exit, relatively unscathed after his encounter with the brutal highwayman. Eddy Grant's *Electric Avenue* pumps out from under the Westway, a fitting enough soundtrack for his departure.

Danny sighs wearily. 'Oh well. Better make a move, I s'pose. Gotta pool tournament later.'

He stands, and cracks his knuckles, his previous good humour withdrawn.

'Come and see me in the Warwick in about half an hour. And

bring that forty quid.'

He starts to walk away and turns back.

'Don't make me take it out on your nose, son. I'd hate to ruin those good looks of yours!'

A trio of street drinkers appear from the lower entrance and amble over to the nearest vacant bench. They set out the afternoon's entertainment from a blue carrier bag. Two men and a woman with coarse, monotone voices, perfectly anaesthetised to the outside world. There's a certain fascination in watching what they do. The click of the ring-pull. The woman upending the can to her parched mouth. The men, dirty and unkempt, but possessed of a strange integrity, like soldiers back from a hard-fought campaign. Part of me wishes I was over there with them. Freed of all moral responsibility and things I don't want to do.

Alone among the fag butts and the empty crisp bags, I think about my future. New York seems a long way off. An impossibility. My whole career erased as if it never happened. Now I'm in even more debt. I'll have to max-out the credit card I've managed to keep hidden from Justine in order to pay Danny.

But there is a consolation. In an hour from now all these worries will be gone. Chased away by the smoke off the silver foil. A date with the magic dragon.

11

Moorcroft looks like Michael Caine in *Educating Rita*. The same rustic beard and suede jacket. Bleary eyes, hinting at late nights and chronic self-abuse. He's put on weight, too, since I last saw him. No longer the trim, athletic type, hustling for a place at the bar.

He greets me with a lopsided grin and sticks out a hand. 'Good to see you, Joe. Been a long time, fella.'

We shake hands firmly. I feel generous towards him, charitable even, in spite of my general aversion to interviews and previous record for standing him up. But I couldn't keep avoiding him. Justine went out of her way to re-schedule the meeting, so I'm expected to comply. He mentions the traffic, the onerous task it is to drive through central London with a dodgy tail light and a stiff neck. I remember his fondness for the scrum, that strange hankering some men have for wrestling a ball in inclement weather.

The young barman steps up, debonair in crimson waistcoat and black bow-tie. Moorcroft scans the optics, scratching his beard with indecision.

'What you having, Brian?'

'Er – sparkling mineral water, please.'

'Seriously?'

'I'm driving, fella.'

What happened to the Moorcroft of old? The lager-drinking raconteur who could sink twelve pints in a single session and still make room for a curry. Age and infirmity must have caught up with him at last.

We adjourn to the back bar, with it's smooth wood panelling and book-lined walls. I've never understood musicians who say they don't like hotels. Try sleeping in a Transit van for six weeks. Besides, hotels have a special place in the history of rock and roll. Countless acts of vandalism and debauchery have been recorded since it all began. Rock musicians are a pretty lame bunch these days. You can't imagine Phil Collins dropping a TV from the fifteenth floor of the Sheraton, or wheeling in hookers on a tea trolley. The whole scene has become sanitised. Now they're all up for Knighthoods and OBEs, queuing up to get a pat on the back from the Queen.

Moorcroft sinks his bulk into a plush leather chair and tries to relax. He stares at my glass with a raised eyebrow.

'What's that you're drinking, Joe?'

'Orange juice. I'm on a health kick. I buried a dead rat in the garden the other day and it nearly killed me.'

Frowning distractedly he takes out a notebook and pen. Moorcroft's always been morose and sardonic, not a man given to huge displays of emotion. Today he's looking older. Wisps of grey hair poke from the open collar of his shirt. Broken capillaries line his coarse red cheeks. With his untidy beard and hulking weight he looks more like a defeated Viking than the award winning music journalist he's supposed to be.

The Q & A begins. Moorcroft sips his mineral water, eyeing me cautiously.

'How's your family, Joe?'

'Fine, thanks.'

'How old's your daughter now – five, six?'

'Nine in a couple of weeks.'

'Really?' He shakes his head in wonder. 'Christ. Where's the time go, eh?

Inching forward in the chair, he switches into journalist mode. You can almost see the transition. The strange light shining in his watery eyes. The harnessing of some primeval force deep inside.

'So what's the story, Joe? You seemed to have slipped off the radar lately.'

'I'm taking time out for a while.'

'From the band?'

'Yeah. It's a kind of, sabbatical, if you know what I mean.'

He nods vaguely, rolling the pen between his fingers. I'm not sure how much he does know, but it's unnerving. A game we're playing, where he has an unfair advantage. And all the time I'm sitting here like a dummy, waiting for him to make the first move, knowing that whatever I say could end up in print.

'Goldstein issued a press release saying you wouldn't be with the band on this tour. Can you say anything about that?'

'It's still under negotiation.'

'But they're using a stand-in at the moment, is that right?'

'Apparently. No one bothered mentioning it to me though.'

He scribbles a few words in his notebook and looks thoughtful. The old style journalism, drinking and hanging out with musicians, gaining insight into the lifestyle so he can write it up later for the fans. As résumés go, Moorcroft's is pretty impressive. Bob Dylan. Hendrix. The Stones. Most of the big names over the last three decades. It's his style, I suppose. His ability to put you at ease, regardless of what ends up on paper.

'Remember the last conversation we had?' he says, the grin on his face strangely unnerving.

'Which one?'

'You phoned me from a pub a few weeks ago. Ranting about the state of the British music scene. The pretentious wankers living in Notting Hill.'

'Did I?'

His grin broadens. 'You said some other stuff too. Unprintable, mostly. I guessed you'd had a skinful at the time.'

I'm horrified. One more potentially damaging lapse in self control. This terrible habit I've picked up lately of calling people up after a few drinks and having conversations I can't remember. Hugh Hanley's apoplexy at the bill I ran up in Paris last year (which even exceeded the bar bill by two-hundred pounds!) Justine, barring me from using the landline after nine o'clock at night after the last statement came through, my random broadcasts itemised all over it.

Moorcroft finds it all amusing, but he has no idea what I've been through. The trauma of losing my job. Humiliating run-ins with the doctor to placate Justine. Only pride keeps me from falling apart completely. The knowledge that whatever else transpires, I'm still someone of note. Joe E Byron – Indie Guitarist of the Year, two years running. The guy who penned Alright By Me, our highest entry on the US Billboard. And the chisel-jawed hustler who stripped to the waist in an advert for Russian vodka that flickered briefly over Times Square.

'How's your acting career? Anything come of that?'

'I've had a few offers. Cameo roles. Walk-on parts. Nothing I really want to get involved in.'

'You played a vampire junkie once, didn't you?' His eyes glint mischievously. 'Do much research for the role?'

'Funny you should mention it, Brian, but no, I didn't actually.'

My brief excursion into the world of film making, over before it began. I couldn't stand it anyway. Having to be on set at five in the morning, standing around in the cold for hours on end. All the luvvies droning on about their agents and who'd been in Rep. But the reviews were good. I had *the look,* they said. I had talent. Charisma.

He mentions the new album. I'm not sure how much I should give away, uncomfortable with the questioning. Do I admit that I was unhappy with the production, the artwork for the cover? Moorcroft's a journalist. He's trained to look for nuances and body language. If I look too cagey or ill at ease, he's sure to write it up and everyone will know how I'm feeling.

'I wanted to use other musicians on certain songs, to give the album a different feel. But that idea got vetoed.'

'What was it like working with Scott Levine?'

'It was, different.'

'In what way?'

'We didn't have the same freedom as before. We had to be more disciplined. More focused.

'Didn't you tell Sian Moore there'd been arguments about the sound right the way through?'

'I don't remember saying that, Brian.'

He sits back, chewing the end of his pen.

'What about the rumours that have been going around? That you were dropped from the tour because you were unreliable?'

'Who said that?'

He smiles vaguely. 'Is it true?'

Now Moorcroft's revealed his hand, we don't have to go through this evasive bullshit anymore. I tell him my version of the call from the lawyer representing the Management Group. Justine's attempts to get me reinstated. The basic injustice of the whole thing that's left me sitting at home doing nothing.

'You pulled out of the tour because of illness?' he says, surprised.

'That's right.'

'Do you mind me asking what it was?'

'Some kind of virus, I think. I'm on a course of antibiotics as we speak.'

He taps the pen against his lower lip, frowning. Right now I could use a drink, a little livener to help me cope with this tedious ordeal. Nearly three weeks off the booze and I'm still feeling nervous and edgy. Even in a place like this, surrounded by music and cuisine and all these well-heeled geriatrics enjoying their retirement.

The last of the heroin I scored from Danny is gone. All burned off on the silver foil. I can't believe his attitude. His refusal to supply me with more on moral grounds, like some twisted social worker. What kind of a dealer is that?

'Drink, Brian?'

'Er – No, I'll stick with this thanks.'

The barman's guileless face implies discretion. He knows how to look after his clientele without betraying their identities or their drinking habits. Maybe the harassed waitress has told him who I am. Famous musician in exile, forced to hang out in these salubrious places.

'Same again, sir?'

'Minus the mineral water, thanks.'

I can almost taste the alcohol. The closer you get to the pumps and the optics, the greater the lure. It's a visceral thing.

The smell of paint to an artist. The perfumed kiss to a lover. Only will power and the threat of divorce papers stops me from giving in completely.

'See that bloke over there?' I point Moorcroft out to the barman. 'The one with the beard and the dodgy jacket?'

The barman nods, intrigued.

'He once downed a bottle of tequila and went swimming in Hampstead Pond – in November.'

'Who is he?'

'He's a dinosaur. A throwback to the sixties. I'm helping him remember where he was when Janis Joplin died. But keep it under your hat or they'll all want a piece of him.'

Orange juice in hand, I ease back into my seat. Moorcroft watches me solemnly, his bulk wedged into the red leather chair. An air of brooding melancholy clings to him, visible in the myriad lines in his face. He stares at my drink quizzically.

'Didn't have you down as a small ships man, Joe.'

'What's that?'

'Uncle of mine in the merchant navy, liked a drop. Got a ninety-nine year ban working on anything with a bar onboard. Didn't stop him drinking though. Took six coppers to get him out the George one night. Old bugger was seventy at the time.'

The story lightens the mood a little, but Moorcroft's scrutiny makes me wary. Music journalists are a different breed. No wonder they don't figure highly in popularity polls.Like wolves, you never know when they're going to turn on you and savage your name in print.

He clears his throat and gazes at me inscrutably. The spark of something remotely ambitious gleams in his pale blue eyes.

'Alright if I ask you a few personal questions?'

'Sure. Fire away.'

'James T made a reference to your drug problem a while ago. Can you tell me about that?'

'I don't have a drug problem.'

'But you went into rehab a couple of years ago, didn't you?'

'For a rest, yeah. I was suffering from exhaustion when we came back from Hungary.'

He scratches his head, nonplussed. 'Why would James T make a statement like that if it wasn't true?'

'You tell me, Brian. Why'd he wear pink leather trousers to the Brit Awards? Why'd he put a *T* in his fucking name?'

Moorcroft swallows this simple truth without comment. I'm surprised at his naivety. How could anyone trust the claims of a man who wears leotards and feather boas, convinced he's the next Freddie Mercury?

'What happened on the last tour of the States? Didn't you have to pull out three dates from the end because of health problems?'

My memories of that time are sketchy. We'd been on the go for months, playing festivals and arenas all over Europe, supporting bands we were basically blowing off the stage. America came at the wrong time, a huge and costly venture dreamed up by the new management when we'd have been better off staying at home. I give Moorcroft the condensed version of events and await the next question.

'What about the documentary Cy Bender made that caused so much trouble? The scene where you're openly talking about using heroin.'

'I don't remember that.'

'But you must have seen it, surely?'

'Sure. I watched it once or twice. It wasn't an accurate depiction of life on the road. More like Cy Bender's home movie he could show all his friends. A lot of things were taken out of context.'

The scene in question bugs me to this day. Backstage after a gig in Memphis. The band in varying states of exhaustion, like athletes after an arduous track event. Bender, the irritatingly pretentious film-school graduate and supposed fan. Master of those long, tracking shots of dimly-lit corridors and people staring vacantly out of windows.

The interview segment was worse. I let my guard down at the wrong moment. One casual remark that should have been edited out and the bastard left it in, knowing it would cause controversy as soon as it came out.

'You know what it's like on the road, Brian. Things get exaggerated. Once you get a reputation it stays with you whether you deserve it or not.'

'So you didn't have a problem?'

'No more than anyone else. I just ended up the scapegoat. And that's the truth.'

The opulence of the hotel bar brings back exactly how much I've lost. Here I am, rehashing the details of a sordid life, when I should be writing songs and performing, finding different ways to enhance my career.

'Let's talk a bit about Hugh Hanley. It's no secret the two of you didn't get on. I wondered if that had anything to do with you being dropped from the tour?'

'Look – can we stop all this talk about me being *dropped*, Brian. I told you. I was ill and had to cancel the flight to New York.'

'But there were tensions between the two of you, weren't there?'

'Yes, there were.'

'Can I ask why?'

'Well, basically he's a selfish asshole with no consideration for anyone but himself.' The statement's out before I can retract it. Moorcroft's eyes glint with a perverse kind of pleasure. He takes a few seconds to savour the moment before launching his next attack.

'Is it true he employed a minder to watch you while you were in New Mexico?'

'No, it isn't.'

'So that was just a rumour as well then?'

'I did go missing once, but the tour manager came and found me. All that minder stuff was invented by James T to make me look bad in the press.'

Moorcroft makes a few notes, scratches his beard and looks up.

'Wasn't there an allegation of some sort against Hugh Hanley?'

'Which one?'

'That he withheld the news your mum was in hospital so the tour could continue?'

'That's right.'

'He really did that?'

'Yeah, he did. I don't know why you're so surprised, Brian. He was pulling stunts like that all the time.'

The true nature of my resentment against Hanley remains unspoken. Sure, his contribution to our success can't be underestimated, I accept that. Without his influence, we might still be playing pubs and small clubs. But his blitzkrieg mentality clashed with everything. As an artist, I found it impossible to grow. My energy, my creativity, even my willingness to go on stage night after night, stifled by the man's gross insensibility.

His behaviour around my mum was appalling. I didn't realise until we got to Milan, where I had a message to call my sister. The shock of finding out she'd been in hospital for three days and he knew all about it almost finished me there and then. One more example of the utter ruthlessness of the man. I knew then that he was capable of anything.

Moorcroft sips his mineral water. The broken blood vessels in his cheeks stand out like grid lines on a map.

'Tell me about your relationship with James T?'

'What d'you want to know?'

'The songwriting partnership. How did that come about?'

'I wrote most of the songs on the first four albums. He just came up with a few ideas.'

'But the credits were Cochran/Byron, weren't they?'

'That was part of the reason I left. I wanted more recognition.'

'I thought you pulled out through illness?'

'Same difference, Brian.'

His constant snipes at my leaving are becoming tedious.

The truth is, if I hadn't been kicked out I'd have left anyway. Either that or murdered James T in a fit of outrage.

'How did this thing with the initials come about?' Was that a marketing ploy, or something you all came up with?'

'That was Cochran's idea. I think we were in Scandinavia or somewhere. He started calling himself James T Cochran.Then he dropped the surname altogether and insisted on using the T version from then on.'

'What does the T stand for?'

'Twat, probably.'

Moorcroft laughs softly, the first genuine sign of humour since we've met. He jots something in his pad and looks up. 'You two were so close at one point. What happened?'

'I got tired of listening to him moaning about his girlfriend. His hair. How he was going to sell all his possessions and live in Japan.'

The truth is a little different, but it hurts too much to go into detail. James T was the best friend I ever had. We did everything together. Took the same drugs, slept with the same women. Then something happened to change all that.The takeover bid by Warner. The sudden influx of cash after signing to a major label. Who wouldn't be overwhelmed? But success has its downside. Egos clash all the time. Overnight, you become this media-hogging tyrant, expecting everyone to jump to your every command.

We move on to Kurt Cobain's recent brush with mortality in Rome. Moorcroft looks genuinely touched, recalling all the artists he's known who burned out on the road.

'Remember Roskilde in '87?' he says gravely.

'Vaguely. Was I there?'

'Oh, you were there all right. I came and interviewed you backstage after the gig. Don't you remember?'

My memory of the event is hazy. Teenagers with face paint and silly hats. Torrential rain on the Saturday afternoon before we came on. I don't recall Moorcroft even being there.

'So what did I say that was so memorable?'

He smiles faintly, shaking his head. 'It wasn't so much what you said. It was how you looked. There were a few people concerned about you that day, fella, I can promise you.'

Roskilde, a brief pit-stop on a frantic tour of Europe. Part of Hugh Hanley's plan to take us to the stars and beyond. I'm embarrassed to think that Moorcroft's recollections of the event are clearer than mine.

'That was a bad year for me, Brian. I kept getting these chest infections and headaches. I was on all kinds of different medication at the time.'

He shifts in the chair, eyeing me solemnly. 'When you first came on the scene, I thought you were one of the best bands around. I really did. You had it all. The look. The music. But I saw the mess you were in that day, fella. No wonder they were taking bets you wouldn't make it past thirty.'

The waitress sweeps by with a distracted smile. I wonder what she makes of Moorcroft and me, enjoying a little tête-à-tête in the cosy back bar like father and son.

I drain my glass and set it down firmly on the table.

'Well – as you can see, Brian, I've cleaned up my act now. I've even got myself a personal trainer and we workout three times a week. How's that for dedication?'

He smiles dubiously. I can't resist the urge to rib him a bit more.

'So what's next for you – retirement?'

He laughs. 'I doubt that very much. I've been asked to write a book, actually.'

'What kind of book?'

'Sort of, memoir, if you like. A look back at all the chaos I've been involved in over the last thirty years.'

'Will I be in it?'

He grins slyly. 'Who knows. Who knows what'll come up when I sit down to write the thing.'

The notebook snaps shut.

'Well, it's been good talking to you, Joe. I'll keep you posted. Let you know when the article's coming out.'

We shake hands, Moorcroft taller than me and considerably wider, but lacking vitality. The watery eyes and weary manner give him that ground down, beaten look. Perhaps writing a book will suit him during his retirement, stuck on some lonely, deserted sheep farm in Wales, tapping away on an old typewriter.

His battered Citroen pulls away from the forecourt, trailing a buckled number plate and a bulbous tow-bar. Sadness descends. Moorcroft represents music and bright lights, the realisation of

a dream that's turned sour. One more part of my life that's gone
forever.

12

Alice calls one sunny afternoon. We sit in the garden and watch the kids play – the two of them like sworn enemies forced to share the same space. One of the drawbacks of being a child, you forfeit your basic human rights – even to your own toys.

Justine looks on anxiously, ready to intervene. 'Let Ben play with your Power Ranger, please, Jake. There's a good boy.'

Jake stands his ground, resistant to any form of coercion. I'm on his side. Why should he give up his prized star-fighter to some snot-nosed kid in dungarees?

Alice is buzzing with some great news she can't wait to share with us. We hover expectantly, bathed in her radiant smile, while the kids fool around on the lawn pretending to be space cowboys.

'Come on then!' Justine says impatiently. 'What is it?'

Alice looks over coyly. 'Well, I was going to tell you earlier, but … We're engaged!'

'Oh, my God! That's fantastic!'

We delight in the good news, as if nothing like this has ever happened before. But Alice does look fabulous, even to my jaundiced eyes, the prospect of marital bliss giving her an enviable glow.

'Come on then,' Justine says excitedly. 'let's see the ring!'

Alice splays her fingers obligingly, beaming with delight. I should have married her instead. We share the same sense of humour. The same love of Chinese food. I hope she's happy with her new man, Mark, I really do, even if he is an opinionated arsehole who sells property in Knightsbridge and drives a second hand Porsche.

She sits back eyeing me with affection.

'You're quiet today, Joe.'

'He's sulking,' Justine says. 'We're going to my mum's later and he doesn't want to go.'

Alice frowns mockingly. 'Not hungover again are you, Joe?'

'He's stopped drinking.'

'Really! What brought that on?'

'I gave him an ultimatum, basically. Stop disappearing for days on end or find another hotel.'

They talk about me as if I'm not there, experts on the shortcomings of the male race. The kids circle each other warily on the grass, looking for the unfair advantage.

'How's your sister, Joe?' Alice says.

'Fine.'

'How would you know?' Justine scowls. 'You haven't been round there in ages.'

One more guilt trip to hit me with when I'm least expecting it. Terry's funeral, a day I'd rather forget. Shaz, almost speechless with grief. Justine having a go at me for getting creamed in the hotel bar after.

'How old was Terry when he died?' Alice says.

'Forty-four, I think.'

'God. So young. Shaz must have been devastated.'

'He wasn't too happy about it either.'

'Joe!' Alice says, feigning shock. 'That's a terrible thing to say.'

The truth is, Terry's death affected me as much as it did anyone. To see someone go from a healthy thirteen-stone down to nine in less than a year isn't a pleasant experience, whichever way you look at it. Months of chemo and heavy medication. Constant trips to the hospital for more tests. God knows how he managed to hold on as long as he did.

'Isn't Shaz a bit ... religious?' Alice says awkwardly. The question hangs in the air like an accusation. Justine tries to explain, how Shaz turned to the church when Terry died. All the community projects she became involved in that helped her through the grieving process. I'm embarrassed. Like admitting you're related to a child molester or an alien, someone operating well outside the socially-accepted norm.

'She must be lost without him,' Alice says. Justine murmurs her agreement, a hint of sadness in her voice.

'The kids loved him. He used to take Sadie and Kayla ice skating in Muswell Hill. Nothing was ever too much for him.' She looks witheringly at me. 'Unlike some people.'

We share a moment's deep and utter loathing. Two people who've forgotten what it's like to have a normal conversation. In company we present a different image, our quarrels restricted to a kind of semi-humorous banter that onlookers might mistake for affection. In private we're estranged, rarely in the same room. And yet something remains to keep us together.

Ben shuffles over, tearfully, and dumps his head in Alice's lap.'

'Oh, what's the matter, darling?' she says soothingly.

'Jake hit me with a stick!'

Justine leaps up out of the chair and makes for Jake, who drops the offending weapon and backs off. The noise level rises accordingly. Soon I'll be sat in an armchair at Miriam's, listening to Eric droning on about cricket, or the new car he's just bought. I wish I had a drink, a few pills. Some form of mild anaesthetic.

Jake is suitably admonished and peace returns. Alice talks Yoga. All the different postures, as demonstrated by the George Clooney look-alike who runs the class in Notting Hill. Naturally, I'm excluded from the conversation, but that doesn't stop me from feeling superior in a smug kind of way. Exercise, the biggest myth of all. One more pointless activity dreamt up by scientists studying heart attacks in middle aged men. The benefits are hugely overrated anyway. Who wants to run round the block three times a week just to earn a few more years washing the dishes.

'Well, I must say I'm feeling pretty good at the moment,' Alice says agreeably. 'I'm eating all the right food. Getting to bed reasonably early. I've even given up alcohol – apart from the odd glass of wine now and then.'

Justine can't resist the opportunity to bring up my recent debacle in Islington. Alice can't hide her amusement.

'How did you manage that, Joe?'

'I don't know. I can't remember much about it.'

'I take it that means you won't be coming camping with us, then?'

'You'd better ask Justine. She's the one who makes all the plans around here.'

'I've got no problem with him going.' Justine snaps. 'It's whether he could stay away from all his precious friends that long. He spends more time at Carla's than he does here.'

Justine looks over, humourlessly, her dislike of Carla overshadowed by her ongoing resentment of me. Maybe I'm too much like my dad. The restless spirit, unable to settle down. Always on the road with his jazz-playing cronies. Justine can't accept it, her boring, middle class upbringing dominating everything. I grew up in a house filled with artists, poets and jazz musicians. Parties at weekends that sometimes went on for days on end. Even with all the chaos and the upheaval, the place was never less than completely alive.

That's something she can't understand. When you've had that level of freedom as a child, rules and regulations are unbearable.

'Jake – put that stick down NOW!'

Justine rises to break up a minor dispute in the middle of the garden. The two protagonists tussle like mini gladiators, watched by a partisan crowd. Traumatised by the noise, I rise wearily and head for the house.

'Two sugars, please!' Alice calls cheerfully. 'Good to see you've been domesticated at last. You'll have to come round my place and wait on me.'

Jake chases me up the garden with his stick. What happened to the sensitivity I've tried to encourage in my children? The love of poetry and books?

'Jake. If that stick hits me …'

'*Ha Ha*!'

'I'm warning you.'

'*Hee Hee*!'

The world is a bad place. You only have to look at your children to know it isn't getting any better. The worse ones graduate from pulling wings off flies to taking out insurgents with laser-guided missiles. It's all in the blueprint. The DNA.

*

A glass of freshly squeezed orange juice sits before me on the worktop. I stare at it begrudgingly and imagine it laced with vodka. No-man's land. The awful place you end up in when your favourite anaesthetic's been taken away.

Sadie roots in the cupboard looking for crisps. She finds a pack of Cheesy Wotsits and leans against the worktop, watching me with all-knowing eyes.

'*We're* going camping with Alice,' she says.

'Yes, I know you are.'

'*You're* not though.'

I stare at her in disbelief. 'What is this – gang up on fathers day?'

She shrugs, crunching a Wotsit. I'm intrigued by the insurrection, the way they've all got together secretly to ease me out of the frame.

'Don't you want me to go?'

Silence.

'I'll stay at home with the cat, shall I? Live on baked beans and peanut butter sandwiches.'

She ponders the inside of the crisp packet, unimpressed. 'Can we go to the pub on the way back from Nanny Miriam's?'

Amazed at her front, I hold up the glass dramatically.

'D'you know what this is, Sadie?'

'Orange juice.'

'That's right. I've been drinking it for the last three weeks, in case you hadn't noticed. D'you know what pubs are for?'

'What?'

'Sanctuaries for people like me to get away from boring old relics like Miriam and Eric. And shitty campsites with no hot and cold running water where you have to walk two and a half miles to find a toilet. So the answer is no. We can't go to the pub on the way back from Nanny Miriam's.'

*

Justine comes in with a tub of clothing and squats down by the washing machine. Thin white knickers peek seductively above the waistline of her jeans. For a moment I'm transfixed, forced to consider manual relief as an alternative to the bedroom.

'There's a letter for you on the hall table,' she says.

'Who from?'

'How the hell should I know? Open it and find out.'

Irrational fear grips me. More demands from credit-card companies. Threatening letters from building society managers for loans I took out ages ago with no intention of paying back.

Tearing open the envelope reveals a far worse ordeal. I scan the contents with a rising anxiety. At the top in ominous black letters is C.O.D.A.T. – Community Outreach Drug and Alcohol Team.

Justine appears beside me.

'What is it?'

'Call-up papers from the Foreign Legion. Have a look yourself.'

She reads quietly, absorbed by the results of her own handiwork. Dropping the letter to her side, she fixes me with a look of pure victory.

'That's it, then.'

'I'm not going.'

'Oh yes you are.'

'Why? I mean, what's the point? I can sort myself out, can't I?'

'How many times have you said that? How many times have you stood there and swore blind you're going to change?'

'But I have changed! I'm not drinking, am I?'

'You're going and that's the end of it.' She yells upstairs to Jake and Sadie. 'Get your coats on, we're leaving in five minutes!'

You'd think she'd be grateful for all the effort I've put in lately. The ordeal of meeting Brian Moorcroft in the Park hotel – sober! What else does she want from me?

She grabs her bag and heads for the door, throwing me a backward glance.

'I haven't mentioned any of this to mum. You seeing a counsellor, she'll only start worrying.'

'You mean she doesn't want a degenerate for a son-in-law in case the neighbours find out. That's more like it.'

'That isn't what she thinks at all. Are you driving or am I?'

'You can.'

'Right. Let's all try and be civilised for once, shall we?'

I find a small lump of hash in my jacket pocket. Enough to roll a joint when I come back from Miriam's. Maybe my luck's about to change. A comet will strike the earth and cancel out all future appointments. Hugh Hanley will fall through a great big hole in the ground.

Whatever happens, there's always Danny. And if he won't come up with the goods I'll ask around. The streets are awash with the stuff. The whole damn city, crying out for relief.

Oblivion.

13

304 is a beat-up old doorway between a jewellers and a cake shop. The sign behind the frosted glass has an obscure logo and a brief rundown of the opening hours. I press the buzzer and wait. Two teenage girls catch my eye and I turn away, ashamed at being caught outside such a sordid place.

'Hello?'

The female voice on the intercom rescues me from further embarrassment. I mumble my name and the time of my appointment and step inside. Muffled voices at the top suggest a busy working space, perhaps an office. There's even a tall pot plant at the top of the stairs with thick, green leaves.

I'm halfway up and a thin, middle-aged woman appears. She looks down at me with a curious half-smile, as if my turning up is part of an amusing private joke.

'Who's your appointment with, please?'

'Val Moody.'

'And just remind me who you are again?'

'Joe Byron.'

She motions me through to a room at the end of the landing that smells of fresh paint. 'Take a seat in there, Joe. Val will be with you shortly.'

The room is fairly Spartan – a few chairs, a bookcase and a portable TV. The window faces onto the main road, the only means of escape should you be traumatised enough to jump.

I sit and wait.

Posters line the walls. A consumer guide to illicit substances, from cannabis to crack cocaine. I tick them off mentally, one by one, an instant reminder of dingy bed-sits, hotel rooms and backstage parties all over the world. Relapse Prevention looks even more ominous, a swirl of circles and arrows making some complex theoretic point. The trick must be to learn this stuff verbatim, so when you're tested by the examiner you'll have all the right answers. *'Mr Byron – for a possible ten points – what are the effects of benzodiazapine on the central nervous system after consuming a litre of vodka?'*

My natural cynicism kicks in. These places are for losers, perfectly suited to rehab because of their low self esteem. For whatever reason, they've dropped out of the system. Lost the ability to look after themselves, the desire to integrate with other people.

'Ah – there you are!'

I sit upright. Standing in the doorway is a large, jovial-looking woman, mid to late forties, with short white hair. She puts out a plump, ringed hand and we shake hands formally.

'Sorry you had to wait, Joe. I'm Val Moody.'

'Nice to meet you, Val.'

'Can I get you a tea, coffee?'

'Er – no, I'm fine, thanks.'

'Won't take a minute? Kettle's just boiled?'

Reluctantly, I accept, and she wanders off along the corridor, leaving me with a view of her formidable behind.

The urge to run comes over me. Flee this strange place and get back out on the streets again. These people aren't for real. What can Val Moody possibly know about *my* problems? The closest she's been to a hard drug is the flu jab she had last Christmas! I don't need her help. I don't need anyone's help. The whole thing's a big misunderstanding, cooked up by Justine to wear down my resistance.

Val comes back with a bright red mug of coffee and a large white folder tucked under one arm.

'There you go,' she says warmly. 'Hope it's not too strong.'

The door clicks shut and we're alone with the drug posters and the muted traffic. She sinks into the chair facing me and lays the folder on her lap with an audible sigh. For a moment her energy seems to flag. I get a glimpse of her workload, the huge responsibility she faces dealing with people like me.

'Welcome to C.O.D.A.T., Joe. Any idea what we do here?'

'Not really.'

'OK. Let me give you some background details before we start the assessment.'

Her smile is pleasant, almost cherubic, in a heavily made-up face She reminds me of an aunt who used to beam down at me when I was a kid, anointing me with lipstick kisses and eau de cologne.

She flicks through the first few pages of the folder, reciting health and safety regulations before moving on. C.O.D.A.T., she informs me, breezily, is an organisation set up to help those with addiction problems. The ethos is friendly and non-invasive, offering the client practical and emotional support to ease them back into society. Therapy groups run several times a week, including a course on anger management and learning to be assertive.

'Any questions?' she says with a smile.

'These groups – are they compulsory?'

'None of the services we provide are compulsory. All our clients are here on a voluntary basis and can leave at any time.'

'So I could walk out now?'

She laughs politely. 'Well, you could, but I hope it won't come to that.'

The room is stifling. You can almost imagine desperate clients crashing headlong through the glass to escape the interrogation.

'Any chance you could open a window, please?'

'Of course. Don't want you passing out before we get started, do we?'

She rattles the top opener and a current of fresh air lifts the net curtain. Sinking back into the chair, she fixes me with the same reassuring smile.

'So. How do you feel about being here today, Joe?'

The classic opening gambit to put suspects under pressure. Gazing at the window, I think about my response. Danny always says deny everything. Stick to a pre-planned story they can't break down. The old criminal mantra, repeated over and over. *I didn't do it. I wasn't there.* Danny's issues are usually with the police, but I'm sure the principle could be applied just as easily here.

'My wife referred me, actually. I came along to please her.'

Her smile fades. The faintly condescending look she gives me confirms my naiveté. 'Well I hope that won't stop you considering what we have on offer.'

I shrug, vaguely, enjoying the role play. We're on good terms here, me and Val, having this cosy little chat about my future with the breeze blowing in and the smell of fresh paint.She looks highly efficient too, in her blue serge jacket and starched white blouse. Like an umpire for a bowls tournament.She's probably dealt with hundreds of cases like mine. Serial relapsers looking for the get-out clause.

She turns a page in the folder.

'Have you had any form of treatment before?'

'Couple of years ago.'

'Where was that?'

'Somewhere in Kent. I was kicked out after two weeks, for smoking a joint in one of the bedrooms.' I get a perverse pleasure from relaying the details, watching her face for a reaction.

She nods slowly, her puffy cheeks reddening with either embarrassment or the warmth of the room. After a long pause she closes the folder and sits back, eyeing me carefully.

'Why don't you tell me a bit about yourself, Joe?'

'What d'you want to know?'

'Anything you like. How about your family?'

Talking about the kids seems reasonable enough. If Justine was here, she could fill in the details about missed birthdays and ruined school holidays. The piss-poor state of my track record at home. But Justine's not here. Instead it's me, forced to defend myself to some woman I've never met before.

Talking about my family opens up difficult areas. I grow bolder and allude to the problems of married life, having a changeable income and a job that takes me away for long periods. Bitterness creeps in. Morbid reflection over what could have been.

'What did you do before you were married?'

'I was in a band.'

'Really? What kind of band?'

'Indie rock, I suppose you'd call it. We made a few albums. Toured the States. That kind of thing.'

'My goodness. Quite successful, then?'

'We could have been bigger. The management let us down in the end. That and the singer, who turned into a complete asshole – excuse my French.'

Her passive smile is strangely off-putting, completely ignoring the scale of my resentment. Years on the pub circuit, honing my craft, to have it all squandered by a *prima donna* frontman who thought he was the next Jim Morrison, and a coke-fiend manager who lost sight of his vision.

'Did you stop playing when you got married?'

'No?'

'Sorry, I just thought – '

'It's my job, my livelihood. It's all I've ever done. I did have to stop recently because of health problems, but it's only temporary. I'll be back, soon as I'm feeling better.'

'I see. And how does that affect your family?'

'How does what affect them?'

'Well, I presume you're away a lot?'

'Quite a lot, yeah.'

'I wondered how they felt about it.'

'I don't know, I never asked them.'

She frowns, as bemused as I am. 'Well, you must have had quite a time. The music business is well known for its excesses, isn't it?'

'You could say that.'

'Plenty of opportunities to give in to temptation.'

'If you're that way inclined.'

'But you're not.'

'No comment.'

She chuckles, indulgently, to herself. 'I have a nephew who loves music. He's just been to see Oasis at the Hippodrome. Is that your kind of thing?'

'Not really. I'm more into Hardcore Techno at the moment.'

She nods meaningfully. 'So, your career's on hold for a while, is it?'

'I'm taking a break at the moment. Kind of in transition, 'til we get a few things sorted out.'

'I see.'

She doesn't see at all. Being in a band is like being married. You're with each other all the time. The smallest and most innocuous character traits get magnified out of all proportion, especially when you're on the road. That's why bands break-up.

'Sometimes it's hard to adjust.'

'To what?'

'Life in general.'

'Can you expand on that?'

'Well, normal things like shopping and paying bills. Taking the kids to school. I never had to do any of that stuff before. I always had someone do it for me.'

'What – a sort of housekeeper, you mean?'

'No. My wife. Justine. She does everything.'

The more questions she asks, the harder it is to be truthful. My glamorous life on the road, overshadowed by too many bad memories, things I'd rather not talk about. Val's nice enough, but she's a complete stranger. And the fact she has my case history balanced on her lap puts an even bigger barrier between us.

'Is your coffee OK?' she says.

'Fine, thanks.'

'We did have a pack of chocolate biscuits lying around the office somewhere, but I think Sarah ate the last one. Sorry.'

She tells me about a job she had years ago, working with underprivileged children, and how sad she felt when she left. I can relate this to my own situation in a way. Being separated from something you love, from the people you've spent half your life with. Ending up sidelined and eased out of the picture by people who don't have a clue.

A sudden thought occurs to me. 'Er – is everything I say in here confidential?'

'Yes, of course.'

'You don't write up lots of notes my wife gets to see?'

'Oh, goodness, no. The only notes I make are for office use only. Nothing breaches your client confidentiality, I can assure you.'

She tells me about a former 'client', careful not to reveal his name. Some luckless reprobate who set up his own cleaning business after years of chronic drug abuse. I relax. Val Moody isn't the monster I thought she'd be. She even seems to care about these reformed clients of hers, who've turned their lives around with a little help from the drug and alcohol team. It's actually quite relaxing, sitting here drinking coffee, listening to her prattling on. But you have to remember where you are. These seemingly kind and considerate people are all part of the same conspiracy.

'You said you had to stop because of health problems,' she says cautiously. 'Was that in any way related to the job you do?'

'Kind of.'

'Was it anything in particular?'

'I got rundown from touring non-stop. Kept picking up chest infections and stuff.'

'I see.'

She gazes at me serenely, her whole demeanour free of antagonism of any kind. I'm tempted to open up a bit more, and fall willingly into her neat little trap. At least give the appearance of being gullible – something I'm not.

'I suffer from insomnia. I come home from a tour and sit up all night trying to unwind. It's OK for the first couple of nights, then it starts to get tedious.'

'Do you take anything to relax?'

'I used to take sleeping tablets, but Justine put a stop to it. We had this, sort of, disagreement over the dosage.'

She nods reassuringly.

'What about alcohol?'

'I don't drink.'

'Oh, I thought – '

'I stopped a while ago. I haven't had a drink for nearly four weeks now.'

'I see.' She looks baffled. 'Is that something you do regularly – stopping?'

The trick question, thrown in to confuse me. I take my time answering.

'Yeah, I suppose it is.'

'But you always start again?'

'Well, I do. But then I stop again whenever I want to. I don't feel it's that much of a problem, really.'

'And what's the longest you've gone without?'

I cross my legs and fidget uncomfortably. Her tone has a bland insistence that's hard to ignore.

'Six months or so.'

'And how did you feel?'

'Fine. No problems at all.'

She changes tack again, back to the successful clients who've turned their lives around. This girl who came off alcohol and drugs and is now a trainee counsellor. The man with the cleaning business, who seems to be a personal favourite of hers and can do no wrong. She talks with great pride at their achievements, as if they're members of her own family.

One word keeps coming up again and again. I remember it from my brief stay in Kent. An awful word that conjures up images of penitents in austere monasteries, living on bread and water.

'Sorry – did you say *abstinence*?'

'That's right. Many of our clients have long-term addiction problems. Staying clean is vitally important if they're to make any progress at all.'

'What about weed?'

'Sorry?'

'Cannabis.'

'Not unless it's prescribed by a doctor.'

I think on this. The huge void in my life that would be left by the absence of drugs and alcohol.

'I couldn't do it.'

'You couldn't do what?'

'Give everything up. I'd go mad, slowly.'

She smiles, humouring me. 'No one's asking you to do anything, Joe. This is an assessment, that's all. Let's deal with one thing at a time, shall we?'

She watches me with the same empathic look, always restrained and professional. I wonder about her home life. The doting husband and quiet nights in by the TV. Dreams of retirement where they'll grow old together and travel the country with walking boots and flasks of tea.

'What does your wife think about you coming here?'

'It was her idea in the first place. Personally, I think it's a scam to get me to do more housework, but I could be wrong.'

She clasps her hands on the folder and looks at me intently.

'Have you been married long?'

'Eight years this July.'

'Well, at least you remembered the date. I've given up expecting my husband to remember our anniversary. I have to drop little hints a few days before and he still forgets.'

I smile vaguely, my eye drawn to the drug charts on the wall. Syringes and pills. Tar-stained foil and heaps of white powder.

'Do you like cooking?'

'Sorry?'

She hands me a flyer with the C.O.D.A.T. acronym stamped at the top.

'We run a drop-in centre at St Anthony's on a Saturday afternoon. There's table tennis and Pool. And a decent size kitchen. Call in and see us sometime, if you like.'

The flyer looks innocent enough, apart from the venue being a Catholic church hall. Perhaps the whole thing's a front for religion, and Val is really a Christian Fundamentalist, looking for converts.

Saturdays are out, I tell her. We always take the kids to Justine's parents for the afternoon. Privately, I'm dubious about the whole thing. The drop-in centre sounds like a soup kitchen for down-and-outs, not the place for a celebrated musician with a few minor problems at home.

The fringe benefits are great, she tells me. We spend the next few minutes discussing boiled rice and other culinary delights. According to Val, the Chinese lady who takes the cookery class once a month is really very good. I feign interest, relieved in a way that we're talking about something else. But the subject holds no interest. What do I care about foreign cuisine? If I'm hungry, Justine can always rustle up an omelette, or phone out for a takeaway. The last thing I'm going to do is break out the pots and pans myself.

She shuts the folder, two podgy hands resting on top. 'Well – that's about it for today, Joe. I hope it hasn't been too taxing for you.'

'No, it's been, interesting.'

Whatever she's gleaned from our cosy little discussion, I hope it helps her, because it sure as fuck hasn't helped me.

I push back the swivel chair and stand, eager to be on my way. She raises a cautionary hand to stop me.

'Er- before you go, shall we make an appointment for next week?'

'Next week?'

'That's right. Is that not convenient?'

I sink back in the chair, deflated.

'How about Thursday – is that alright?'

'Thursday's fine.'

'Are you sure? You look a bit, uncertain.'

'No, it's … I wasn't aware this was going to be a weekly thing, that's all.'

'Like I said at the beginning. It's entirely voluntary. We don't make you do anything you don't want to.'

I mumble my compliance. She makes a note for the following Thursday, welcoming me into the fold with a distinct air of victory. The deal has been struck. I'm the latest C.O.D.A.T. initiate, primed and ready for the next phase.

The woman in the office smiles vaguely at me as I head for the stairs. Again, I get the feeling the whole thing's a set-up. Behind the unobtrusive scenery is a huge machine, gearing up to get me. The abstinence police, closing all escape routes, making it harder and harder for me to come up for air.

14

Carla thinks I'm being paranoid. She tells me this casually as she heats up a value curry in the microwave.

'Nobody's out to get you. It's all in your head.'

'But you didn't see it This woman had a fucking dossier on me. Now she wants me to go back next week.'

'So don't go. What's she going to do, take out a court order on you?'

I'm looking for sympathy in the wrong place. Some people can't relate to anyone's problems but their own.

The microwave pings. She removes her steaming hot curry with a tea towel and stares at it resentfully.

'I don't know why I bothered. I'm not even hungry.'

'Give it to next door's cat.'

She looks up, mystified. 'Cat's don't eat curry.'

'Ours does. Fucking thing eats anything – especially rats. I had to bury one down the garden the other day in a plastic bag.'

'Thanks.'

'What?'

'Talking about stuff like that when I'm about to eat.'

My dealings with the abstinence brigade are forgotten. The serious business of food takes over. Carla treats mealtimes as a chore, something to be endured rather than enjoyed. Baked beans on toast. Value packs and microwave dinners. Anything to cut down on washing up.

She prods the yellow rice, listlessly, with a fork. After a few token mouthfuls she sighs, arching her back with a grimace.

'What's the matter?'

'My back. No matter how I sit, it's still painful.'

'Lie down then.'

'Oh, you're so funny.'

'What about the painkillers the doctor gave you?'

'They don't work. The cortisone injections didn't either.'

'There must be something you can do, surely?'

'There is. He's recommended acupuncture in a few weeks time.'

'Acupuncture? Didn't you have enough problems with needles before?'

She stares at me evenly. 'I'm not even gonna dignify that with an answer.'

'Suit yourself. What's for dessert, anything interesting?'

I do worry about her health sometimes. The damp flat, the agoraphobia. Years of addiction taking their toll. She might feel better about herself if she got out more often. I keep telling her but she won't listen. The world's most glamorous vampire, stuck in this tomb all day long.

Danny comes up in the conversation. I relate the incident on the Green, where he relieved the poor student kid of his possessions. She shakes her head disapprovingly.

'What were you doing with Danny anyway?'

'I ran into him outside the Arcade and couldn't get rid of him.'

She looks at me dubiously and pushes her plate away. I think of the line in *Jaws,* where Hooper asks Brody's wife if he can finish her dinner.

'Don't you want the rest of it?'

'I'm not hungry.'

'You really should eat more, Carla.'

'And you really should mind your own business.'

'Is that any way to talk to your friends?'

'Huh. Some friend you are. You only come round to smoke all my blow.'

The sonic pounding of helicopter blades comes from high above the rooftops. Carla looks up with a scowl. 'Fucking things. Spying on people like that. Why don't they go looking for real criminals?'

'What, like Danny?'

'Yeah right. That's all I need. *Him* round here performing.

'Her cynicism amuses me. But Danny does have some strange quirks, that's for sure. What kind of a person fires up a stolen chain-saw in the hallway to see if it's working? The one time I've seen Carla lose her legendary cool, screaming at him to get out before she called the landlord. And yet, somehow, I can still see the pair of them together. The flawed diva and the desperado, on the run from the millicents like Bonnie and Clyde.

The helicopter moves on, to recce another part of London. I'm plagued with the thought of abstinence. Booze has been my best friend, my reason for being, ever since I can remember. How am I supposed to cope without it?

'How did you feel when you came off the gear?'

She looks at me strangely. 'Why?'

'I'm curious to know, that's all.'

She thinks. 'I just had enough, I suppose. My whole life was going to shit at the time. Everyone hassling me for money or drugs. I couldn't seem to get away from it.'

'What about booze?'

'What about it?'

'Did you give that up as well?'

'I never had a problem with it. I could always take it or leave it,' she smirks at me. 'Unlike some we know.'

A stream of images plays back from the past. Rimmer's apartment in San Diego. The two of us getting through a huge amount of heroin and cocaine. Then me having to leave one morning to hook up with the band in San Francisco, feeling like someone had skewered out my insides.

Carla scowls at the mention of Rimmer. 'I could never understand why you hung around with him. He used to give me the creeps.'

'Why?'

'He was just one of those people. He had that look. I never felt safe around him.'

'Was it Rimmer who got you on the gear?'

'No?'

'So who was it, then?

She reflects, a distant look in her eye. 'I met this guy who'd just come back from Thailand. He was into everything. Stolen credit cards. Money laundering. We just, sort of, gravitated towards each other.'

'And he was bang into the gear?'

'Yeah, but you wouldn't have guessed to look at him. He was always smartly dressed. Well spoken. Plenty of charisma.'

I picture the two of them, hand in hand in some exotic location, breaking up the romantic interlude to play hunt the dealer.

'How come you never told me him before?'

'You never asked.'

She makes a roll-up from her dented tobacco tin, her forefinger burned brown at the knuckle from smoking down to the filter. I wonder at Rimmer's dubious influence. The way he'd turn up unexpectedly at gigs and parties like the Angel of Death. Lure you back to some seedy apartment, there to administer his potions and cocktails. How persuasive he was. How persistent. And how easy it was for me to go with him without the slightest resistance.

'I did an interview for Brian Moorcroft.'

'How is he?' she says, with a smirk. 'Still drinking Guinness?'

'Mineral water by the looks of things. He said he saw me backstage at Roskilde in '87. Said I looked dreadful.'

'Was that before or after your little outburst at the Brit Awards?'

'Before. Why?'

'No reason.'

Why are people so fixated on the bad things I've done? Surely everyone's entitled to make mistakes every once in a while. Brian Moorcroft trying to make out I'm some kind of degenerate junkie. Now Carla, reminding me of some harmless bit of banter between me and Rick Astley after I'd tucked-in to the free champagne.

'I need a favour,' Carla says.

'What's new?'

'Don't be like that. I need a lift to Kensal Green.'

The last time I took Carla to Kensal Green, we ended up in this drug emporium with three black guys and a bored teenage white girl. The girl turned out to be the daughter of one of the black guys, who'd come along for the ride. You had to marvel at the way Carla dealt with these people. Her belligerence and guile. Her total disregard for danger. With headlines like 'Crack War Murders' and 'Shootings In Ladbroke Grove' you have to be careful who you mix with. You could get taken out for the slightest thing.

'So what's the deal?' I say deviously. 'Can you get me some dazzies?'

'I'll try.'

'You said that the last time.'

'Look – don't hassle me. I said I'd try, didn't I?'

She toys with her bangles, unusually coy.

'There is one other thing.'

'What's that?'

'I want you to come in with me.'

'What for?'

'It's just a precaution, that's all.'

'Against what?'

'Look – it's no big deal, or I wouldn't have asked you. Will you do it, or not?'

Carla's made a lifetime's work of getting other people to do her bidding. Manipulation, solicitation. It's what she does best. You find yourself going along with it out of sympathy, knowing deep down you're being shafted royally.

*

The deal turns out to be a straightforward transaction on a housing estate. The guy who answers the door looks like Anthony Perkins in *Psycho,* and has the same chronic vagueness and nervous disposition. He greets Carla with a sickly familiarity, and I can see at once why she wouldn't have wanted to be alone with him. All the time they're talking I'm aware of the surroundings. The smell of rancid food. The tacky, lithographic prints on the wall. It seems I've spent a lifetime in these places. Drawn to the magic dust, the whispered promise. Always chasing the feeling I had years ago when I first started out, and failing consistently to recapture it.

We descend the wrought-iron staircase and head for the car. Carla notes my silence and nudges me.

'What's the matter?'

'I thought you were gonna ask for the pills.'

'Sorry. I forgot.'

Maybe I should get a hat and become a chauffeur. Drive all the stoners round London, looking for the best deals. There's no end to it. The utter thoughtlessness of some people.

15

The Girl turns Nine today. She has that unmistakeable regal air, common to all highly evolved species, and treats the whole event as somehow beneath her. I can't believe how grown up she is, how calm and self assured. Having missed whole chunks of her formative years I feel a sense of obligation. This is a chance for me to fit in and prove I belong. Make up for all my previous absences by being here for her and not running away.

Justine hands me a triage of red balloons, festooned with streamers. 'Before you disappear, tie these to the front door, will you?'

The balloons are emblazoned with silver stars and a garish number 9. I feel slightly stupid holding them, like a man attached to a practical joke.

'What happens if the wind gets up and I take off?'

'Wouldn't be the first time, would it.'

Fred next-door watches me tie the balloons to the front porch. He puts down his trusty shears and takes a breather from trimming the hedgerow

'Someone's big day, Joe?'

'Sadie, Fred. She's Nine today.'

'Got your work cut out there then.' He winks at me. 'Still – put a few balloons up then it's off to the pub, eh?'

'Not today, I'm afraid. Too much to do.'

Fred's a sociable old chap really. His days in the Parachute Regiment are long gone, but the stories he tells are good. Throwing pork at the Muslims in Egypt. Defeating the Germans at El Alamein. Christ knows what he makes of me, the louche bohemian, coming home at four in the morning with a road cone on my head.

'Got over your bout of sickness, have you?' Fred says with a twinkle.

'What was that, Fred?'

'Justine said you weren't too good the other day. Laid up in bed with a fever or summat.'

I grasp the hidden meaning. Another of Justine's pointed references to my disappearance in Islington. That's what happens when you upset the home help. They tend to get their own back in underhand ways.

'Probably all that foreign food,' Fred says, with a scowl. 'We went abroad a few years back. I caught the lurgi from some seafood restaurant we were in. Coming out both ends it was. You off on your travels again soon?'

'Not for a while, Fred. I'm, sort of, resting at the moment. Doing a spot of gardening and helping out with the kids. It's a tough job but someone's gotta do it.'

Fred nods solemnly. I'm not sure how much he's gleaned from Justine. The true extent of our arguing and bickering. Yesterday, I went out to get a paper. Because I was half hour late getting back, she wanted to know where I'd been. There's no escape. The fallout from past misdemeanours keeps coming back to haunt me.

*

Party time for the Birthday Girl. The chosen ones sit around in the front room listening to Michael Jackson. The adults hang around in the kitchen and the hallway, keeping out of the way. Jake dribbles a mini football between the legs of bemused guests, undeterred by Justine's exasperated yells from the kitchen. I can understand his reluctance to conform. When you've heard the same thing so many times before it loses the power to shock. You become immune.

Justine appears in the doorway. 'Jake, why don't you take the ball out in the garden.'

'In a minute.'

'Not in a minute. Now, please!' She looks at me, red-faced. 'Er – any chance you, could, sort of, help me out round here? Make sure everyone's got a drink or something?'

One of the mothers is standing alone by the window. With her thick black glasses and neat wedge of dark hair she looks like Thelma from *Scooby Doo*. I sidle up to her with a touch of forced nonchalance, acutely aware of my menial role.

'Enjoying the party?'

'Yes, thanks.'

'Can I get you anything – drink, crisps?'

'I'm fine, thanks.'

We watch the birthday girls chattering away in their private huddles. I feel distinctly awkward, lacking any social inclination without a shot of something to give me the courage.

'You're Sadie's dad, aren't you?' she says, glancing nervously up at me

'For my sins, yes, I am.'

'I've seen you at the dance class on a Monday night. I take Rebecca.'

Now we've worked out the background details, we can relax and talk shop. The rigours of teaching Salsa to a bunch of temperamental nine year olds. Thelma seems quite sweet and approachable, not too pretentious like some of the other mums. I begin to warm to her.

'We've got something in common then. We're both used to standing round waiting for the dance class to finish.'

She looks at me strangely, biting her bottom lip. I wonder if I've offended her in some way.

'Was it something I said?'

'Oh no, it's just …' She fingers her wine glass, reddening visibly. 'I feel embarrassed to say it, really.'

'Go on.'

She screws up her face, wincing with the effort.

'It's just … I've got one of your records at home and I wondered if you'd sign it for me?'

The initial shock wears off. I grow two inches taller in my

Cuban heels.

'Which one?'

'Sorry?'

'Which record?'

She grimaces. 'Something about … dancing, I think.'

'Dancing with Tall Girls?'

'Yes – that's the one!'

The mechanics of seduction is a strange thing. No matter how out of practise you are, the urge is always there, lying dormant like a virus. Thelma seems in awe of my faded celebrity. With only one Top Ten hit in this country it's hard to think why, but you can't knock her commitment. She has that glazed over look common to teenage girls in the grip of adulation, I don't have to try too hard to impress her because she knows who I am. I'm the poster on the wall. The living, breathing embodiment of rock and roll, masquerading as the in-house entertainment at a children's party.

One question remains.

'Were you a big fan – of the band, I mean?'

'Er- kind of.'

'Is that a yes or a no?'

'Well – please don't hate me for this but I was really into Depeche Mode.'

I'm mildly offended but try not to show it. Michael Jackson sings Rock With You in the background, the song's hypnotic beat and towering vocal filling the room. We had the same dream. Five tours of the States in ten years. Thousands of miles covered in a CJ Starbus. For what? To end up burned out and disillusioned, minus a job at the end of it. Nothing more career enhancing than the odd blowjob in the toilet, or a complimentary line of cocaine from some eager to please fan.

'Do you still play now?' she says.

'I'm moving more into production these days. People are queuing up to work with me. It's finding the time, you know?'

We connect on some deeper level. Here among the balloons and the streamers, the party girls arranged demurely along the twin sofas. I'm overcome with a strange desire to tell her everything. All the sordid details of my previous incarnation. My stalled career. Joe E Byron – rock star par excellence, who terrorised half the known world for more than a decade. Destined to be remembered for a walk-on part in a movie no one saw and a drunken assault on airport security staff at Heathrow that made the Front Page of *The Sun*.

'You've lived such an amazing life,' she says, gazing up at me through her thick, black rims. 'You've been to all these places. Met all these fascinating people.'

I'm humbled by her excessive praise. This sweet, impressionable little housewife from suburbia, who's probably never been north of Romford. How can she possibly know what it's like to be me? The excitement of signing to a major record label after years in the shadows. Finding out our third single had entered the Hot 100, peaking at sixteen. She shakes her head incredulously, willing me to go on, but the truth would only taint the picture. The truth about life on the road with its long hours of sustained boredom. The constant quest for things to do. And every excess under the sun catered and paid for, encouraged and fanned wherever you go.

Alice joins us, fixing me with an odd quizzical look as if my game's been rumbled. 'Justine's bringing the cake out in a few minutes. She asked me to let you know.'

'Joe's been telling me all about his days in the band,' Thelma says, smiling warmly.

'Really? Did he tell you about the time he got stuck in a lift with Luther Vandross?' Alice strolls off with a distinct air of victory. Thelma watches her go, sipping her wine timorously. She turns to me, puzzled.

'Did you really do that?'

'What?'

'Get stuck in a lift with Luther Vandross?'

'It was Alexander O'Neil, actually, but that's another story. Can I top up your wine for you?'

We move towards the second phase of our relationship, close enough to be lovers, our growing intimacy held in check by other people. She talks a bit about herself, her family.

'Are you married, Thelma?' I say casually.

She looks up, wide-eyed. 'What did you call me?'

'Sorry. Slip of the tongue. You just look like someone I used to know.'

She frowns hesitantly. 'I am married, yes.'

'Happily?'

'Yes … Why?'

'No reason.'

The Cake Ceremony begins. Sadie sits in the corner, eyes shut, a conical party hat angled on her head. Her friends gather around her in their best party frocks, quietly expectant. Justine enters with the cake, bearing nine pink candles and, at a prearranged signal, the unholy choir sings 'Happy Birthday'. The star of the show sits perfectly still, entranced by the outpouring of love from all corners of the room. With a tentative smile, she leans forward and blows out all the candles in a single breath.

I look round and Thelma's gone.

'Piece of birthday cake?' Alice says, gloating.

'No thanks, I'm watching my figure.'

'What did you say to get rid of Rebecca's mum so quickly?'

'Nothing. We were getting along fine until you came along.'

She narrows her eyes, peering at me mysteriously. 'Everything OK?'

'Fine.'

'Sure?'

'Yeah. Why wouldn't I be?'

She nibbles at her cake, sighing pleasurably. I get the feeling I'm under scrutiny.

'Justine says you've been getting some help. You know. For your drinking. Is that right?'

'I've been seeing this counsellor, that's all.'

'I hope you don't think I'm prying.'

'Course not.'

She squeezes my arm tenderly. 'Chin up. You'll be OK. I know you will.'

I nip upstairs during a lull. The bathroom cabinet holds out a vague hope. Sifting through the cluster of bottles, creams and potions, it strikes me I'm looking for a miracle. Nothing. Not even an aspirin. That's what happens when you live with someone who doesn't need pharmaceuticals. My usual hiding places reveal nothing, not even the residue from a cellophane wrapper, or the stub of an old joint.

I go back down and rejoin the party, a smile on my face like terminal lockjaw.

Justine calls me into the kitchen.

'Where have you been?'

'Upstairs, in the bathroom. Is that alright?'

A small child races through the hall, his mouth smeared with chocolate. Justine gives me a sudden directive. 'Take the pizzas out of the oven and cut them into slices, will you? And after that you can empty the bin.'

'Anything else?'

'No, that's all.'

'You don't want me to clean the windows and wax the car while I'm at it?'

She ponders a suitable answer before turning away.

I smoke a cigarette, alone out on the front step. Music and laughter filter from inside, the soundtrack to something poignant and familiar that one day upped and left me. I'm happy for Sadie. She's got all her friends here and everyone's having a good time. But, for me, the party's over. I've nothing left to say to anyone. Including the 'happily married' Thelma.

*

Jake wants his favourite bedtime story *The Magic Kingdom*. The youthful hero wanders through the dark forest, fighting off dragons and werewolves, to arrive at the Giant's Castle. There he must free the Princess, held prisoner inside, before the Giant comes round from an evening on the crack-pipe and batters them both to death with a tyre iron. Jake gets the sanitised version, of course.

'Stop reading it like that!'

'Like what?'

'In that silly voice!'

'Why? Don't you think Peter sounds better with a Scottish accent?'

Before we get to the bit where the last and most fearsome dragon appears, Jake interrupts with a question.

'Can we go to the park tomorrow?'

'Er – what happened to the story?'

'Can we?'

'No.'

'Why not?'

'Because I'm busy. Do you want to hear what happens to the dragon or not?'

The story concludes. Jake's eyes stay open by an act of will. I lay my hand, gently, on his forehead and stand up.

'Goodnight, little man.'

'Mmmm'

I leave the door ajar and quietly head downstairs.

Justine's still clearing up from the afternoon's soiree. She should try catering for rock musicians instead, wading through empty beer bottles and discarded sandwich wrappers, the remnants of a backstage party that went on ten years too long.

'Where's Sadie?' I say.

'Staying at Mikela's.'

'What – on her birthday?'

Justine looks at me irritably. 'She wanted a sleepover with her friends. I told you all this ages ago'

She jettisons a plate of mini sausage rolls into the bin and takes a cloth to the worktop, glancing up at me between lunges.

'You were getting very cosy with Rebecca's mum earlier. What was all that about?'

'She wanted my autograph. We were one of her favourite bands apparently.'

She throws the cloth into the sink and dries her hands. I feel insignificant suddenly, like I'm being ignored.

'Why did you tell Alice I was seeing a counsellor?'

She looks up, bemused. 'She's my friend. Why wouldn't I tell her?'

I don't have an answer.

'Anyway, she thinks it's a good idea.'

'What – like a frontal lobotomy?'

'Don't get down on it so quickly, you've only been once.'

'That's enough, isn't it?'

She leans back against the worktop with a sigh, her cheeks flushed from exertion. In spite of the troubled mood I'm in, a cunning plan begins to take shape.

'Listen,' I say softly. 'Seeing as we're on our own tonight, why don't we – '

'Don't even think about it.'

'You haven't let me finish!'

'Joe, please. I'm tired, and I've still got all this clearing up to do.'

I sit resentfully and stare at the wall. My daughter turned nine today and I was there to witness the celebrations. I even blew up a few balloons and handed pizza out, all without a drink or a drug to get me through the ordeal. You'd think there'd be some form of recompense.

'Look. I'm really grateful you helped out today,' she says wearily. 'It meant a lot to Sadie, having you here. Please don't spoil it.'

'I'm not spoiling it.'

She comes closer and folds her arms, a troubled look on her face.

'Can I ask you something?' she says.

'What?'

'Where did you go the other night?'

'What night?'

'The night we went to mum's. You borrowed the car when we came back.'

'I went over to see Cribbs. I told you.'

She mulls this over.

'Please don't lie to me. I'm not stupid.'

'I'm not lying to you. Jesus Christ – what is this?'

'So you're not taking anything?'

'No?'

'What – nothing?'

'I smoke the odd joint now and then. What's wrong with that?'

There's a theory that people close to you want to believe you're telling the truth. But when your lies have been exposed on so many occasions before, you don't have the same leverage. You have to rely on belligerence and denial to convince them.

She turns to go and hesitates. 'You had a phone call last night.'

'Who from?'

'Some girl. She left a number for you to ring.'

'Did she leave her name?'

'Naomi, I think.'

A wild surge of enthusiasm grips me. This could be it. The opportunity to do something positive towards my career after so many setbacks.

Justine looks back, sadly, from the doorway. 'All I ever wanted was for us to be together as a family. I don't think that's too much to ask, do you?'

She turns and walks away. I feel compelled to follow her but something stops me. I'm struck by the huge gulf of understanding between us. The fact that we share the same house but we're rarely in the same room. Part of me wants to make it up to her for all the things I've done. All the lying and the cheating, the reckless diverting of funds. The other part wants to rebel. Tear everything down around me and leave in a cloud of dust.

I ring the number out in the hall. A man answers, bluntly, the trace of an accent I can't place. Funny how you get an instant mental picture of someone from the sound of their voice.

'Is Naomi there, please?'

'Who's calling?'

'Joe Byron ...'

A rash of nerves sets in. I've done nothing to get things moving since first hearing the demo. No calls to producers. No hassling contacts for free studio time. But this is a real opportunity. A chance for me to turn it all around.

16

We sit in the blue room, me and my learned confessor. She has that quiet, inner confidence typical of people who know things you don't. The posters look less intimidating this time, there's even a hint of peach air-freshener to spruce things up. But the warm welcome and businesslike handshake leaves me feeling uncomfortable, the guest on some obscure chat show, brought on under false pretences to tell a few entertaining lies.

'So, how have you been, Joe?'

'Fine, thanks.'

'Any news since I last saw you?'

I tell her about Sadie's party, my promise to Justine that I'd stick around and not run off to the pub. She coos in admiration, as if this is a real bona fide achievement.

'Well, I'm sure your daughter appreciated you being there. Did you find it stressful?'

'Not really. I blew up a few balloons and doled out the pizza. Did my bit as resident DJ.'

The drug poster catches my eye. Cannabis, heroin and crack cocaine. Not the kind of thing you'd want hanging on your living room wall for your kids to see. California comes to mind. A ceaseless orbit of strange people, all gravitating towards the same thing. And in the centre of it all, Rimmer, conducting operations from his sleazy boardroom.

'How's the drinking?' she says. 'Are you still? ...'

'Absolutely. It's been six weeks now.'

She claps her hands with pure joy. We share the good news. Six torturous weeks on the wagon, with nothing stronger than orange juice to calm my nerves.

'That's fantastic!' she says admiringly. 'How do you feel?'

How does she think I feel? Can't she see the brass band playing outside? The banners draped up and down the high street?

'I feel great. No problems at all.'

She beams across at me, her chubby, ringed fingers clasped in her lap. I wonder who the real woman is behind the starched, white blouse and the sixties hairdo. How she came by her current job, counselling a bunch of misfits who've wandered in off the streets.

She asks about my family. The camping trip bothers me, although I can't think why. Talking about it highlights all the tensions at home, the reasons I wasn't invited in the first place.

'So they're going without you?' she says.

'Looks that way.'

'Did you want to go with them?'

'Not really. It's just the principle. They're all off having fun and I'm left behind with the cat.'

The truth is, I'm relieved. Three nights in a tent listening to Sadie moaning about insects, and Jake thrashing around in his sleep. Not my idea of a weekend break. But the slight still hurts. Being excluded by your own family when you're doing your best to toe the line.

'What does your wife think about you stopping drinking?'

'She hasn't really said.'

'But she must see it as a positive development, surely?'

'She gets stressed easily, with the kids and everything. We don't get much time to sit down and talk.'

More sober platitudes follow. The benefits of living drug free in a world of gym referrals and mineral water. I reach for the chocolate chip cookies and try to relax. Val's voice is smooth and beguiling, the true professional giving me the hard sell. She reminds me again about the classes they run. Anger management and assertiveness training. The drop-in centre on a Saturday afternoon. All this with a zealous light in her eyes that's strangely disconcerting.

'We have a Men's Group that meets on a Tuesday afternoon,' she says eagerly. 'I wondered if you'd be interested in that?'

'Sorry, I had enough trouble with the last one I was in.'

'You were in a group before?'

'The band … I told you about it last week.'

She titters quietly, hiding her embarrassment. The perfect hostess, with her clop of white hair and matching baubles. But there's a limit to how much I can take in. The slick promotional tour. Success stories from previous clients. All these are smokescreens for what's really going on.

'Do you have any other hobbies, apart from music?' she says.

'Sorry?'

'Any interests? Anything else you like to do?'

'I like reading.'

She raises an eyebrow. 'And what sort of things do you read?'

'Sartre. Camus. People who knew the score about this world.'

She smiles demurely. I feel a sudden rant coming on, inspired by my current surroundings.

'Camus believed in the pointlessness of existence. We're all just cogs in the machine going nowhere.'

'Is that what you believe?'

I shrug and make a play for the biscuits. 'Do you mind?'

'Of course not. Help yourself. That's what they're there for.'

The chocolate chip cookie dissolves quickly, a powerful drug in itself. I settle back in the chair for part two of our discourse on modern philosophy.

'You *can* change your beliefs,' she says, frowning thoughtfully.

'Really?'

'Oh yes. That's one of the first things we teach people here.'

My focus starts to drift beyond the window. Val's gaze is pleasant and non-threatening, encouraging me to open up. 'Well I found out the hard way. You put your trust in people and they let you down.'

'Can you give me an example?'

'Sure. How long have you got?'

She smiles politely. Self righteous anger wells up in me.

'It's right across the board, isn't it. Even your own parents let you down in the end.'

'Did your parents let *you* down?'

The sugar hit recedes. Instinctively my hand reaches out to feed the craving.

'My Dad took me to the cinema one day when I was a kid. He left me in the queue with total strangers while he went off drinking with his mates. It's, sort of, stuck in my mind ever since.'

She shifts in the chair, her navy trousers stretched over large, meaty thighs. A weightlifter's build, I think distractedly. Broad shoulders and a rotund but pleasantly feminine face.

'What sort of relationship did you have with your dad?'

'Pretty good. When he was there.'

'Was he away a lot?'

'He could be away weeks, months at a time.'

'What did he do?'

'He was a jazz musician.'

'I see. And do you still – '

'He died four years ago from a heart attack. He was forty-nine.' The words are out before I can stop them. Painful memories, pushed away at the back of my mind.

'I'm sorry, I didn't realise.'

'That's OK. It was a shock at the time, but I'm over it now.'

The obituary notice lies in a box at home. *Saxophonist who took improvisation to new heights of emotion.* A faded, black and white photo of the great man playing a solo. Eyes shut, lips compressed around the instrument's mouthpiece. His death troubles me in ways I can't comprehend.

'I didn't even cry at his funeral. Do you think that's a bad sign?'

She angles her head sagely. 'No, I don't believe so. We all grieve in different ways. Sometimes the process is delayed by shock, or some other trauma. That doesn't make the experience any less meaningful.'

Her response has a mild soothing effect. But I'm wary, never having talked about these things to anyone before.

116

'Do you think bad luck runs in families?'

'In what way?'

'Well, my dad died young. My mum spent time in a mental institution. Not exactly reassuring, is it?'

'And you think this has some bearing on your future, do you?'

'Wouldn't you?'

Her eyes glint softly. 'I think you can waste a lot of time and energy in speculation. Of course, certain things are hereditary. There's nothing much we can do about that. But I think it's far more beneficial to see yourself as an individual with choices. Not just the victim of a cruel genetic lottery.' She looks at me intently. 'Do you mind me asking why your mum was in hospital?'

'She's manic depressive.'

'I see.'

'Every so often she goes nuts, and they cart her off to the funhouse for ECT.'

'That must have been difficult for you.'

'You get used to it. I just found it embarrassing when I was growing up. Knowing she wasn't like other kids' mums. But they say it runs in families, don't they. Out of me and my sister, I definitely drew the short straw.'

'What makes you say that?'

'I've had the lithium and the largactyl treatment too. Doctors and psychiatrists tampering with the inside of my head. It's fate. Destiny. That's why I choose to self-medicate.'

'You think that drinking and taking drugs helps your mental state?'

'Sometimes.'

I could tell her about the chronic stage fright I used to suffer. The bigger the gig, the worse it got. In the end, medicating heavily before the show became the only answer. Half a bottle of tequila and several lines of coke later, I'd venture out behind the curtain to face the crowd. In truth, I was a liability. A Frankenstein's monster, ready to implode.

'How are you finding the break from your job?'

117

'Great. I'm working with this girl at the moment, producing her first album. Then there's a solo project I want to start. Plenty of options really.'

She nods, courteously, a slight questioning look in her eye. Talking about Naomi brings up more uncertainty. The promise of a meeting that may or may not come off, depending on her job prospects sailing round the Med. Then there's the other problem. Trying to secure Cribbs's involvement when he's rarely in this country.

'You talked about boredom being a problem. What happens when you're at home?'

'I improvise.'

'In what way?'

'Watch TV. Do crossword puzzles.' My sarcasm eludes her. I shrug. 'I've never been too good at sitting in a chair doing nothing.'

What's the point in elaborating, she wouldn't understand? I've spent the last ten years in different time zones, having my senses scrambled, my metabolism rearranged. But even I have to concede the gig's been worth it. Every moment on stage a bid for immortality. A waltz with the gods. How can you give all that up and go shopping in Sainsbury's?

'I've been thinking about getting fit,' I say casually.

'Really – in the gym?'

'Round the block on a mountain bike, more like. I'm not *that* keen.'

She nods agreeably, missing the absurdity of the statement, the unlikely spectacle of me cycling anywhere. I drift back to the distant past. Hugh Hanley introducing us to a crowd of sixteen thousand in Madrid one night, a beautiful orange sunset lighting the evening sky. We opened with a Hendrix cover and the crowd went wild. Something happens that you can't explain. The crowd is your heartbeat, your lifeblood. It drowns your senses and sucks you in. You yearn for its embrace and, when you're starved of it too long, you sink into despondency.

Everything changed when I heard Electric Ladyland. Before that it had always been The Beatles and the Stones, and my father's extensive jazz influence. Hendrix spoke another language. After hearing him, I knew what I wanted to do, and who I wanted to emulate.

'Do you smoke?' she says.

'Religiously.'

She smiles. 'Well, it's good to be health conscious, isn't it?'

'I wouldn't know, I've never tried it before.'

We share the joke in the relative safety of the blue room. Val's subtle, ingratiating humour jollies me along, her podgy face brushed with cheap foundation and good living.

She views me from another angle.

'Where do you see yourself a year from now?'

'I don't usually think that far ahead.'

'But if you could, where would it be?'

'On an island in the Caribbean, probably. Surrounded by flunkies bringing me drinks on silver trays.'

She smiles faintly. I sense the change in direction, the clever little trap she's set for me to fall into. I decide to play along, seduced by her makeshift confessional.

'Justine thinks I'm selfish.'

'In what way?'

'She says I always think of myself first. Not a good trait when you're the father of two small children.'

'And what do you think?'

I can't answer, reminded where I am and what's at stake.

'Do you resent being at home?'

The question surprises me. 'Sometimes.'

She nods, her silence goading me.

'Justine forgets some of the sacrifices I've made. The money I put down on the house.'

'You see your contribution in financial terms, do you?'

'No I don't. I'm just aware I've been away a lot over the years. I've tried to make up for it in other ways.'

'Like blowing up balloons on your daughter's birthday?'

'That's right.'

She eases forward sombrely.

'How old are you, Joe?'

'Thirty-two.'

She mulls this over, nodding her head at some profound inner truth.

'I went to a funeral last week. Someone who attended our group last year. He was only thirty-five.' She pauses. 'The police had to break down the door of his flat. He'd been there for three days, apparently.'

The net curtain flutters. I feel an odd twinge of unease, my resistance somehow linked to this anonymous death.

'Every day, people die like this,' she says gravely. 'It's heartbreaking for those left behind. Family and friends who have to pick up the pieces.'

'Yeah, I know what it's like.'

'You do?'

'My granddad was an alcoholic. I remember the trouble it caused in our family.'

She hesitates. We've moved away from the tea and biscuits into uncharted territory. I feel I should lighten the mood a little.

'Gotta die of something, I suppose. Might as well go out enjoying yourself.'

She stiffens visibly. I move to correct my error.

'What I meant was, it's a choice you make. Like smoking forty a day, or jumping out of an aeroplane. You can't spend your whole life avoiding danger. You might get cancer, or walk in the road and get hit by a bus.'

'Yes, it is a choice, I agree.' She falters. 'For most people. But not everyone has that luxury.'

We sit in silence, either side of an impasse. I think back over my tenure as band member and journeyman player on the international circuit. The Olympian excesses of life on the road. *NME's* cover shot one year, of the four of us in our New York Doll's phase, complete with ripped t-shirts and black eyeliner. James T's arm slung around my shoulder, his grinning face close to mine. The photo didn't quite reveal what went on behind the scenes. The competitive side to our self-destruction. How we bonded, instinctively, over the champagne and the cocaine, the endless miles.

'I'd like you to do something for me, Joe.'

'What's that?'

'I'd like you to keep a diary next week.'

'A diary?'

'Write down how you're feeling at different times of the day. It's a good exercise. Helps you to see how certain thought patterns come up again and again.'

'Then what – read it out to you?'

She laughs softly. 'No, it's just an exercise. Writing things down is actually quite therapeutic. You'd be surprised how much it helps. But we can discuss how it went at next week's session if you like.'

Now I get to record my innermost thoughts for posterity.Page after page of twisted observations to confirm what I knew all along. I'm a bad seed. A chronic backslider. Fiends like me don't belong in nice people's houses.

She glances distractedly at her watch. 'Well – unfortunately that's it for today. Are you happy to continue with this arrangement?'

'It's fine by me.'

'Good.' She stands with a resurgence of warmth. 'Then we'll see you at the same time next week.'

We shake hands.

'And don't forget the diary,' she says, beaming happily. 'Write it all down. It'll help, I promise you.'

The stairs creak on the way down, a kind of trapped, musty smell lingering in the vacuum. I can't wait to get out. Away from the stifling walls and the graphic posters. Val Moody's subtle manipulation that's hard to resist.

17

Lake Washington Boulevard, Seattle. The newsreader talks about a body being found by an electrician carrying out repairs at a house. Pictures of the property flash up, a modest dwelling with a small balcony and open garage below. A reporter stands in the street outside and describes how the occupant, one Kurt Cobain, killed himself with a single shotgun blast to the head.

'Fuck.'

Justine appears in the doorway. 'What's up?'

'Look at this.'

More pictures of the house flash up. Interviews with music journalists and people who knew him. The sense of loss affects everyone, including me.

Justine sits, quietly absorbing the details.

'When did it happen?'

'No idea. They think he was lying there for days.'

'Was it an accident?'

I look at her in bewilderment. 'He blew his brains out, for Christ's sake.'

The death of such a major international artist leaves a huge hole, a void that can't be filled. I'm numb with shock, unable to grasp the implications.

'You OK?' she says softly.

'Not really.'

Nirvana thrash around on stage in a clip from one of their early performances.

'I suppose there'll be some kind of enquiry,' she says.

'What good will that do?'

She stands. 'Oh well. I'll put the kettle on. Can I get you anything?'

Her sudden concern for my welfare catches me by surprise. The shock of Kurt Cobain's death inadvertently bringing us closer together. The realisation that it could have been me, perhaps, shipped home from some foreign country in a body bag.

The shock wears off, replaced by a leaden sadness. How do you mourn someone you never knew? Someone whose success affected your career in ways you couldn't have imagined? Before Nirvana, British bands were welcomed all over the States. As soon as they exploded on the scene you couldn't get a look-in, unless you had the trademark grunge image with the grubby trainers and the tousled hair.

Justine brings in the tea. I keep seeing the house in the news clip. The terrible finality of what happened inside.

'What made him do it?'

'Who knows?' she says blithely. 'He was obviously depressed about something.'

'But to put a shotgun in your mouth and pull the trigger. How fucked-up do you have to be to do that?'

She shrugs, clearly preoccupied, before turning to face me

'Listen – I know it's probably not the best time to discuss it, but I spoke to Hugh earlier.'

'Oh yeah.'

'Now that the tour's finished, he's willing to go into mediation.'

'About what?'

'He's organising a meeting where we can all sit down and discuss the future. There's been some major changes in company policy over the last year or so, and he wants us all to be aware of that.'

I'm speechless. One of the most talented songwriters of the last twenty-five years has topped himself and I'm forced to listen to this corporate bullshit. Since when did boardroom politics have anything to do with music and creativity?

'You don't seem too enthusiastic,' she says flatly. 'I thought you'd be pleased.'

'About what – being sold out to that scheming wanker?'

'But it could get you reinstated. I thought that's what you wanted?'

Now she's the intermediary for Hugh Hanley and Goldstein Enterprises. They've somehow talked her into wearing me down.

'OK, we'll talk about it later,' she says, sitting back. 'How did it go with Val Moody?'

'Great. She wants me to keep a diary.'

'A diary – what for?'

'So I can record all my innermost thoughts. See if there's a pattern to the way I'm thinking.'

'And that's supposed to help, is it?'

'According to her it is.'

I'm incensed at Justine for instigating the whole thing and erupt. 'It's a complete waste of time. Sitting there drinking coffee. Eating chocolate chip cookies like a plum. What's it meant to achieve?'

'It's good for you.'

'How?'

'It gives you something positive to aim for.'

'Like what? I can run my own life, can't I?'

She gives me a deeply ironic look and we settle into uneasy silence. The death of Kurt Cobain hangs over us like an omen. I think of all the things he achieved in the short time he was on the planet. Dazzling album sales. Artistic credibility. The harrowing scream at the end of Where Did You Sleep Last Night. And all for what? To ensure he joined the elites. That exclusive batch of rock 'n' rollers who bowed out early at the age of 27.

'I'm going into production,' I say bitterly.

'You're what?'

'I've spoken to Naomi and Cribbs. They're up for it.'

'What about the band?'

'Fuck the band. D'you see them looking out for me lately?'

She folds her arms, rigidly, and stares at the table.

'OK. Do what you want.'

'What does that mean?'

'It means, do whatever it is you have to do. Just promise me you won't go making any sudden decisions about the band until after the meeting. Please?'

I'm suspicious of her tone, the unusual levels of tolerance she's showing towards me. Maybe the winds are picking up after weeks in the doldrums. The sombre mood is about to change. There won't be that awful, underlying tension following us from room to room.

*

The news is full of tributes to Kurt Cobain. Sitting here with my mug of tea and carpet slippers, it's hard to feel much of a connection. Cobain blew his brains out with a shotgun, ending a lifelong cycle of illness and addiction. I'm laid up in suburbia, with all my addictions on hold, every little thing I do under observation.

Sadie reaches for the remote.

'Don't even think about it, Sadie.'

'I want to watch *Blockbusters*.'

'You can watch *Blockbusters* some other time. This is real life. Real people. OK?'

Pictures of Cobain as a child are flashed up. The programmers draining every last ounce from the subject while the item's still hot. I wonder how my own children would react if it was me. Would they be sat around in mourning, tearful and inconsolable, or would life go on as before?

'Sadie.'

'What?'

'Would you miss me if I was gone?'

'Where are you going?'

'I'm not going anywhere. I'm just saying.'

'Saying what?'

'Well … would you miss me if I wasn't around anymore?'

She shrugs, the question beneath her. The dilemma takes on a painful significance. I need reassurance, the knowledge that

I'm loved and needed by those closest to me.

'I love you, Bunches. You know that, don't you?'

'I love you too, Daddy.'

Her monotone, pre-programmed response isn't enough. How do you win back your children's affections when you've let them down so many times? Horse riding lessons and party frocks don't quite do it any more. She's reached the age where she wants something else, something I'm clearly not able to give her.

'Bed early for you, Sadie,' Justine says in her strict adjudicator's voice. Sadie sits up, horrified.

'Why?'

'Because I said so. I con't want any arguments either.'

'But Daddy said I could stay up a bit longer.'

'No I didn't!'

'Yes you did! You said earlier!'

I'm stunned by the blatant lie, but impressed, equally, by the simple ingenuity. Perhaps I should side with her more often and practise leniency instead of hopelessly trying to impose discipline. Kids understand the way it has to be. The good cop, bad cop syndrome parents employ to get the job done. I just don't want her to resent me when she gets older. I want her to have good memories too. Not just the ones of me lying on the sofa, sweating and shaking, and crawling up the stairs on my hands and knees.

Sadie slinks off to bed with a truculent 'Good night!' I'm left alone, briefly, while Justine oversees the final stage of the operation. Maybe I'm getting used to it. The stay-at-home husband, temporarily out of a job, reduced to a kind of eunuch status. All my bad habits are gone. The booze, the pills, the heroin. Nothing but the odd joint now and again, a concession permitted under the new regime.

The phone rings.

Justine strides along the hall, cursing me for not answering it.

'It's for you!' she says bluntly.

'Who is it?'

'Go and find out!'

'Sometimes you get a feeling, a kind of presentiment or

warning for what's about to happen. Even before I've picked up the receiver I know who it is on the other end.

'Hello?'

'How you doing, Joe? Thought I'd give you a call. See how you were.'

The urge to hang up comes over me. The familiar, jet-lagged voice triggers powerful emotions pushed down below the level of consciousness.

'What d'you want?'

'Courtesy call, mate, that's all. You've heard about Kurt, I take it?'

'Yeah, I heard.'

'I couldn't believe it. I was, like, devastated when I heard the news.'

He mumbles on in the same vein. Something about a night club organising a candlelit vigil the following evening, and would I like to come along. Typical of him that he'd want to make a big deal out of it, as if he knew Cobain personally.

We slip into old friends mode and talk about the last few weeks as if nothing's happened. Even the tour fails to get a mention. After a few minutes of this, he's forced to humble himself and confront the truth.

'They told me you were getting some kinda treatment, Joe. How's that working out?'

'Great. I'm on a health kick now. No pills, no booze. Nothing.'

'Justine OK?'

'She's fine.'

'And the kids?'

'Kids are fine too.'

He mumbles an affirmative, shamed, perhaps, by his own guilt. I'm not in the mood to listen. What can you say to someone you spent the last ten years with trying to change the world, only to have them shit on you, remorselessly, from a great height?

'Well, better go, I suppose,' he says quietly. 'Take care of yourself, Joe.'

I wander into the front room in a daze. Justine looks up enquiringly.

'What did he want?'

'Some nightclub have organised a vigil for Kurt Cobain. He thought I might wanna go along.'

'The great James T called to ask you *that*?'

'He called to find out if I was still breathing. That's what he called for.'

I can't get over the fact that he actually sounded genuine. A kind of awkward humility in his tone as if he actually cared what happened to me after all. Something else too. Regret for the past, the future. And the most troubling thing of all, the sense that he was somehow paying his last respects. Saying a few pithy words to someone already long gone and forgotten.

18

An exodus of waterproof coats and welly-boots. The deserters traipse down the front path. Sadie, smiling happily, in the yellow NY baseball cap I brought back for her after the last tour of the States. Jake with a fishing net propped on one shoulder like a makeshift rifle. And Alice, waving excitedly at me from her Vauxhall Estate, as if I'm going with them. I wave back, slightly embarrassed, watching Justine load their bags, wondering if she'll miss me.

We iron out the last minute details through the passenger window, me on one side, the happy campers on the other. Justine takes me through the itinerary, one step at a time. I get the feeling she's leaving behind a wilful adolescent.

'You realise I'm trusting you to stay here on your own, don't you?'

'What am I gonna do, blow the place up?'

'You know what I'm talking about.'

'Justine – you're going away for three days, that's all.'

'That's what I'm worried about. Just don't do anything stupid. And remember to feed the cat!'

Watching them drive away, I'm seized with a momentary regret. I could have gone with them and played the dutiful father, impressed Justine with my skills at erecting a tent. But even before the car has turned the corner my feelings have changed. There's a sense of tension, mild curiosity even. I'm alone in the house, subject to the Law of Chaos. Anything can and will happen.

The place is forlorn without them. No Jake kicking a football along the hall. No Sadie snapping at him to stop in that condescending tone she's picked up from her mother. In three days time they'll be back and life will resume as normal. Until then, I'm on my own, with assorted microwave dinners and a drawer full of clean underwear.

Tacked to the fridge door is a list of requirements, Justine's omnipotent presence following me from room to room. *Don't leave the back door open. Don't fall asleep in front of the TV. Read the instruction booklet on top of the microwave.* I feel like a newcomer to the Twentieth Century. All the things I should have learned have passed me by. I've been pampered, cosseted and sheltered since the age of sixteen, spared the indignities ordinary people have to go through and now I'm paying the price.

Justine's shopping pad lies open on the kitchen table. Rows of sundry items ticked off one by one. *Eggs, mince, spaghetti, onions, milk.* The sheer tedium of the list staggers me. No wonder people go insane. How can you aspire to a higher plane of existence with phone bills and piles of dirty washing, endless trips to the supermarket because you've run out of greens.

I pick up the pen and write resentfully. *All work and no play makes Joe a dull boy.* The ghost of Val Moody looms at my shoulder, urging me to try again. Incensed, I tear out the page and thrown it across the room.

Bitterness sets in, an amalgam of all the things I've been trying to suppress for so long. I don't have a band. I don't have a job. My family have all run off and left me. The only alternative is to extract some form of revenge. Perform some meaningful act that will purge me of all these awful resentments and leave me feeling whole again.

A sudden impulse comes over me. I dash upstairs, and wrench open the wardrobe door, pulling out the stage outfits that survived the last clearout. The bohemian rock star look, circa 1985. Silk shirts and paisley waistcoats. Crocodile-skin boots with two inch heels. Collecting them up in my arms, I head for the garden, filled with a wild and jubilant exultation.

A few splashes from a can of lighter fuel and up they go. Red and green silks turn a mottled blue, iridescent sparks leaping upward, whipped away by the wind. The smell of something unwholesome fills the air. My illustrious career gone in a cloud of toxic, black smoke.

*

Carla's problems distract me from my own for a while. We share an intense few minutes discussing the plumber from Soames. The copper pipes he's left in the hallway. The canvas bag, like an animal carcass, with all his greasy tools inside.

'Eight o'clock he was round here, ringing the bell,' she says. 'As if I didn't have enough to put up with.'

'So where is he now?'

'Gone to get more fittings. If he doesn't come back soon I'm phoning the landlord.'

Now we can add tradesmen to the long list of undesirables. Ordinary life, eating up all the precious hours we've been given, and not a break in sight. We share a similar aversion in that respect. All those mind-numbing intervals where nothing much happens. A tedious endurance filled with plumbers and carpenters and TV repairmen, waltzing through the house to ransack your dignity.

We adjourn to the front room, awash with pale sunlight and discarded magazines. Carla snatches up the remote and *GMTV* flashes on. Eamonn Holmes interviews a dumpy, middle-aged woman about the time she spent with some religious cult in Arizona.

The front door slams. Footsteps echo along the hallway, followed soon after by hammer blows and the rending of metal. I'm horrified.

'Jesus! How much longer you gotta put up with that?'

Carla grimaces. 'Not much longer, that's for sure!'

She takes out a small nugget wrapped in clingfilm from her

silver tobacco tin. The lighter flame softens the resin between her thumb and forefinger, making it crumble to the touch. No matter how many times you've seen the ritual before, there's always an element of excitement, like watching a woman undress in a dimly-lit room.

'Can you take me to Exmoor Road?' she says.

'What for?'

She looks at me quizzically. 'To sign-on, of course.'

The hammering ceases. She stares at the wall with utter contempt. 'God, I wish I still lived in Ealing sometimes.'

'Why? What was so good about Ealing?'

'I didn't have to put up with this shit for a start. Can you take me or not?'

Eamonn Holmes concludes his interview and turns to the camera, ready with the smooth Irish charm. Carla zaps him smartly with the off-button and stands.

'Come on then, let's go.'

'What about the plumber?'

'He's got a key, he can let himself out'

Armed and resolute in her fur-trimmed coat and thigh length leather boots, she confronts the poor man in the hallway.

'How much longer d'you think you'll be, I've gotta go out for a while?'

He mumbles something unintelligible, a short, wiry little man in grubby, blue overalls. Carla looks at him coldly.

'I just don't understand why it's taken so long. I mean presumably you heard about this weeks ago from the letting agent?'

Anxious to get away, he makes another excuse. Carla stands by, unmoved, the capacity for forgiveness not high on her list of personal attributes.

'It's just not good enough,' she says. 'I wouldn't get treated like this if I lived in Knightsbridge, would I? You'd be round the same day!'

We drive through the Grove in silence. I think of all my favourite watering holes, out of bounds because of Justine's embargo. The Prince Albert. Finch's. The Warwick. You can picture the hardcore drinkers and stoners hidden inside, intent on hedonism at all costs.

'D'you ever miss it?' I say.

'Miss what?'

'The lifestyle. The gear.'

'Sometimes.'

The stigma must be hard for her, especially coming from a privileged background like she does. Some transition. Flying all over the world with the cream of the country's recording stars, to this – living on state benefits in a rundown tenement, forced to sell a bit of dope now and then just to survive. I'm intrigued by the concept of her signing on.

'What's it like in there?'

'In where?'

'The dole office.'

She checks her face in the mirror. 'It's a dump. What d'you think it's like in there?'

'Do they ask lots of questions?'

'Like what?'

'I don't know. "How are you today, Miss Burns? Was that a monster spliff I saw you smoking outside?" '

She gives me a jaded look and reaches for the door. 'Ten minutes, OK?'

I watch her cross the road and head for the entrance. I'm eight weeks without a drink and nothing has changed. The newfound well-being I'm supposed to be feeling has failed to materialise.

Carla comes back. I search her face for signs of moral degradation.

'How'd it go?'

'How did what go?'

'Signing on. Anyone interesting in there?'

'Oh sure. Couple of Saudi princes. Few members of the Royal Family. Come in with me next time and see for yourself.'

She rolls a cigarette from her tin as I pull away. I tell her about the ritual burning earlier, the decision I've made to sever links with the band. She seems genuinely surprised.

'You burned your clothes?'

'Yeah. I thought it was, kind of, symbolic.'

'Of what?'

'New beginnings.'

An idea occurs to me. What if we were to stop off somewhere and have a drink? A kind of celebration to mark my transition into the solo field. Justine would never find out. No one need ever know, except me and Carla.

'Fancy a drive over to the Metro?' I say.

'What for?'

'See if we can track down Cribbs. Turn Naomi into a global superstar.'

'Is that a good idea?'

'What – Naomi?'

'No, going into a bar. I thought you weren't drinking?'

'So? I just fell off the wagon.'

'And what will Justine say about that?'

'Who cares!' I stare at her irritably. 'What are you – a social worker?'

At the back of my mind lurks a sobering thought. Maybe this isn't such a good idea after all. I can still see Justine's face, peering at me, dubiously, from the passenger side of Alice's car. But what have I gained from this period of enforced sobriety? What good has it done me? I was better off before, finding my own levels of equilibrium from the back street chemists I used to frequent. And look what's happened to my music, my motivation. I've hardly played a note in weeks.

'Just the one, then we'll go,' I say seriously. 'Happy with that?'

'Whatever.'

The deal is on. I feel inspired. Better than I've felt in ages.

19

I come to on the floor. The features of the room don't register. Cream walls with faint, hairline cracks under the coving. Pale orange curtains filtering in the light. Then it hits me. The books in the recess. The paintings on the wall. They're mine. I'm at home. Only it doesn't feel like home. It feels like another planet, somewhere I really shouldn't be.

A key rattles in the lock, the sound amplified along the hallway. I try to sit up and a searing pain shoots across my eyes. The wrecking ball in my head, bringing down walls and opening up new avenues of torture.

The front door jars against the chain. A woman's voice calls my name, repeatedly. The voice is familiar, insistent, an omen of things to come.

Forcing myself up off the floor, I stagger out into the hall, feeling my way like an earthquake victim.

I unhook the chain and open the door. Standing there, oddly impressive in a red dress suit and silver coiffure, is Miriam. We stare at each other with mutual surprise.

'Joe!'

'Hi, Miriam.'

'Justine asked me to drop by to see how you were. I couldn't get in. Are you all right?'

Blisters of sweat break out on my brow. The pain in my head intensifies.

'Can I come in?' she says expectantly.

'Er – I've only just got up. Can you gimme half an hour?'

'I'd really like to come in now, Joe, if you don't mind.'

I feel my way, gingerly, back along the hall, her heels striking the wooden floor behind me.

In one panoramic sweep, we take in the carnage together. Cigarettes and ashtray by the hearth. Empty wine bottles on the coffee table. Records scattered over the carpet. A stale and murky aura lingers, like the fog in a dingy pub.

Miriam opens the curtains and daylight floods in. A mishmash of record covers lie strewn at her feet. Black Sabbath, Steely Dan. Freddie King – live in Texas. The aftermath of a party where all the guests have long since gone.

She hovers by the coffee table, frowning distastefully.

'What's this?'

My heart freezes. Hanging from her fingertips is a strip of blackened foil. I feel like the victim of a horrible game. Someone has crept in during the night and rearranged all the furniture, left incriminating evidence behind to destroy me completely.

'No idea, Miriam. Maybe Justine left it there before she went away.'

She drops the foil on the table and stands back with a grimace of distaste. The pounding in my head gets worse, a siege to the castle walls, complete with battering rams and poisoned arrows.

'Look – I'll clean all this up in a bit, Miriam, no problem.You don't have to stay.'

She turns to me in a daze. 'I was … I was going to cook you some breakfast.'

I manage a weak grin through the sickness. Miriam, frying up eggs, bacon and sausage, while I run round getting rid of the evidence. The wine bottles and the ashtrays. The strip of blackened foil. Remnants of a debauch I can't even remember.

She rocks the wine bottle on the table, reading my mind.

'I thought you weren't drinking?'

'I'm not.'

'So what's this?'

'I had a few friends round last night. They stayed a bit later than planned.'

Maybe she believes me. All those occasions in the past when she's taken my side. The time she caught me smoking weed in her shed and I talked my way out of that. Now I need her help more than ever.

She steps back from the table, glancing nervously about the room. 'I'm really not happy about all this, Joe. I mean the room, the mess. What's Justine going to say when she gets back?'

'I'll clear it up in no time. They don't get back until tomorrow.'

She looks puzzled. 'Didn't you get the message?

'What message?'

'Justine tried to phone you last night. Sadie's had an upset stomach. They're coming back today.'

There are times when you know instinctively that the game is up. Whatever you try to do to change the outcome won't make any difference. All I can do is get Miriam out of the house before she finds something else to hang on me. Hope she won't say too much to Justine.

With some coaxing, I manage to get her out of the front room and into the hallway. Her hollow complaints ring out ahead of me, full of disappointment and regret.

She turns to me with a troubled frown. 'What happened, Joe? I thought you were doing so well lately?'

'I'm fine. Honest, I am. I just had a bit of a late night, that's all.'

With a solemn goodbye, she clip-clops down the steps in her stubby red heels and turns right by the post box on the corner. Eric's probably waiting in his brand new Cavalier, listening to Radio Four and daydreaming about the Test Match at Lord's. They'll probably discuss what's happened in detail. The degenerate son-in-law who couldn't stay clean. Too sick to be there for his own family.

The sense of impending disaster grows by the minute. Like standing at a railway station, waiting for a train to arrive. When it does, the carriages will be filled with people carrying briefcases and depositions, documentary evidence of all the terrible things I've done.

*

I call Carla to find out what happened. She fills in the missing details. The drive over to see Cribbs at the Metro Bar. My sudden decision to have one small drink when we got there. I'm appalled, unable to remember any of it.

'What was I drinking?'

'Lager.'

'Nothing else?'

'I don't know! You had an argument with Cribbs and insisted we leave. Then you dropped me back home and went on somewhere else.'

'Where?'

'How do I know? I wasn't holding your hand all night.'

The implications sink in. The horror of not knowing where you've been or what you've done. Strains of Islington all over again.

I mention the foil Miriam found on the coffee table. Carla sounds as bemused as I am.

'So who did you score from?'

'I don't know!'

'Well think back. Retrace your steps. Where did you go when you left me?'

'I can't remember!'

'What nothing?'

'No! Nothing! Nothing at all!'

Hangover cures don't work. I've tried them all. The long glass of cold water before bed. Full English breakfast the morning after. Nothing quite matches the hair of the dog for levelling out the edges but you've got to have the stomach to keep it all down. Sleep is the best option. I once crashed-out for thirteen hours straight on a flight back from Singapore and woke up feeling reborn.

I sit at the kitchen table and stare at the cat. He looks up from his water bowl, patently disinterested in my physical condition. Stomach cramps. Sweat oozing from every pore. The spectre of death stalking me wherever I go.

One thing's becoming clearer. When Justine gets back, I need to be somewhere else. Put some distance between me and the fallout.

20

I make the call from a phone box on Holland Park Avenue.
Sadie answers and for the next few minutes we have this bizarre
conversation to determine who I am and the exact purpose of
the call. I put up with it a while longer before losing my temper.

'Sadie, just put Mum on, will you? I need to speak to her
now.'

'She doesn't want to talk to you.'

'Why not?'

'Because you burnt a hole in the carpet with a cigarette. You
could have burnt the whole house down, too!'

A leaden weariness descends on me.

'Sadie, just get Mum, will you, please?'

Alone here in this dank, piss-stained phone box, I'm
reminded of all the trials behind me. The shameful sequence of
events that brought me to this point. Waking up in a strange bed
with some deranged woman in Islington. Losing my job through
no real fault of my own. Doctors and drug counsellors, droning
on about addiction, expecting me to live without my best fried.
How has it come to this? A life that started out with so much
promise and opportunity. Maybe it's all down to genetics. The
unconventional upbringing I had as a child.My errant father,
who was never around. The best sax player of his generation,
who abandoned me in a cinema queue one afternoon to go off
carousing with his mates.

'What do you want?'

I'm shocked from my reverie, heart beating fast.

'I just wanted to talk to you.'

'What about?'

The speech I had prepared vanishes. I try another angle. The innocent victim, left alone to fend for himself.

'I'm not interested,' she says. 'You've broken the terms of the agreement and that's it.'

'I've done what?'

'I'm not arguing with you. You've gone back on everything we talked about. Drinking. Taking drugs. I'm sick of it.'

'Listen, I can – '

'You're not talking your way out of it this time. It's over. Finished. And if you try coming round here I'll call the police.'

I can't believe the effrontery. A few drinks in your own home and suddenly you're being treated like a monster. 'So that's it then? You're just going to kick me out like that?'

'Oh – you think I should have you back after what Mum found, do you?'

Any fight I might have had drains out of me.

'Listen, Justine – '

'No, you listen. You brought that *filth* into the house. After all we talked about. All the promises you made. That's how much we mean to you, isn't it?'

'Look, I'm sorry, OK? Gimme a break. Please.'

But the guilt trip won't work, flung back at me with extraordinary venom. She reels off a list of all the things I've done. The awful disappointment I've been as a husband and father. And worst of all, the criminal neglect of two young children.

'I went out of my way to help you,' she says. 'And you've thrown it all back in my face. I can't take it anymore. Go and destroy yourself somewhere else!'

The blur of the dialling tones cut-in. I see where I am. Alone in an airless phone box, the word 'fuck' scratched in the glass by some maladjusted loser. Where do I go from here? Carla's spare room? Cribbs's sofa? Neither option sounds too promising. Misfortune has bad connotations, after all. Once you hit the skids even your friends stop talking to you.

I make a second call.

'Shaz? Listen, I'm in a bit of a dilemma ...'

Cars flash by. People in the street. An old woman searching her handbag with a look of abject consternation. I push my foot against the door to let in some air and get a flashback to New York in the Eighties. An irate taxi driver in Brooklyn, throwing up his arms at a jay walker, yelling, *'Hey, buddy! There's something wrong with the picture here!'*

There's something wrong with the picture here, too. I've stepped out of a nice, comfortable home, with a wife and two beautiful kids, into a nightmare. My skin's crawling with unidentified toxins. My brain's been cleaved in two. And yet I can't escape the nagging thought that keeps recurring. If only I'd bought a few cans and drunk them at home she might never have known. I might have got away with it.

'Shaz – you still there?'

The honest approach is usually the best. I tell her everything, except for the bit about Miriam finding the foil on the coffee table. She's philosophical, understanding. The good Christian, always there for others in times of trouble.

'I can't do it for long, Joe, I've got the kids to think about.'

'Yeah, I know, Shaz, but this is an emergency. She's kicked me out on the streets. I'm homeless.'

After a tense pause, she gives in. Relief washes over me. My kind and caring sister, saving me from destitution.

'Thanks, Shaz. I appreciate it. I really do.'

Wandering the streets, hungover and filled with remorse, I'm vaguely aware of pedestrians passing me by. A couple come out of the newsagents and pause to cross the road. The woman catches my eye and appears to recoil visibly as if she's seen something of particular distaste. I move on, quickly, pondering the mess I'm in, the complete and utter breakdown of human resources. One minute planning the future, the next alone and abandoned, paying the price for one colossal moment of stupidity.

21

The tube is packed with android commuters. They hang on plastic handrails and stare into space. The red-haired girl next to me is reading a paperback. She rocks gently with the motion of the carriage, ignoring the two jabbering city boys to her right. All of us, lost among the driftwood. Bemused travellers heading east in the most inhumane conditions possible, packed together without an inkling why.

Shepherd's Bush looms. The girl with the paperback gets off, her faded denim and red hair lost in the crowd. A big black mama takes her place, staunch and immovable in layers of synthetic black. I gaze at her, admiringly, in my semi-catatonic state. With inner strength like that you could cope with anything. Face up to your problems instead of always running away.

The doors whoosh shut and the carriage jerks forward. If Hell had a soundtrack, this would be it. The clanging and grinding of steel wheels careering into nothingness, half the population of London on board. Soon the noise is deafening. Bearable for the average commuter maybe but not for a refugee with a terminal hangover.

Blackness gives way to bright, fluorescent light. The train slows and the glazed brown tiles of Holland Park Station appear in the carriage windows. Relief wells up in me that, at last, the nightmare is over.

Breathing in traffic fumes and recycled air I exit the steps, all my worldly possessions slung over one shoulder. Memories of the last few hours play over in a painful loop. Calling in at the house to collect my things. Being given a few tense minutes to decide what to take and what to leave behind. Justine watching me coldly from the doorway.

'Get your things and go. I don't want you here any longer than necessary.'

'Can't I see the kids and say goodbye?'

'Don't you think you've caused enough trouble already?'

Eight years of marriage dismissed as if it was nothing. Barred from seeing my own children. Even the memories don't seem like mine, hidden away in a box marked, *'Not to be opened.'*

A small, blue-eyed urchin opens the door. I gaze down upon him with a mixture of sadness and affection.

'Hello, Charlie.'

'Are you coming to stay at my house?'

'Yes. But only if I can eat all your sweets.'

Charlie looks bemused, mildly suspicious even. Maybe he still remembers the rooster's claw I brought back for him from New Orleans one Christmas. I've never seen Shaz so upset. Even the normally mild-mannered Terry had a go at me in the kitchen after dinner.

Shaz greets me in the hall, looking subdued and weary. She notes my holdall with a frown. 'Is that all you've brought with you?'

'What did you expect – a suitcase? I had five minutes to grab a few things and get out before Justine slapped an injunction on me.'

We stand awkwardly in the narrow hall facing each other. Shaz already has that look of advanced martyrdom.

'I've made up a bed for you in Charlie's room,' she says quietly. 'Go and put your bag up, I'll make you a coffee.'

'Don't I get a kiss? A hug?'

She steps forward and, almost reluctantly, we embrace. I'm overcome. The first real human contact I've had in ages and it affects me deeply. We part, slightly embarrassed. I try to summon up any reserves of charm I might have left, an essence of the exuberant younger brother, always ready to entertain.

'Thanks, Shaz. You're a real lifesaver. I don't know what I'd do without you.'

My room is sunny and bright and crowded with toys. Small model planes hang from the ceiling, suspended by lengths of cotton. In one corner there's a mini drum kit. Next to that a white plastic table and chair. The bunk beds are made up perfectly without a crease in the matching duvets.

The view from the window reveals the small garden with its patchy lawn and makeshift washing line. Strangely I'm disappointed. After all the heartache she's been through I would have wanted something better for Shaz and the kids. A bigger house, maybe. More money. Without Terry she's had to resign herself to second best, the kind of dire situation no-one wants to end up in.

*

A mug of coffee sits on the dining table, presumably for me. Shaz is out the back, pottering around in the kitchen. The unmistakable blare of Kids TV comes from the front room — that perennial head-fuck that can triple a hangover by proximity alone.

Fragments of my former life begin to haunt me already. Jake climbing all over me while I'm trying to take a nap. Sadie gazing virtuously up at me while she hammers me at chess. Even the thought of Justine has a certain poignancy, an added twist that makes the whole thing more unbearable.

Shaz joins me at the table.

'Have you eaten?' she says.

'I had a pork-pie earlier.'

'Would you like to eat with us, or were you planning on going out?'

'I'd love to eat with you. I just didn't want to push my luck so soon.'

Strange how quickly you can adapt to new surroundings. One minute traumatised by eviction, the next looking forward to a home cooked meal.

'Where's Kayla?'

'At her friend's. She'll be back soon.'

'Does she know I'm staying?'

'Not yet.' She looks at me firmly. 'Joe – I think we should get a few ground rules out of the way before we go on. Is that OK?'

'Sure.'

'First of all, this isn't a hotel. I don't want you coming in at all hours, waking everyone up.'

'No, course not.'

'Secondly, I've got the kids to think about. There's things like bedtimes and school runs. I don't want any major disruptions to their schedule. Is that all right?'

'Shaz – You won't even know I'm here. I promise you.'

'I just felt it needed to be said.'

The lecture over for now, she sits back. At least she hasn't laid the God trip on me yet. Scriptural verses from the Bible on how to toe the line. You have to make allowances, I suppose. Bereavement does strange things to people, taking away the capacity for rational thought. She was leaning that way before Terry died, but his death must have pushed her over the edge. As a topic for conversation we tend to steer well clear. To Shaz, my heathen views are unacceptable. A lifelong student of Sartre and Schopenhauer, I don't believe in anything, least of all the man with the long, white beard sitting in judgement of us all.

Kayla looks older than I remember her. She waltzes in with pale, spindly legs and frizzy-blonde hair. The bag on her back looks almost bigger than she is.

Shaz calls out. 'Kayla. Come here, please.'

Kayla turns reluctantly and shuffles over.

'Isn't there something you've forgotten?' Shaz says. Kayla gives a perfunctory smile.

'Hi, Uncle Joe.'

The merits of communication. Children following parental rules at all times. I sit on the sidelines listening, the perennial dropout, with nothing relevant to say.

Shaz explains that good old Uncle Joe is coming to stay for a few days. But Kayla needn't worry. Everything will carry on as normal. The domestic routine won't alter one little bit. I try to make light of the situation. 'I've moved all my things into your room, Kayla. You'll have to sleep on the sofa for a few days.'

With a dubious smile, she wanders off, the oversized bag swaying on her hip. Shaz watches her go, pensively.

'I do worry about her sometimes. She keeps everything on the inside.'

'She'll get over it'

Shaz looks at me incredulously.

'I meant kids are resilient. They bounce back.'

Sadness pervades the whole house. Terry's boisterous spirit no more than a memory, something left behind for the rest of them to cling on to. I wish there was something else I could say, some meaningful gesture that would make it all better.

'Charlie OK?'

'He's fine.'

'Does he mind me staying?'

'Of course not. He thinks it's great you're sleeping in his room.'

She folds her arms and looks at me expectantly.

'Come on then … Tell me what happened.'

Other people's problems are always so much easier to deal with than your own. Especially when the wound goes so deep you can't bear to think about it. Shaz understands. The pressure of living at home and conforming to other people's expectations. All the arguments between me and Justine. In my current state the whole thing's too painful to talk about. Too draining. But I do owe her some kind of explanation at least.

'I went out with Carla, had a drink in the Metro and that was it. I woke up in the front room the next morning.'

'I thought you'd stopped drinking?'

'I did – for six weeks.'

'What made you start again?'

'Boredom, I suppose.'

Miriam's sudden visit plays like a horror movie in my head. The front door jarring against the chain. That shrill voice ringing out along the hall. I touch on the worst aspects, the vagaries of losing your mind at inopportune moments. Shaz looks at me curiously.

'Can't you remember anything?'

'Nothing at all.'

'But how did you get home?'

'No idea. I was blitzed. Out of it.'

There seems little point in hiding the truth. As soon as she speaks to Justine she'll find out and I'll be implicated anyway.

'There is something else ... Miriam found a strip of foil on the coffee table.'

She looks puzzled. 'Foil?'

I glance behind me to make sure the kids aren't listening. 'It's a drug thing ... You know ... for chasing smack.'

Her frown deepens. I can't believe her naivety, the fact I've got to say the word out loud.

'*Heroin.*'

'You mean you were – '

'No! *I* wasn't using it. Someone else must have brought it into the house without me knowing.'

The whole drugs thing puts me in a bad light. But Shaz knows how it is, with my job and everything. She's read enough about me over the years to know I'm no saint. This is all about damage limitation. Doing what you can to protect your reputation before it's trashed completely.

'It wasn't my fault, Shaz. Justine's blown the whole thing out of proportion.'

'Do you think she'll have you back?'

'Not this time. You should have seen the way she looked at me when I went round to pick my stuff up. She wouldn't even let me say goodbye to the kids.'

Thinking of Jake and Sadie opens up a well of guilt and remorse that's too black to contemplate. They're the innocent ones in all this. Stuck between two warring factions. Two people who can't agree on anything except their total inability to be in the same room.

'So what are you going to do?' she says.

'About Justine?'

'About everything.'

I can't answer. The truth is I don't know.

Charlie's intrigued to be sharing his bedroom with his favourite uncle. He shows me his planes – Spitfires, Hurricanes and a Japanese Zero – hanging from the ceiling. I suggest he adds a few bombers to his collection to make it complete. He look up at me innocently.

'Have you been on a plane before?'

'Lots of times.'

'What's it like?'

'Depends who you end up sitting next to. The last time, I had this big fat man next to me, taking up all the room.'

'How fat was he?'

I spread my arms and puff out my cheeks. Charlie grins with delight.

'Has Jake been on a plane, too?'

'A couple of times. But he wouldn't have remembered much about it, he was too young.'

Charlie thinks. 'Is Jake coming to my house?'

'Er – not today. He's at home with his mum. Wanna play a game or something?'

We sit on the floor like Navaho Indians and spin the globe he got for his last birthday. For some reason the places he'd like to visit are populated by huge, scary monsters with limb-tearing capabilities and mad, bulging eyes.

'Have you seen a Spiderpig?' he says.

'Not recently. What is it?'

'It's big and it lives under the stairs.'

'Does it eat people?'

'Yes.'

'Would it eat me?'

'No.'

'Why not?'

'Because you're made of big green bogeys!'

I adjourn to the bathroom – the window ledge bristling with cacti and lush, green pot plants. The glass fronted shower cubicle seals me inside, the grime from Saturday night's debauchery washed effortlessly down the plughole. An illusion of cleanliness. The guest in someone else's home, everything you touch on loan. The soap, the shower gel – even the cleansing jets of hot water. All offered on a precondition that you behave yourself and don't cause any fuss.

*

The Asian proprietor follows my movements with deep suspicion. Maybe he sees something I don't. The potential for trouble maybe. Some basic dishonesty I've yet to see in myself.

I wander the aisles with a keen sense of unease. Foreign tinned-goods line the shelves. Bags of pasta and exotic flavoured rice. The chill from the freezer cabinet gets in my bones, moving me swiftly on. The strains of an Arabic dirge serenades me behind the shimmer curtain, making me think Beirut or Marrakech.

Death Valley looms up ahead. Rows of imported lagers and beers stacked floor to ceiling. Vodka in five different languages. I only came in looking for shaving foam and razors, but the temptation is too great. Shaz would never know. I could down a couple of cans on the way back and hide the others in Charlie's room. The internal debate goes on, an exchange between former lovers.

A saying from rehab comes to me, one of the many they used to scare us into submission. *'No mental defence against the first drink.'* Maybe they were right. There is no defence. I'm caught in the grip of something beyond my control.

The Asian proprietor rings in the items, his gaze darting between the till and the goods on the counter – shaving foam, razors and a half bottle of Vodka. There's something vaguely disturbing about this odd little collection, but I can't work out what it is.

'Anything else?' he says abruptly. I buy an *Evening Standard* to complete the subterfuge. He folds the paper, slips it in the bag and takes my money, and in that moment we share a lingering distrust, reinforced by decades of cultural misunderstanding.

Holland Park looks cold and unfriendly, a continuum of the atmosphere I left on the tube. People are too consumed with their own lives to worry about anyone else's That collective indifference you find in any big city, deepening feelings of loneliness and isolation.

A quick blast of vodka changes everything. The taste is foul, metallic, burning my throat and the lining of my stomach. Then something mystical happens. A strange chemical reaction. A warm glow that spreads from the core outwards.

Tomorrow I'll stop.

Buy Shaz a box of chocolates and some flowers.

Call Justine and make restitution.

The chink, chink in the blue bag reassures me, jollying me along. Good old Russian vodka. Cheap, odourless and easily concealed.

The sickness has gone. I feel better already.

22

Emma has one of those soft, baby-doll voices, with a curious, heart-warming lilt at the end of each sentence. She feeds my details into the computer and we wait for the response.

'Sorry about the delay,' she says sweetly. 'These things are so slow sometimes.'

'No problem, Emma. I can wait.'

The alcove we're in gives the illusion of privacy. Someone shuffles papers at a nearby desk. A phone rings on the far side. I try to pretend I'm someone else. A businessman, or company director. Some well meaning entrepreneur trying to create jobs for the unemployed.

'How much was it you wanted to borrow, Mr Byron?'

'Four thousand, eight-hundred, please.'

Always ask for less than five thousand, Carla said. That way you don't need to produce evidence of income and mortgage statements as a guarantee. What's five grand anyway? I've squandered more on clothes and thought nothing of it.

'And what's your occupation?'

'Musician.'

'How much do you earn?'

'Difficult to say, really. My earnings tend to fluctuate.'

'Could you say roughly?'

'On average, I'd say about a grand a week. I'm waiting for an overseas contract to be finalised at the moment, so I need something to tide me over until then.'

She nods, reassuringly, tapping the details in with her podgy fingers. I feel I should capitalise on this unique opportunity to make myself known.

'Do you like music, Emma?'

'Yes, I do.'

'What's your favourite band?'

'Blur.'

'Really? Funny you should say that, I know Damon quite well. He lives round the corner from me.'

I picture Emma in a pair of fishnet stockings and a Basque, hoovering up a fat line of toot from a glass-topped table. I'm standing behind her, hands on her ample hips, pumping away like a beast. Somehow the imagery doesn't compute. I feel like shit, my personal life in disarray.

We wait for a new document to load. Emma frowns at the screen, her dainty chin resting on her freckled fist.

'Patience is a virtue, Emma.'

She smiles vaguely. 'Oh, I don't have much of that, I'm afraid.'

'Me neither. It's one of my major failings, so I'm told.'

They say money is the root of all evil, but that's only true if you've got fuck-all. When you've spent your whole life squandering what you've earned in clubs and bars and seedy bordellos you begin to see the need for some restraint. I should have paid more attention to the financial side of things when I was younger, instead of letting other people take control. Apart from buying the house with Justine eight years ago, I've done nothing to safeguard the future at all.

In the end it comes down to expectations. When you're just starting out and someone slips a grand in cash in your back pocket telling you to go out and have some fun you tend to think all your problems are over. The gravy train will keep rolling on forever. For over ten years, all my life consisted of was clothes, records and drugs, and getting to the next soundcheck on time. Now I'm in the same state as everyone else. Ground down by fate. Forced to look for handouts with an air of desperation.

'Ah, here we are!' Emma says. 'Looks like everything's gone through.'

'The money's in my account?'

'It is, yes.'

A surge of elation grips me. I stand, smiling expansively, the most agreeable person in the world.

'Thank you so much, Emma, you've been extremely helpful. I'll have a word with Damon and see if I can get you a free ticket for one of their gigs. Either that or you can come to one of mine... Have a nice day now!'

I leave the premises nearly five grand better off. The thought of all that money in my account instils in me a fleeting happiness, consolation for all the heartache I've suffered in the last few days. I'm alone now. Freed from the responsibility of marriage and children, the indignity of having to earn a wage. What else can I do but celebrate?

23

Lunchtime in the Prince Albert. A motley crew of drinkers sit around the polished mahogany bar, supping ale and chatting amongst themselves. Sunlight kisses the wood and the pint of Stella idling before me. My six week brush with sobriety is over, ended on a whim a few days before. I'm mesmerised by the simplicity, the sense of ordinariness about the whole thing. No one looks surprised. No one comes running up, urging me to reconsider. I'm back, reintegrated into the fold as if I'd never been away.

The moonfaced barmaid comes over. She has this palpable aura of sadness that adds to her charm. I used to fantasize we were lovers, forced to meet in secret locations. Then I upset her one night with some offhand remark and things were never the same.

'Did you miss me?' I say, hopefully.

'I didn't know you'd been gone.'

'It's my yearly sabbatical. I take six weeks off to unwind, then it's back to the grindstone like everyone else.'

The old boy along the bar waves a finger and, dutifully, she wanders off. Her first customers of the day – me, the old boy, and an assortment of regulars. There's a timelessness to the scene that lends to the attraction. Like a soap opera on TV where you can pick up on conversations that were going on months ago. People you thought had died, or been barred by the landlady, turn up and mingle brazenly. Spend enough time in these places and the atmosphere seeps into your pores, becomes a part of you that's hard to resist.

Irish Mary totters in around lunchtime, her broad Belfast accent ringing round the bar. She has the look of a car crash victim, dishevelled and permanently out of sorts, garish make-up over wrinkled, parchment skin. I can't resist a little harmless repartee.

'Top of the Marnin' to you, Mary! Where've you been, we were just about to send out a search party!'

She winks at me, mischievously, fishing in her handbag for her deluxe plastic purse. The actress in her takes over. That urgent need to perform to the crowd, whether it's a handful of regulars or a heaving mob on a Saturday night. And, like all consummate performers, she never gives less than her best shot.

The barmaid loiters by the optics, hands behind her back like a playground monitor. I think I'm in love but I can't be sure. It feels like love but it might be something else. Lust or boredom maybe.

'Ever been to California?' I say.

She shakes her head.

'It's beautiful. Plenty of sunshine. Beaches that go on for miles. We could go together someday.'

A tired smile flickers and fades away. She polishes the bar with a cloth. Each small, circular motion brings us closer together.

'Don't you ever get bored?'

'Of what?'

'Working in a bar. Reprobates like me coming in, annoying you all the time.'

'Sometimes.'

'Well at least you're honest. That's a quality that's missing these days, don't you think?'

Irish Mary's shrill laugh rings out from the other end. I shared a taxi with her one night and learned more about her arthritis and the noisy kids in Flat 11 than in countless sessions propping up the bar. But the barmaid's hard work, a reminder I'm not so well known around these parts. In Japan, we were mobbed at the airport, literally descended on by hordes of screaming teenage girls. Here I'm just another punter, shamelessly trying it on.

'What do you do when you're not working?'

'Sleep, generally.'

'What about your social life? Don't you go out?'

'Not much.'

'That's terrible. You should come out with me one night.'

'I don't think so.'

'Why not?'

'I don't think my boyfriend would like it.'

Maybe it wasn't the offhand remark that did it last time. Maybe it was the drunken pass I made at her one Christmas Eve. My life's been filled with similar incidents, nearly always landing me in some kind of trouble. The flight to Stuttgart after a late night boozing session in Pimlico, where I upset a taxi driver with a joke I made about his wife, then nearly got thrown off the plane for insulting a stewardess. Why do people take offence so easily? Can't they appreciate the warped sense of humour that comes from supping a few ales?

The sleazy barman joins us from the back bar, his trademark fringe angled stylishly over one eye. He grins amiably. 'Hello, mate! Ain't seen you for a while. Been abroad?'

'Busy at home.'

'Touch of decorating was it?'

'Something like that.'

He shakes his head ironically. 'Women, eh? Do one room they want the whole house done. Pint of Stella?'

The view from a bar stool is all encompassing. You get a unique insight into the world without even moving. The serious issues of the day discussed at leisure, like the *Sun's* Page Three Girl or who's next on the pool table. Serious drinkers cherish the quiet moments, a kind of meditative pause before the real rabble come in.

But somewhere in the background is the nagging sense of loss, of having something of inestimable value and throwing it away.

The barman lingers, focusing in on me with a silly grin.

'How's the band?'

'Sorry?'

'The one you were telling me about the other night. You trashed some hotel in L.A. Ran through the corridors with no clothes on.'

I stare at him blankly. I don't remember telling him anything about the band, or the incident he's referring to. But he has that perverse, stubborn streak you can't ignore, and clearly expects me to fill in the details. One of the downsides of drinking too much and forgetting what you've said.

'Shame about Kurt Cobain, wasn't it,' he says. 'Ever meet him on your travels?'

'No, I didn't.'

'All that money and fame. Didn't do him much good, did it.' He flicks his fringe from his eyes and ponders. 'Funny lot, pop stars, aren't they. What was the name of that geezer on *Top of the Pops* a few years back, prancing round with half a tree hanging out his back pocket?'

'Morrissey.'

'That's the one. They get paid for that shit, too, do they? Jesus. I'm in the wrong job, mate.'

Booze – the antidote to all human failings. No matter how bad things are, you can always seek solace in the glass. That sublime state of immunity from the outside world. From other people.

The sleazy barman leans closer, a strange imploring look on his face.

'Listen – you're in with the local dance crowd, incha?'

'Who?'

'Trendies. Ravers. Cruising up the M25 looking for warehouse parties.'

I stare at him in confusion. He lowers his voice urgently.

'Your mate, Danny. You was in here with him the other night.'

'So?'

'I was wondering. You know. Maybe you could have a word with him.' He glances nervously around. 'Sort me out a couple of them love-hearts everyone's talking about.'

I can't believe it. The first time I've set foot in the place for weeks and already I'm being accosted by shameless drug-fiends looking for pills. I should be at home, repairing the cracks to my ailing marriage. Ringing round contacts, looking for work.

*

We sit around the table with a pack of playing cards. Four of us. Three irreverent building site workers and me. The perfect number for a little late afternoon fun. I'm pleasantly wasted, in an easygoing and non-confrontational way. Who wants to end up fighting the bouncers or being ejected by the landlady when you can sit back and enjoy the atmosphere? The goal is simple. Get quietly and honourably slaughtered before sauntering back to my lonely room.

The heavily-tattooed lump shuffles the pack and calls us to order. 'Right! You know the rules. First Jack names it. Second sips it. Third drinks it. And fourth pays for it. All drinks must be doubles. Got it?'

The game commences.

Philosophy measures everything against impending death. We're all on a limited run here anyway so what's the point in seeking attachments? Your last day on earth and the chances are you won't even know it. This game we're playing has no more relevance than the raucous chatter drifting round the bar, but its existence gives it meaning. We're unified by it – the four of us – driven to see it through by forces beyond our control.

'First Jack!' yells the tattooed lump and a satisfied murmur goes round. Player number one, the man with the scar on his cheek, ponders the Jack of Hearts as tension mounts round the table.

'What'll it be, Mo?' the lump says.

Mo scratches his chin and looks up with a malicious smirk.

'Tia Maria and coke!'

A collective groan goes up at such a devious choice. But we all know the rules. First Jack chooses. Second sips, Third drinks, and Fourth pays.

As the cards are dealt, poignant memories surface, triggered by the banter round the table and the noise from the bar. Haunting scenes from life on the road. A roll-call of sound engineers, roadies and assorted hangers-on – limos waiting to whisk us away to a nearby hotel. The glamorous life I used to lead, played out in flashbacks and dreams, snatched so cruelly away by the monster of fate.

'Second Jack!'

The crowd roars.

Player number two smiles lazily, the Jack of Clubs upturned beneath his leathery face. He knows the score. To drown in alcohol is a vocation. You need to be suited to the task, like an astronaut to space travel. You have to understand the pitfalls, the dangers. The likelihood that you'll come home from the pub one night to find the locks have been changed, your long-suffering wife has taken a lover.

'Third Jack!'

The illusive Jack of Spades lands in front of player number three – a mean-looking dwarf in a lumberjack shirt who shakes his head in grim disbelief. 'Unbelievable,' he says. 'Fucking unbelievable.'

The tattooed lump reminds the dwarf of his sworn duty. He *must* down the drink – in one, at the game's conclusion, witnessed by the rest of the committee.

'Rules is rules, me old cocker,' the lump says heartily. 'Rules is rules.'

The cards are dealt again.

My mind drifts. Playing Spoof with Kamikaze Bob in the Warwick. Bob, the easy-going telephone engineer from Gravesend, who rammed his ex-wife's car outside the family home, earning him a hefty fine from the judge and the Kamikaze nickname from Danny. The summer of 1990. Jake had just been born and the World Cup was on. I'd come back from a tour of Sweden, and was on reasonably good terms with Justine. Memorable days, gone forever.

'Fourth Jack!'

The crowd roar again.

The Jack of Diamonds sits upturned on the table – in front

of me.

'Tough luck, son!' the lump says, clapping me on the back. 'Double Tia Maria and coke for me mate here. And don't hang about – you're paying!'

Rising graciously from the chair, I excuse myself from the table. The lump watches, carefully, unofficial timekeeper and referee. The regulars at the bar step back to let me through, as if the whole thing has been choreographed beforehand.

The moonfaced barmaid looms conveniently.

'Listen, love, I need a favour. See that big bloke over there ...'

The outside air is cool and welcoming. My quick exit out the back door seems to have gone unnoticed. Just to make sure, I pick up the pace, from a sedate stroll to a light jog, dodging the odd pedestrian on Lancaster Road. The pitfalls of fraternising with these building site types are serious. You could get your head kicked-in for the slightest infraction. But it was worth it for the adrenalin rush. That one sublime moment when you're out there on the wire.

*

I put the key in the lock and enter, closing the door quietly behind me. The hallway and staircase are in shadow, silence pervading the whole house. Making my way through to the kitchen, I collide with an armchair and curse under my breath. For a moment I imagine I'm at home, that the vague outlines of the room are familiar.

A light goes on in the stairwell.

I'm caught, like a thief, with the cupboard door open, one hand on a bottle of Pimm's.

Shaz appears in a dressing gown, and peers at me with sleep-filled eyes.

'What're you doing?'

'Looking for the teabags.' I shut the cupboard door. 'Don't mind me. Go back to bed.'

'Joe – it's one o'clock in the morning. Where have you been?'

'I met a few friends in Knightsbridge. Had a few ales.' I grin helplessly, amused at my impression of Withnail. She stares back at me, unimpressed.

'I told you I didn't want you coming in waking everyone up.'

'Shaz, please. I'm gonna listen to some music on the headphones for a while. Then I'll go to bed.'

'Why can't you go now?'

'Cause I'm wide awake. I told you before, I don't keep the same hours as you. Remember?'

She wrestles with the dilemma, uncertain.

'Please don't make any noise.'

'I won't. Honest. I'm just gonna chill out down here for a while before I get my head down.'

I listen out for the creak of her feet on the staircase.

The stair light goes out.

Now we're alone. Me and the bottle of Pimm's, left to our own devices.

24

Shaz stirs mixed herbs into a wok, the portable TV on in the corner to keep her company. I still can't get used to the transition, the fact that I'm here and not at home. The past intrudes, catching me at odd moments. Painful thoughts, triggered by snatches of music and conversation, the spicy, cooking smells coming from the pan.

'Corkscrew, Shaz?'

'Should be in the left-hand drawer.'

Maybe she likes having a man in the house, even if it is only her dissolute brother. We can all sit round the table and pass the bread rolls, discussing *EastEnders* like a proper family.

'Sorry – can't find it.'

She sifts through the drawer and finds the corkscrew, laying it on the worktop with a disapproving glance at me.

'Wine glasses?'

'Top cupboard above the microwave.'

I take two glasses and open the bottle. She looks up pensively.

'Joe – is that really necessary?'

'What?'

'Drinking with your dinner. Can't you just have water instead?'

'It's red wine. What's wrong with that?'

She turns back to the stove, stirring vigorously. Two fluted glasses sit on the worktop along with the cheap Beaujolais bought from my newfound chum, the Asian proprietor. I don't understand her reaction. Wine is an appetiser. The perfect accompaniment to any meal. If I'd wanted to be really antisocial I'd have brought vodka, as well as the replacement bottle of Pimm's, and downed it from the neck of the bottle.

I pour myself a glass and hover the bottle over hers.

'Shaz?'

'No thanks.'

'Sure?'

'Yes, I'm sure. Could you lay the table for me, please?'

I'm a little fazed by her attitude, the long silence to put me on the spot. What's a few glasses of wine when you've been around the world and drank with the best. Even Hugh Hanley used to comment on my tolerance, this inbuilt capacity I seem to have to keep going when everyone else has faded away.

We sit at the table, Charlie and Kayla like graduates from finishing school. None of the bickering and rowing we had in our house at meal times. Maybe that's where I failed as a parent. Giving in too often. Being overly lenient when all they needed was a good old-fashioned clip round the ear.

Shaz says Grace.

Red tea-lights burn softly in the alcoves. Nina Simone sings a soulful lament. Shaz has this nun-like serenity on her face, her hands clasped, devoutly, together. How did this strange religious obsession come about? The need to pay lip-service to a worn out ideal. We grew up in the same house, listening to Louis Armstrong and Errol Garner. Art and culture reigned supreme. With all the atheists and agnostics in our family you'd think she'd have known better. But right now I'm not that bothered. I'm the guest, enjoying her hospitality. As long as the wine flows freely, I can put up with anything. Even religion.

'Bolognese is great, Shaz. You got the sauce just right.'

'Thank you.'

'Bon Appétit.'

We touch glasses – my cheap Beaujolais and her still water. She avoids my eye, noticeably distant since we all sat down. A continuation of the atmosphere in the kitchen when I opened the wine. In the best Christian tradition, I try to be agreeable. Did Kayla learn anything new at school? I ask. Has Charlie shot down any German bombers in the back garden lately? Charlie grins infectiously. We're the best of mates, sharing bunk beds in his toy-filled room. But something's missing. Where's the raucousness and the fooling around? The irrepressible spirit of rebellion I've tried to encourage in my own children?

'Dessert?' Shaz says.

'No thanks. That was sublime. If I'd known you were *that* good a cook I'd come round more often.'

Kayla and Charlie clear the plates away without a murmur. The wine bottle glints in the flickering light, the level already well below the halfway mark. My thoughts are subdued, melancholy. I've been drinking solidly for days now, topping up every now and then in order to function. The trick is to appear normal, to hold a conversation without slurring your words. Sometimes it works, sometimes it doesn't.

Shaz toys with her glass, thoughtful. 'You didn't tell me you'd been seeing a counsellor.'

'Who told you that?'

'I spoke to Justine earlier.'

I shrug, irritably.

'Don't you want to talk about it?'

'What's there to say? It's a sham. We just sit in a room and talk about drop-in centres and how to cook rice.'

She says nothing. I sense a conspiracy.

'What else did Justine say?'

'She thinks you should go back to the doctor.'

'What for?'

'Because you're drinking again.'

'What – a couple of glasses of wine with dinner? What harm's that gonna do?'

I drain the glass and pour another. The wine has a bitter, acidic taste, not my usual choice, but welcome at a time like this. More pressure. Shaz and Justine ganging up to get me to do things I don't want to do.'

'Why should Justine care what happens to me anyway? She was the one who kicked me out in the first place.'

'Of course she cares. You're still her husband.'

'Not for much longer. She'll get one of Hugh Hanley's

lawyers on the case and I'll get shafted completely.'

Nina Simone's plaintive crooning starts to lose its appeal. I need something more upbeat to enhance the effect of the Beaujolais.

'Can't you put something else on?'

'What's wrong with this?'

'It's depressing. Got any dance music?'

Reluctantly, she changes the CD – a busy instrumental with violin and cello. Soon I'm hopelessly lost in the past. The stark realities of life in Ladbroke Grove, the longest I've lived anywhere since I left home as a teenager. The year we bought the house, I ran into Dutch during the Carnival, and we shot speed in his flat in Powis Square. Up all night listening to Black Uhuru and the Clash, watching the festivities outside his window. Sadie came along in May the next year. A cute little baby with a screwed-up face and a sprig of black hair like the holly on a Christmas pudding. I celebrated fatherhood with a night at Subterranea and two grams of high grade coke. Less than a year later, Dutch was dead of a heroin overdose, and I was off touring the States, so immersed in the drug scene myself I failed to notice the warnings.

'D'you think I'm selfish, Shaz?'

'In what way?'

'Justine says I'm the most selfish person she's ever met.'

She ponders. 'I think it's been hard for you, doing what you do. You've had to, compromise.'

'How d'you mean?'

'Well. All the travelling you do. The fact you're hardly ever home. It doesn't lend itself to married life exactly, does it?'

Her face is composed and agreeable, no trace of sarcasm in her tone. But the accusation is there all the same. You could have done things differently, she's saying. You could have stopped being a degenerate for one brief moment and made a few subtle changes.

'I always felt Dad was partly to blame,' she says.

'What for?'

'Being away so much. Being so unpredictable.'

'He missed a few of my birthdays, too, you know.'

'I'm not just talking about birthdays. I'm talking about everything else. You grow up thinking it's normal to live like that.'

'What – listening to Charlie Mingus at five years old?'

She looks pained, reluctant to answer.

'You know what I mean. As soon as he came back, he was off again. We hardly ever saw him.'

My memories of him aren't quite the same. To me he was always a giant, the one person I tried to emulate when I was growing up. His effortless charm and style. The fact he could talk to anyone, no matter who they were, and somehow make them feel they were the only person in the room. I hated him too. For dismissing my talent. Belittling my achievements when I was starting out. One day I showed him the gold disc we got for *Romance on the Dark side,* and he just looked at it, blankly, and nodded his head.

'Remember when he used to take us over to the Hamilton's?' she says. 'And they'd let us play in their swimming pool?'

'Only because you pestered him all the time.'

'I loved that house,' she says dreamily. 'The lane and the fields. The cakes Mrs Hamilton used to make with the blob of jam in the middle.'

'They must have felt sorry for us. The ragamuffin kids with holes in their shoes.'

'We weren't that bad.'

'We weren't exactly well off either, were we?'

I learned a lot of things from my father. His insistence on living in the moment and partying hard. His firm belief that any kind of responsibility kills the creative spirit – as evidenced by his cavalier attitude to marriage and children. I think I felt my mum's pain from an early age, her sadness when he was away, her inability to cope on her own whenever her illness worsened.

'Do you miss him?' I say.

'Yes, of course I miss him. There's hardly a day goes by when I don't think about him. It's just been so hard what with everything else that's happened.'

Some people are able to process grief internally. Shaz is good at keeping it hidden, but occasionally it reveals itself in the darkening shadows on her face and the distant, yearning in her voice. Her strength is admirable in a way. Losing Terry so soon after Dad, with no booze or pills to get her through it. No crutch, other than her faith in God and the church and all that waffle. Perhaps that's what we've got in common. Neither of us can cope with reality.

The violins pick up the tempo, like a storm at sea. She turns to me gravely.

'Will you promise me something?'

'What's that?'

'You'll try to get some help as soon as you can.'

'For what?'

'Your drinking.'

I sit back, deflated. 'Shaz, I've got a lot of problems right now and drink isn't one of them'

'How can you say that? How can you say that when you've lost your job, your family?'

'Is it money you're worried about?' I say indignantly. 'You want me to give you something towards the rent?'

'No of course it isn't the money. That wasn't what I meant at all.'

I'm tired, drained by the trauma of the past few days. Shaz's concern is tinged with disappointment, as if besides letting Justine down, I've let *her* down in some way too.

I pour more wine, consumed by an urgent need to escape.

'Listen, d'you mind if we continue this discussion some other time?'

She shakes her head. 'No, I've said all I needed to say.'

'Thanks, Shaz.' I stand wearily, taking the wine and the bottle. 'Oh – d'you mind if I make a phone call?'

'No. I told you, you don't have to keep asking.'

Sometimes you do things without knowing why. There's a part of you that knows it's wrong and wants to stop, and another part that won't listen. Each step along this path makes it harder to find your way back. Like a road where all the lights go out, one by one, until all that's left is darkness.

A woman answers. The same hard voice as before. She asks me to wait and calls out raucously, behind her.

Danny comes to the phone. I mumble my way through a coded request, aware of Shaz hovering somewhere in the background. He sounds angry, belligerent. Why should he help me out? he says. Why should he go out of his way for some pain-in-the-ass junkie who only calls when he wants something? Then his raucous laugh to show he's half-joking.

'One last time, Joe, and that's it. You listening?'

'Yeah sure, Danny. I hear what you're saying. I appreciate it, I really – '

The bastard hangs up.

Shaz looks up from clearing the table. 'I'm making coffee, would you like one?'

'No thanks. Thought I'd nip out for a bit. Get some fresh air.'

The lie comes easily. In fact, it isn't really a lie at all, but a mild distortion of the truth. Sometimes, you need a little extra. A little something to take your mind off your current problems. And with nearly five grand tucked away in a building society account, I have the means to make that happen.

25

A routine glimpse in the mirror behind the bar and there he is. The angular face and the brooding lower lip. Eyes like radars taking everything in. The urge to escape comes over me. A sudden realisation of what I've become. But it's too late. I'm trapped here, waiting, resignedly, to serve out my destiny.

He comes over and stands beside me, looking me up and down. 'What's happening, son?'

'Nothing much.'

'Get 'em in, then. All that running round I've been doing for you lately.'

He orders a bottled Heineken from the painted doll behind the bar, and cheerfully announces that I'm paying. Our elbows connect. His creased black leather and a touch of gold at the wrist. The imprint of a faded tattoo.

'What's the score then, Joey-boy? You look a bit down in the boots.'

'I'm fine.'

'Off on another world tour soon?'

'Not quite.'

'That's a shame, you could've taken me along.' He sees the barmaid and leers. 'How you doing, darlin'?'

The barmaid uncaps his bottle and saunters off, her lime green cardigan trailing cotton at the hemline. He watches her with a covert grin.

'Would you give it one or what?'

'I doubt it.'

His eyes narrow. 'Why not?'

'She's not my type.'

He shakes his head. 'I swear there's summat wrong with you lately. Must be all that hanging round with George Michael and Elton John.'

Such charm and charisma Danny has. It oozes from him like radioactive waste from an arms dump. But it's his volatility that's the real problem. By the time you've worked out what mood he's in it's usually too late. All that pent-up aggression and paranoia, drink-fuelled testosterone from the terraces. I should have arranged to meet him in some back alley instead, and spared myself all this.

Two workmen in fluorescent yellow jackets come in and head for the pool table. The taller man racks the balls and scatters the pack with an explosive break. The second man, short and muscular, chalks his cue and eyes the table. He looks familiar, but I can't work out why.

I turn to Danny. 'Did you manage to get it?'

'Get what?'

'You know ... What we talked about on the phone.'

He takes a leisurely drink, eyeing the barmaid. 'Slight problem there, Joe.'

'What's that?'

'Bit of a drought on at the moment. Nothing much coming in.'

My disappointment merges with the music, the impact on the pool table. The plans I had to find a nice, quiet corner of the universe and get pleasantly wasted are put on hold.

He lays his hand flat on the bar and winks at me. 'Have a quick blast on this if you want.' He takes his hand away. 'Don't be greedy though, eh?'

Lying there on the polished mahogany is a small, rectangular wrap. I try to contain my eagerness.

'What is it?'

'Charlie. Good stuff, too.' He leans in, conspiratorially. 'And if you can come up with the spondoolies, I might invite you over the Manor House later. Mate of mine's just had a blinding batch of E's come in.'

Flushed with a mixture of excitement and anxiety, I palm the wrap, discreetly, wait a moment, and head for the Gents.

Drug etiquette is a strange thing. The rules vary depending on your present company and where you happen to be. Toilets and restrooms are the preferred location because of their privacy, providing the user with a quiet place to indulge his habit without an audience looking on. Five-Star hotels or ten-dollar flophouses – it's all the same. Nothing else matters but ingesting the contents and getting the drug in.

With a heel against the broken cubicle door and a knee on the toilet lid, I unfold the edges of my pristine wrap. A small amount of fine white powder lies within. A quick dab with a finger convinces me it's the real thing – a distinct, bitter taste, faintly medicinal. I rack out a line on the cistern, and bend, eagerly, to the task, all my problems temporarily forgotten.

Coming out of the Gents, newly revitalised, I head past the pool table. The short, muscular bloke in the fluorescent yellow jacket looks up and catches my eye. We share a brief moment of recognition.

Danny welcomes me back with a knowing grin. I take a drink, casually, tendrils of powder still lodged in my nose.

'Come on then,' he says. 'Let's have it.'

'Huh?'

'Don't fuck about. The wrap I give you. Where is it?' He stares at me with mixture of horror and disbelief. 'Don't tell me you've done all of it?'

'Sorry, Danny, I thought – '

'I don't believe it! Forty quid's worth in there and you've done the fucking lot!'

I'm speechless, my mouth hanging open. For a moment my life hangs in the balance. The thought of what Danny might do to me is offset, slightly, by the coke running through my system, but it's a thin consolation. I make a humble and heartfelt apology, promising I'll go straight to the cashpoint and reimburse him accordingly.

He starts laughing, rocking on his heels. 'Fell for that one, didn't you, son – eh? Should have seen the look on your mug!'

Relief gives way to mild irritation. Danny might be the supplier of all things chemical, but his sense of humour leaves a lot to be desired.

He asks about Carla, when I last saw her and who she was with. I tell him about the boiler man. Her hostile reaction to him as he ransacked her flat with a greasy spanner. He frowns.

'Was she on her own when you went round?'

'Apart from the boiler man, yeah.'

'She mention anyone else?'

'No.

He thinks this over. 'What about the landlord?'

'What about him?'

'Well – she could be shagging him, too, couldn't she?'

I disengage from the conversation, tactfully, amazed at the workings of his rabid mind. My gaze is drawn to the pool table again. The short, muscular bloke bends to take a shot. He sights along the cue, his coarse, pockmarked face revealed under the light.

Realisation dawns with a sudden chill. I remember where I've seen him.

'I ever tell you about the job I did for a landlord in Hackney?' Danny says. I tear my gaze away from the pool table, preoccupied.

'Huh?'

'Some foreign bird and three kids, lounging round in pyjamas, eating toast. Almost felt sorry for 'em - till we clocked the four lodgers hiding in the back room. They had to go, mate. Straight out the door, no messin'!'

A pool ball slams in a corner pocket. I'm overcome with an urge to leave immediately.

'Danny, I really need to – '

'Then there was this geezer in Brick Lane, near where Carla was living. I chased the cunt down three flights of stairs and out into the road and me fucking shoe come off. I couldn't believe it!'

He soon tires of me and renews his acquaintance with the doll-faced barmaid. I turn my back on the bar and try to immerse myself in the music. UB40's King comes on – one of the most haunting songs I ever heard. I think of the bowling alley in Streatham Hill where I first met Justine. All the things we did together, the places we went. The cocaine and the booze acts as a buffer, stopping the pain from getting through, but it's always there in the background, waiting, no matter what you do.

'Fancy the Manor House then?' Danny says.

'Sure. Go now if you like.' I drain my Beck's, and put the bottle on the bar.

'Hold up, son. I ain't ready yet.' He looks at me strangely. 'What you keep looking over there for?'

'Where?'

He nods in the direction of the pool table.

I'm filled with a strange foreboding, warning lights that flash on at the edge of my vision. I know who he is. The mean-looking dwarf from Friday's drinking session in the Prince Albert. Sat there waiting for his double Tia Maria and coke while I did a runner out the back door.

'I've gotta go, Danny.'

'What for?'

I mumble something about a prior appointment, meeting an old friend of mine in Finch's. He flashes me one of his dangerously unhinged looks.

'Fuck's the matter with you?'

'Nothing.'

'You call me up saying you wanna meet me. Then you do all me gear and fuck off. You're out of order, son. Bang out of order.'

The dwarf comes up to the bar and stands a few feet away, sifting change in the palm of his huge hand. The more I look at him, the worse it gets. He isn't a dwarf at all. He's short, but physically imposing. A compact piece of granite hewn from a rock face. What he lacks in height, he makes up for in menace.

'Game of doubles, mate?' Danny says cheerfully. The dwarf shakes his head. The barmaid serves him, the sleeve of her green cardigan unravelling along with my poor mind. I see the future clearly. The dwarf's huge fist pounding me mercilessly. The scream of an ambulance siren as I'm carried through the streets to the local infirmary.

The dwarf takes his drinks and turns to go.

'Like the jacket, mate,' Danny calls out. The dwarf stops and looks back.

'Do what?'

'The jacket. Proper job, innit? Won't have trouble seeing you in the dark, will we?'

The Landlady strolls by – sunburned ex-pat with a vicious temper. For a moment she looks like an ally, someone to resolve the situation before it disintegrates completely. She disappears behind the bar, and we're left alone with the action unfolding.

Danny fixes the dwarf with an easy grin. 'Come on then, mate. Game of doubles. Best of three for twenty-quid.'

'I'm not interested.'

'Why not?'

The dwarf turns his radar on me coldly. 'Ask your mate. He'll tell you.'

Danny looks to me for an explanation. I can't move, rendered immobile by a mixture of fear and cocaine.

The dwarf moves off.

'Oi, mate?' Danny calls out. The dwarf stops, his shoulders like steel girders welded to a thick, porcine neck. Turning slowly, he fixes Danny with a look of contempt.

'What *is* your problem?'

'I was talking to you,' Danny says reasonably. 'You walked away.'

Like the scene from a movie, the next few seconds happen outside time. The dwarf puts the drinks on the bar and strolls over, thrusting his face up inches from Danny's. In spite of the height difference, Danny looks slight and unprepared.

'You got summat you wanna say to me?' the dwarf says angrily. Danny laughs and puts his hands up in a gesture of surrender and, for a moment, the tension's diffused. Then, with lightning speed and unbridled ferocity, he darts-in and head-butts the dwarf right on the button. Stunned, the dwarf staggers back and, like a drunk performing some hopelessly uncoordinated dance routine, crashes into a table and drops to the floor. The barmaid shrieks, calling for the landlady, who's already marching out from behind the bar gesturing wildly.

'Get out! Get out! I'm calling the police!'

Swiftly, we head down Kensington Park Road, seeking the anonymity of the early evening crowd. Behind us a pub in disarray and a man in need of urgent medical attention. A vague sense of unease troubles me, a nagging thought that the whole thing was my fault, that I could have done something to prevent it happening.

At the next junction, Danny stops. He stares at me, breathing heavily. 'Let's go back.'

'What for?'

'Do the cunt properly.'

'Danny – you've gotta be joking! We've got to get out of here, quick, before we get arrested!'

Carla used to say I had a calming influence on him, but after tonight I'm not so sure. Somehow I convince him not to go back and finish the job on the dwarf and his mate but it isn't easy. The violence in him is disturbing. I can't get the thought of it out of my mind. The sight of that big lump squirming on the carpet, his nose pushed across his face, somehow wasn't enough. Danny wanted wholesale retribution.

*

Two hulking bouncers watch the crowds disperse, arms folded, ready to go home. Danny's nowhere to be seen. The girl I was with has vanished, carried away by some unknown rival with better dance moves and a flat in Chelsea. I'm alone and miles from Shaz's. Alone, with no money and no cigarettes, a disconnected tribal rhythm still playing in my head.

But so what?

This is it

Everything's beautiful. Nothing else matters but this. Love in its purest form. The peak of a snow covered mountain. All the joys and wonders of the universe encapsulated in a little white pill.

I wander the streets in a rapture, side-stepping gangs of youths on their way back from the frontline. Past the taxi rank and the foreign takeaways, waves of unconditional love emanating from my being.

This is it.

No more missiles and barbed wire fencing. No more tanks rolling in Tiananmen Square. The backstreet chemist's have found the answer. Peace on earth and goodwill to all men.

I walk for miles in this blissful state. Tree-lined avenues with wide pavements spring up. Huge Georgian flats set back from the road. Some of the buildings look familiar, like places I've been to before to score crack and heroin, enticed along by the night people – artistes and conmen, prostitutes and drag queens, the strangest coalition to exist on the streets.

The temperature drops. Goose bumps break out on my arms, my skin clammy with dried sweat. The love vibe – so overwhelming only moments ago – has faded. In its place, a cold and desolate void.

The house on the corner looks promising. Wide brick bays and leaded windows beneath a three quarter moon. At the end of a long back garden is a wooden shed.   Easing the latch back, I slip inside. Damp smells overwhelm me through the murky blackness. Obscure shapes appear in silhouette. The handle of a lawnmower. A looming chest of drawers. I stub my foot against a metal container, the noise amplified in the blanket silence, but I'm past caring. I need warmth. Physical comfort.

Sleep.

Wrapped in a rolled up carpet, I slip into a strange, trancelike state. The club we were in – a rambling, country house set in expansive, floodlit grounds. Jungle pumping from every room. Danny and the *Man,* caught in the strobe lights, their chequered faces stark and surreal. And the girl with pink hair and cherry lip-gloss, perched on my knee, eagerly awaiting the rocket ship to the next dimension.

Melody lines from obscure dance tracks play over in my head, the orchestra on a doomed ship. But I'm comfortable here in the darkness, alone with the earthy, oily smells of my newfound home. My first night as a vagrant and already I'm a moderate success. Saved from freezing to death by my own intuition.

26

'Do you know where you are, Joe?'

I'm in a small office, with a filing cabinet and coloured folders on the wall. An attractive woman in her thirties stares at me across a desk. Her name is Roz. I gather this much from the name tag above her left breast.

'Some kinda hospital?'

'That's right. You're in St Luke's. Can you tell me what day it is?'

'Friday.'

'And the year?'

'1994.'

'And who's the Prime Minister?'

'Is this a joke?'

'No, it's an assessment. Could you answer the question, please?'

A fresh wave of nausea hits me.

'John Major.'

'Thank you.'

'Did I pass the test?'

'It isn't a test. I told you. It's an assessment.'

She watches me, closely, rocking in her swivel chair. No smile, or inkling of any warmth beneath a clinical veneer.

'Do you remember who brought you in?'

'The police.'

'And do you remember why?'

'I was sleeping off a hangover in someone's shed.'

She stares at me evenly. I'm overcome with a wild sense of

desperation.

'Look – can you tell me what I'm doing here, please? I need to get home. People are gonna be worried about me.'

A butch looking nurse loiters by the door and fires off a salvo at Roz – something about ward boundaries and patients absconding. They debate the issue using jargon I don't understand, until the woman leaves.

Roz turns to face me.

'Joe – you were brought in under Section 136 of the Mental Health Act. Do you understand what that means?'

'No?'

'It means you're here for your own safety because you were found wandering in a public place.'

'I wasn't wandering anywhere, I was sleeping in a fucking shed!'

'If you're going to be abusive I'll have you removed from this office. Do you understand?'

A terrible fear grows in me. Images of police officers shining torches in my face. Some white-haired old gent in a dressing gown and his timid little wife, watching, bemusedly, as they led me away.

'Listen. Just phone my sister. She'll confirm who I am, OK?'

'We've already spoken to your sister.'

'So why can't she come and get me?'

She runs through the legalities of my stay in her coldly efficient voice. The words *detained* and *assessment* keep cropping up, reminding me I don't have a choice.

'Any questions?' she says.

'Yeah. When can I go?'

'When you've seen the doctor.'

'And when will that be?'

'Monday morning.'

I stare at her blankly. 'You gotta be kidding me!'

'Joe – when you were brought in you could barely even remember where you lived. You were extremely agitated. We have to see how you respond to the treatment.'

'What treatment?'

'The detox we're giving you.'

'I don't need a detox, I just need to get home!'

A row of names are written in red marker on a whiteboard above her head. At the bottom is mine – *Joe E Byron*, a name I no longer recognise. Did I insist on them using the middle initial when I came in, or is this some kind of cruel joke? A sick reminder of my former profession. The jaded rock musician washed-up in this hell-hole without so much as a travelling bag.

'I need something to calm me down.'

She looks up, frowning. 'What about the Librium we gave you earlier – isn't that working?'

I vaguely remember a nurse giving me a pill and a glass of water.

'I need something stronger.'

'I'm sorry. You'll just have to wait until later.'

'Why?'

'Because that's the policy.'

The sense of unreality persists. What can I do? They have all the evidence to keep me detained. Doctor Kahn's notes. My psychiatric history and drug dependency from as far back as 1981. Even the time I spent three days in hospital in Kent with barbiturate poisoning and discharged myself early against the doctor's advice.

'Can I go out?'

'You're on ward boundaries until you've seen the doctor.'

'What? This is ridiculous!'

She closes the file on her desk and stands. 'Right. Let me show you to your room.'

The dormitory along the hall has four single beds curtained-off to give the illusion of privacy. White walls and crisp white sheets. An airless, musty smell lingers.

'Why can't I have a single room?'

'Because we don't have the beds at the moment.'

'I don't wanna share with other people.'

'Well you'll just have to get used to it. This isn't a hotel.'

She leaves me with a wintry smile, hips rolling seductively in tight, blue jeans. If I hadn't felt so ill, I might have seen her as a challenge, someone to bait until I found a way out of this mess. But she's the nurse and I'm the patient. The chances of a romantic encounter between us are next to zero.

*

A morose-looking black nurse drops a sports bag at the foot of my bed.

'Your sister brought this in for you.'

'Is she here?'

'She couldn't stop. She's going to call the office later to find out how you are.'

The gesture contains a positive message of some sort, but I'm too numb to work out what it is.

'Listen, nurse. I'm feeling a bit edgy at the moment. Any chance of something to calm me down?'

'Depends what you're written up for.'

I'm confused. 'Why does everything have to be written up round here? I thought this was supposed to be a hospital?'

'Sorry, I don't make the rules.'

'There must be someone qualified to give me something?'

'Speak to the staff nurse. I can't give you nothing.'

She wanders off, devoid of sympathy, devoid of anything.

I rifle the contents of the sports bag in a state of profound depression. One pair of stone-washed jeans, t-shirts and assorted underwear. One luminescent green wash bag with shaving foam and miniature deodorant. The only consolation is a Walkman and selection of tapes in a carrier bag. I tip them out on the bed. Fleetwood Mac, The Stones, Tom Petty. At least I'll be in good company while I'm locked up in here. Drown it all out with a set of headphones.

An embossed silver photo frame lies at the bottom of the bag. I hold it up, overwhelmed with remorse and sorrow. Two beautiful, smiling faces, snapped by a photographer friend of Justine's in Covent Garden. From now on they'll be watching me everywhere I go. A calculated guilt trip from Justine to remind me what I've left behind.

A man wanders in, hugging himself repeatedly. He looks like an undertaker, thin-faced, with oily black hair. Ignoring me completely he shuffles over to the bed in the far corner and lowers himself down, rocking gently back and forth, staring at the wall. After a while, the sight becomes unbearable.

'Hi, I'm Joe,' I say with forced cordiality. 'Have you been here long?'

Silence.

Instinctively, I withdraw, afraid I'll be infected by the same condition. All the lunatics in one place to contain all the madness and stop it from spreading. Outside in the metropolis the virus is a temporary problem, infecting a small percentage of the population then moving on. In here, you're grounded, forced to run the risk of your own particular brand mutating into another form. Some of us don't have much choice either way, tainted by the hereditary link before we were even born. The chemical imbalance, passed through faulty genes from one family member to another.

I've spent my whole life fearing such an outcome, but here I am. Stuck in the nuthouse like my poor old mum.

27

'Doctor's ready to see you, Joe.'

I leap up off the bed, re-energised by the thought of freedom. Roz notes my new roommate Colin, lurking by the window, and points a warning finger. 'I hope that's not a cigarette you've got there, *Mr Hamilton*. I'll have you back on ward boundaries so quick you won't know what's hit you!'

Along the corridor we go, past the office and through a set of double doors. Roz taps once and opens a door on the left. Inside the small room are a handful of people, all seated. The Committee, waiting, presumably, for me.

A studious looking man in a shirt and tie gets up and offers his hand. 'Good morning, Joe. I'm Doctor Reece. Take a seat.'

So begins my assessment under the Mental Health Act. I'm eager to explain how I came to end up in this grim institution. How the whole thing's been a big mistake. All I did was drop a little white pill and crash out in someone's garden. I should be making records and boarding planes, trying to kick-start what's left of my ailing career. Instead, I'm sharing a room with a suicidal depressive and a bored psychotic. I haven't had a moment's peace since I came here.

The doctor listens with a fixed smile, nodding his head, attentively, to show he's taking it all in. The two dour looking women stay silent, their expressions guarded, as if the slightest deviation might upset the status quo. A young male student-type sits cross-legged in the corner taking notes.

'What kind of thoughts have you been having lately, Joe?' the doctor says.

'How d'you mean?'

'Hear any voices? Anything telling you what to do?'

'No.'

'Any significant changes in your mood?'

'Only anxiety from being in this place.'

He firms his lips and murmurs thoughtfully to himself. The male student type sniffs and scribbles in his pad.

'Do you remember how you came in to the hospital?'

'The police brought me.'

'Any thoughts about that?'

'Not really. I was pretty confused at the time.'

'And you'd been taking ... ecstasy, is that right?'

'Yeah, but not intentionally. Someone must have slipped it in my drink without me knowing.'

He nods agreeably, in no hurry to continue.

'How much had you been drinking, can you remember?'

'A few lagers. Couple of shorts.'

'And before that?'

'Before what?'

'Had you been drinking every day?'

'No. I just went out for one or two and someone spiked my drink. It happens all the time round our way.'

He smoothes his chin, pulling a strange facial contortion with his lower jaw.

'The nurse says you've been having trouble sleeping?'

'That's right. I suffer from insomnia.'

'What about the medication you were prescribed at night?'

'The dose is too low. I told the nurse but she wouldn't listen.'

The student's pen jerks across the pad and stops. Doctor Reece crosses his legs and frowns at the dilemma I've given him.

'I'd like you to stay on the ward for a few days, Joe.'

'What for!'

'So that we can assess the treatment you've been having and see if your mood stabilises.'

'There's nothing wrong with my mood!'

A ripple of unease stirs around the room, as if I've broken

some unwritten rule. But the good doctor's decision is final, inflexible. He stands, hovering amiably above me like I'm his favourite pet.

'That's all for now. See you in ward round on Wednesday.'

Roz catches up with me outside. She seems reserved, almost apologetic. 'You'll just have to go along with it, Joe. There's no point in arguing, you'll just make things worse.'

'Is this legal? I mean, can they do that – keep me in here against my will?'

'Nobody wants to keep you in any longer than necessary. I suggest you calm down and see what he says on Wednesday.'

The next few days loom in my mind with a special dread. Stuck on the ward with all the other fruitcakes. Certified. Certifiable. The only relief a big, fat jar of tranquillisers under lock and key, wheeled out occasionally to wind up the inmates.

I turn to Roz, incensed. 'Do these people know who I am? … I mean, do they? … Have they stopped to think what'll happen when my management company hears about this?'

She gazes back at me, unmoved. 'Joe – why don't you go and have a bath or something.'

'I don't want a bath.'

'Read a book then, or sit in the TV lounge with the others.'

I'm drained by the effort of arguing, the leaden sickness of comedown.

'What about boundaries? Can I go out now?'

'Within the grounds.'

'On my own, or do I have to be escorted?'

'You can go on your own, but don't abuse the privilege.' She smiles demurely. 'If you try and run off we'll find you and bring you straight back again.'

Time in here is a vacuum, like being sealed inside a capsule in outer space. When I came in I was relatively normal, apart from the excess of pure MDMA still left in my system. Now I'm a patient, an inmate. One of those strange, lobotomised creatures you see in television documentaries, shuffling round hospital corridors in ill-fitting clothes. I need something to take the edge off. Sedatives. Opiates. Anything. And if the staff won't give them to me, I'll make a phone call and get them brought in instead.

*

I use the payphone in the lobby overlooking the car park and the grounds. Carla can't believe where I am and immediately blames Danny. I find myself defending him, earnestly, recalling his altercation with the dwarf and our sudden exit from the pub.

'How long are they keeping you in?' she says, cutting me off mid-sentence.

'Until Wednesday, at least. It's a fucking joke. Can you come up and visit me?'

You always know who your real friends are when you start calling in favours. I can hear the excuses turning over in her mind before she's even opened her mouth.

'Carla – can you visit me or not?'

'How am I supposed to get up there?'

'Jump on a bus. Get a taxi. I'm fucking dying up here!'

A young girl with acne slouches past on her way to the ward. She has a permanently switched off look, her features dulled by medication or some other form of post-traumatic shock.

'What ward are you on?' Carla says.

'Allington.'

'So what things do you need?'

At last, a glimmer of sunlight. The thought of some heavy pharmaceuticals to take the edge off my sickness. I start to put in a hushed request and she stops me outright.

'Wait a minute. You want me to come all the way up there just so I can smuggle drugs in for you. What happens if I get caught?'

'You won't get caught.'

'How do you know?'

'Carla. Gimme a break will you? You don't know what it's like in here. I'm surrounded by head shrinks and weirdos all day. I need *something*.'

Why do people have to be so obtuse? Why can't they just do

what you want them to do without making everything harder? Her half-hearted promise to visit me isn't all that convincing. Given her innate selfishness and chronic agoraphobia the chances of her coming all the way up here to see me are minimal. But right now she's the only hope I've got.

'D'you think they'll give you ECT?' she says.

'What?'

'They gave it to a friend of mine a few years ago. She only went in for a rest.'

'Thanks, Carla.'

'Just a thought.'

'Yeah. That makes me feel a whole lot better.'

'Well just hang in there and don't do anything stupid. They can't keep you there forever, can they.'

I linger for a while, gazing out the window. The few patients on the grass verge look like college students on campus. They sit around smoking and chatting, none of the outward signs you'd normally associate with the mentally ill. Perhaps after a while you get used to it. The unendurable becomes routine.

*

Lunch is a pre-ordered serving of cod, chips and peas. The batter looks too flat and lifeless to be edible but I'm hardly in a position to complain. The queue stretches out the door. Patients from the women's ward – some in dressing gowns and slippers, mingle freely with the men. The mood is lively and upbeat, a coffee shop or busy restaurant in the city. Some of the patients even look happy, the contentment of people with nowhere else to go.

The woman opposite me sits chewing her food mechanically. She has a pale, haunted look, as if she's holding it all inside and at the same time doing all she can to maintain her dignity. I can feel her distress, broadcast like radio waves to the rest of the room.

'Food's not up to much, is it?' I say, compelled to make conversation. She cuts, delicately, into her fish, staring at her plate.

'Have you been here long?'

Ignoring me, she guides the fork to her mouth in painful slow motion. They must have dosed her up on some real potent medication to cause an effect like that. Maybe she's had ECT. Ten-thousand volts through the head in the devil's antechamber. I remember what my mum looked like when *she* came home.

A man with hollow cheeks and glazed eyes joins us. He has that strange insular look common to heavy drug users, a look that distances them from all but their own kind. Our eyes meet, and a flicker of understanding passes between us. I'm heartened by his arrival, the opportunities for trade he might bring.

I push my plate away, too sick to eat. Memories from the opium trail beset me. San Diego '86. Hooking up with Rimmer and trawling the bars looking for his dealer. Going back to his girlfriend's apartment and cleaning out her medicine cabinet, loading everything into a syringe and blasting off into orbit.

There must be something fundamentally flawed with such people. Something lacking in childhood maybe. We weren't shown enough love, or given enough toys to play with. Or maybe it's just a general aversion to life. We find out early we can't cope and go quietly of the rails from that moment on.

I leave the happy diners and go back to my room. Nothing penetrates the cloak of despair that's settled in. To compensate, I've found a couple of patients willing to donate their sleeping tablets in return for tobacco. They palm the tablets at medication time and give them to me later, out of sight of the goon squad, who'd have me back on boundaries if they found out. Four 5mg tablets give a reasonable hit, but the effects are over too quickly, leaving me craving more. I fantasise about large amounts of narcotics smuggled in by friends. Handfuls of pills. Syringes filled with heroin and cocaine. Anything to change the way I feel.

A nurse appears in the doorway.

'Visitor, Joe.'

'Who is it?'

'I think it's your sister.'

28

The canteen doubles as a tea-room – post colonial style with arched glass canopy and ornate white chairs. Exotic plant life in the corners gives it a restive, botanical feel, relief from the clinical drabness of the ward.

We sit in embarrassment, neither of us speaking. A white-coated flunky, presumably another patient, serves us coffee and leaves without a word. Shaz looks tired and lacklustre. She tries to make small talk, commenting on the décor, but I'm not really listening.

'What happened, Joe?' she says with a sad smile.

'I don't know.'

'Do you want to talk about it?'

'I'm stuck in a mental hospital, Shaz. What's there to say?'

Her coffee sits untouched, her fingers linked on the table, as if in prayer. I try to see it from her side, coming all the way up here to visit me in this dump. The wayward brother, sectioned for his own safety. Whichever angle I try to use it doesn't work. I simply don't have that level of empathy.

'What's your room like?' she says.

'It's a dormitory.'

'Do you get on alright with the others?'

'When they're asleep.'

She fidgets awkwardly.

'The nurse said you were having some kind of treatment.'

'5 milligrams of Librium three times a day. It's an insult.'

'Doesn't it help at all?'

'It would if they upped the dose. Too much to ask though.

Wouldn't want you feeling better, would they.'

She sits passively, forced to put up with my bitterness.

'Justine asked after you.'

'Oh yeah. Like she really cares.'

'Of course she cares. We all do. Nobody wants to see you in here.'

A man in chef's whites comes in and starts lifting lids in the dimly-lit kitchen area. I feel like telling him to fuck off, that we're trying to have a private conversation. What does he care? He's going home in a few hours. I'm stuck in here until Wednesday.

Shaz sips her coffee, looking at me tenderly 'Charlie misses you. He keeps asking when you're coming back.'

'What did you tell him?'

'I just said you weren't well. You were staying in hospital for a few days.' She pauses, fingering the rim of her cup. 'Have you thought what you're going to do when you leave?'

'Go to the pub and celebrate.'

She stares at me blankly.

'It was a joke, Shaz. I don't know what I'm gonna do, alright?'

The man in chef's whites leaves through a side door. An unnatural stillness descends, like the lull in a war zone. I can't help resenting Shaz for making me grovel. She knows I'm destitute, that after this place there's nowhere else for me to go.

'Can't I stay with you?'

She sighs faintly. 'It's not that easy, Joe.'

'Why?'

'You know why.'

'No I don't.'

She eyes me wearily. 'How do you think I felt when the police rang up, saying you were in hospital? I just can't have that level of disruption. I've got the kids to think about. I told you.'

I stare at the table, sharing her confusion at the way things have turned out. All the other doors have slammed shut. Shaz offers the only lifeline. I want to reach out and grab hold of it without somehow demeaning myself in the process.

'You need help, Joe.'

'I'm getting help.'

Her eyes glisten with tears. 'It's awful. Coming up here and seeing you like this.'

We sit in silence.

She reaches into her handbag and lays a brown paper bag on the table.

'I brought you something.'

'What is it?'

'Open it and see.'

I take a tentative peek inside. One large bar of Cadbury's Fruit & Nut and a thin paperback hidden beneath.

'What's the book?'

'It's a daily meditation. I thought you might find it helpful.'

I'm mildly insulted. As if some pious book could help me, stuck in a place like this. She doesn't have a clue what it's like. The loneliness. The sense of separation from every other living thing. In here it's amplified, cranked up another level. You're reminded of it constantly.

'Ken said he'd like to come and visit you,' she says.

'Who?'

'Ken – the Pastor at our church.'

'Visit me where – in here?'

'Yes. Why do you sound so surprised, he visits people in hospital all the time?'

I'm horrified. Visions of some ageing cleric tramping up the stairs clutching a worn copy of the Bible. I decline, politely, careful not to jeopardise the chance of a future bed.

'Well, the offer's there if you change your mind.' She smiles reassuringly. 'Anything else you'd like me to bring in?'

'A shot of morphine.'

'I was thinking more along the lines of books and magazines.'

A sudden deviousness stirs in me. I'm reminded of all the illicit goods available on the ward.

'Could you lend me some cash?'

'Of course.' She reaches for her bag. 'How much do you want?'

'Twenty?'

She frowns, going through her purse. 'I can let you have ten. Is that enough?'

Years ago when I was a kid I used to steal from my mum. Then, as I got older, I found out it was just as easy to ask for the money instead. I learned the subtleties of manipulation. The right tone of voice. The right facial expression. These things worked where good honest thieving didn't.

She lays a ten-pound note on the table like a bribe. I'm slightly disappointed but try not to show it.

'Thanks, Shaz.'

'I wish there was more I could do,' she says pityingly. 'I feel so helpless seeing you like this.'

Memories from childhood crowd in. Things I've witnessed that I've tried to forget.

'Did you ever visit mum in hospital?' I say. She looks at me strangely.

'Once or twice, why?'

'I remember going up once when I was a kid. She was sat out in the grounds on a bench. It was like she didn't recognise me.'

The memory hurts even now, a kind of rejection I've never been able to work out. 'And all that creeping round the house when she was depressed. I hated it. I was ashamed to bring people home.'

Shaz sits mutely with nothing to add. An indescribably black rage comes over me.

'At least you got the good genes. I got the ones with 'serial fuck-up' stamped through the middle. That's why I ended up in this shit-hole.'

She stares back at me evenly. 'Would you like me to go?'

The hard edge in her tone shocks me. I'm filled with a sudden anxiety, that the session will end and I'll have to go back on the ward.

'I'm sorry, Shaz, OK? It's being in here. Fucks your head up. Makes you say things you don't mean.'

I try to imagine my mother in a place like this. Eating dinner in the canteen. Shuffling back to her room. Waiting for ward round like all the other in-patients. My dad used to say she was two people – outgoing and vivacious one minute, crippled by black despair the next. She's the reason I'm like I am. It's because of her I've spent my life out on the highwire, steeling myself to never look down.

'Remember when we went to stay with Celia and Donald?' I say. 'In that freezing cold house of theirs.'

She smiles vaguely.

'I thought it was a punishment for what we'd done to Mum.'

'Why did you think that?'

I can't answer. All I can see is an ivy-covered house in the country, me and Shaz arriving like little evacuees. The home comforts were minimal compared to the standards we were used to. No cakes and biscuits, no colour TV. Water pipes that groaned horrendously whenever you turned the cold tap on. Uncle Donald, a morose and humourless man given to long periods of introspection with the *Telegraph* and his trusty pipe. He barely said two words the whole time we were there. But there were bonuses. I smoked my first cigarette around that time, whipped from the packet Auntie Celia had left on the dining room table. A moment of pure release, sparked by adversity and a box of Swan Vestas.

'I did love the dog,' Shaz says wistfully.

'Yeah. He had more personality than Donald, that's for sure. Fucking thing bit me once though.'

'I'm not surprised, you were always teasing it.'

We sit with our shared recollections, the awkwardness of the past. I've never found much comfort in it, like some people. I've always preferred the road. The feeling that wherever you are, you'll soon be moving on again.

Shaz stands, reluctantly. 'Well, I'd better be going.' She takes a folded newspaper from a carrier bag. 'Justine asked me to give you this. There's something in there about you, apparently.'

The copy of *NME* unfolds on the table, a bizarre intrusion from my previous life. Drinking orange juice with Brian Moorcroft in the Park Hotel. The jaded rock star, fielding questions he didn't want to answer.

'Have you read it?' I say.

'No. Should I have?'

I mumble a reply, sorry I asked.

We embrace at the table, alone in the dimly-lit room. Shaz stands back with a brave smile, her eyes filled with tears.

'If you want anything else, just let me know.'

'Thanks, Shaz. Thanks for coming up. I appreciate it, I really do.'

I watch her turn the corner in the hallway and she's gone. Like a jacket someone slipped around my shoulders, fear sets in.

29

New Musical Express

Fall of the Young Lions
by *Brian Moorcroft*

I first met Joe Byron at Reading Rock Festival in 1984. Dressed in a rhinestone shirt, torn jeans, cowboy boots, and a battered felt hat over long, dark hair, he certainly looked the part he claimed he was born to play. Although they didn't know it at the time, Eponymous Mouse, the band he'd been with for three years, had just played their last gig with him as guitarist. Shortly after, in response to repeated invitations from Polydor A&R man Chris Billings, he joined the up and coming indie band Surf Mutants and began a ten-year tenure with them. This culminated in the underground classic *Dancing with Tall women,* hailed by Lou Reed as one of his favourite albums.

Surf Mutants, of course, went through several line-up and name changes, to become the ultra-sophisticated Geisha. Extensive touring in Europe and America brought critical acclaim and the promise of commercial success that somehow failed to materialise in their native country. Their biggest UK hit to date, 'Alright By Me', peaked at number 4 in July 1985. Since then, they have remained a little known act over here, albeit with a strong and loyal following built up from their live performances, with fans willing to travel vast distances to see them play. Huge popularity in Japan, Sweden, Denmark and Germany has been some consolation, but a somewhat disappointing outcome for a band once described as 'The doyens of sub-rock, destined for the World's biggest stages.'

But what of Joe Byron, ten years on? I met up with the man in April this year at the Park Hotel, Kensington, just after the release of Geisha's fifth studio album *Insomniac's Café*. I asked him, among other things, about stringent record company policies, rifts with fellow band members and addiction problems that go back a long way. Looking relatively relaxed at first, and sipping orange juice, Joe was his usual laconic self, dismissing questions he didn't want to answer with a mixture of sarcasm and evasion, occasionally being blunt to the point of rudeness.

When asked about his being dropped from the recent sixteen-date tour of the States to promote the new album, Joe at first denied this was the case. After further questioning, he admitted there had been problems within the band for some time, particularly between him and singer James T. Relations with Goldstein impresario Hugh Hanley have also been strained, although the details have never been given. The official reason for Joe's omission from the current tour was ill-health. Many believe the decision was due to Joe's increasingly erratic behaviour and long-term substance abuse.

Brian Moorcroft *You seem to have been keeping a low profile lately, Joe. Can you tell us what you've been up to?*

Joe Byron I've been busy working on solo projects and ideas other people have brought to me. Things I've been planning to do for quite a while, but just haven't had the time due to other commitments.

Goldstein issued a press release, saying you wouldn't be with the band on their forthcoming tour of the States. What were the reasons behind this decision?

I didn't know anything about that decision until a phone call that came through about three days before the tour was due to start.

Before then I'd been ill, due to an infection, and I'd been resting on the advice of a doctor. I can't say much more than that right now because we're still in the process of negotiation.

What about Dekko Wainwright, the stand-in they used, who, ironically, took over from you when you left Eponymous Mouse? Didn't you see this as a deliberate move to undermine your position?

Like I said, I'm not able to comment on that right now.

How about your acting career, that seemed to take off a few years ago? Anything along those lines among the solo projects you've got planned?

Nothing I've found interesting enough to commit to on a long-term basis. For me, music comes first. Anything else is a sideline. I enjoyed playing Slick Chandler in *Certified Undead,* and got good reviews from some of the movie magazines. But the whole process means a total upheaval to your personal life. You have to change your schedule completely. Plus, I'm not too good at getting up at five in the morning, whatever the deal is.

Let's talk a bit about the new album. Weren't there disputes within the band about musical direction, particularly between you and James T? For instance, your preference for using other musicians on certain tracks?

Some of my ideas for the album did get vetoed, yes. There were disagreements about the direction we were heading in. Input from certain sources that I didn't feel were relevant, or even necessary to what we were trying to achieve. I wanted to use a Gospel choir on Redemption, and record them live in the studio, but we couldn't organise it within the time frame we'd been allocated. Little touches like that. Things we couldn't do for different reasons, none of them artistic. I didn't like the idea of being under pressure because of time and money. What goes on the record, stays on the record. You can't change it a few years down the line.

You've been critical before about the management policies of Goldstein, and in particular Hugh Hanley. How much has their influence changed the band's direction since you were taken over in 1987?

We've always maintained artistic freedom to play and record whatever we liked. In the early days, under Bill Mac, we were constantly in debt and always on the brink of going under. There was a feeling of desperation about everything we did. The deal with Goldstein enabled us to break out of that rut and freed us up from that never-going-anywhere mentality that holds so many bands back. But signing with a new management company wasn't all roses. We had problems initially from certain elements within, who thought we were going to be the next INXS or something. That went on for some time. All these unrealistic expectations that we were going to change our act suddenly to please them. Most of the bands they had on their books were mainly derivative. There was no originality in the things they were doing whatsoever.

In a recent interview with a Swedish radio station, James T made several references to your drug problems, a claim that you subsequently denied. How much strain have allegations of this sort put on your relationship with him and other band members?

First, let's get one thing straight. I don't have a drug problem. Yes, there have been incidents where I've been exhausted from touring, and from the insomnia I've suffered with for a long time. And, occasionally, I have overused certain prescription drugs to cope with the demands of life on the road. But none of these allegations have any substance, and shouldn't be given any air time. Especially not by people out to make a name for themselves on the back of the band.

I take it you're referring to the documentary by Cy Bender?

Well, now you come to mention it, yes. That's one example of someone abusing a position of power. Cy was invited along on the last tour of the States we did and given pretty much unlimited access backstage, and look what happened. Things I said were taken out of context and edited in such a way that made me look like a deviant. The entire slant of that documentary was dishonest and misleading.

He did say, later, that you'd abused him verbally at an awards ceremony in Los Angeles. Even threatened him physically if he didn't withdraw the film. Was this another marketing ploy to increase publicity?

Dreamed up by me and Bender, you mean?

Well, no, that isn't what I meant, but go on.

I didn't threaten him at the awards ceremony or anywhere else. That's just paranoia. But maybe that's what happens when you've upset so many people. You start thinking everyone's looking to fill you in.

Your career, to date, has been dogged by scandal and ill-health. Your short stay in rehab in 1992, for instance, that made the music papers, and one or two of the tabloids. How much has adverse publicity of this sort affected your ability to keep playing?

Apart from the odd occasion due to illness, I've never missed a gig, or a recording session. Certainly not because of drugs. People like Cy Bender and James T have made these allegations for their own reasons. I don't have to comment on them to vindicate myself. My record as a musician stands for itself.

OK, let's move on to your relationship with Hugh Hanley. You once likened his style of management to a tornado. Could you expand on that?

Well, for one thing, he doesn't understand the word no. Tell him he can't do something and he'll go out of his way to prove you wrong. This worked well for us in the early days, when we were under his wing, so to speak. We benefited from his unconventional way of getting things done. But we weren't always treated with the right consideration.

Things started to go wrong at some point?

Well, yeah. It all changed when Goldstein signed the girl band DreemZ. He started promoting them as well as us. We got sidelined, and handled by another division of the company who barely knew who we were. There were personality clashes along the way that should have been dealt with differently. Arguments about musical direction, what we should wear and how we should come across in interviews. Stuff like that. I think they were confusing us with one of their manufactured acts who were used to being told what to do.

You've enjoyed success as a songwriter over the years, having also written songs for other artists as well as for the band. Could you tell us a bit about the process, particularly your collaboration with James T?

I've always found songwriting easy, at least in terms of the initial idea. I generally start with a chord sequence, or melody line, and expand on that until it sounds right in my head. Sometimes James T will come to me with lyrics written out and I'll come up with the guitar part. I like to experiment at home and work on ideas I can structure and then take to the band later. *Romance On The Dark Side* came about largely through that process. I discovered outtakes and rough demos on a tape that had been lying around at home and thought they were worth reworking.

Going into the studio is the culmination of that process. You hope to hear your original idea translated into something polished and inspiring. Something people will want to listen to for years to come. That doesn't always happen, of course, but it's worth all the hard work when it does.

How big a role has your wife played in your career to date?

Justine took over as my business manager several years ago, to save me the hassle of thinking for myself. She's great at processing all the legal stuff and renegotiating contracts, arguing with people on the phone. Bit like a female version of Hugh Hanley really, but don't tell her I said that.

Where do you see yourself a few years from now?

Still playing and touring, hopefully. Working with other artists. Having more freedom to branch out in other areas creatively.

Lastly, If you could change anything, what would it be?

I'd probably spend more time at home with my family. Apart from that, I wouldn't change a thing.

30

St Luke's – the land that time forgot. You fill the hours with trivia, listening to music on headphones and mingling with patients in the hospital grounds. The outside world is off limits, unless you're one of the lucky ones, signed out for the weekend to stay with family or friends. The high red-brick wall reminds you where you are, stuck here in this makeshift prison.Nothing to do but think and act like an inmate. The whole day built around medication and the queue for lunch. You see them everywhere. Lost, institutionalised. Shuffling along the corridors with that haunted, vacant look, unable to perform the simplest act without a nurse on hand.

'Joe – visitor for you.'

I open my eyes. The morose black nurse is standing before me.

'Who is it?'

'I think it's your wife.'

Shocked from a trance, I shuffle out to the corridor to investigate. Standing by the alcove, in blue jeans and a black leather jacket, is a sombre-looking Justine. Her mouth drops when she sees me. I'm not the man she thought she'd find. I'm the inmate in a mental institution with a crumpled shirt and long, dishevelled hair.

'Welcome to the Hotel California,' I say, forcing a little black humour. She smiles distractedly, a glimmer of shock in her eyes that she tries to hide.

'Can we go somewhere more private?' she says.

'Sure. Take a walk in the grounds if you like.'

'Are you allowed outside?'

'Long as I stay within sight of the gun towers I can go where I like.'

The Big Man comes lurching along, his enormous bulk almost filling the narrow gangway. He gives me the nod on the way past, a gesture of solidarity from one inmate to another.

She watches him pass by, uneasily.

'Who's that?'

'Bernie. He's the Daddy in here. Keeps everyone supplied with Maltesers.'

The male nurse looks up from his perch by the door. He looks pleasantly surprised to see me.

'Off boundaries today then, Joe?'

'That's right. Check with Roz if you don't believe me.'

'I'll take your word for it,' he says, grinning inanely. 'If you're not back for dinner we'll send out a search party.'

Justine's boot heels strike the metal runners as we head downstairs. A strange, dream-like happiness descends on me. From now on things are going to be fine. Justine will intervene and get me out of here. The nurses will see that it's all been a big mistake and discharge me right away. I'll be free, reunited with my kids again.

We head for the grounds, a strong waft of food drifting over from the kitchens. Two male patients are smoking in a recess, hidden away like fugitives. They look up with obvious hostility, and the wave of happiness I felt on the staircase vanishes. Only a few days ago a patient was stabbed in a random attack by a schizophrenic. Things like that put the experience of being here in a different light. The thought that you might be a target for someone more damaged than you are.

Justine keeps walking, oblivious to the danger. She looks sullen, withdrawn, unwilling to make conversation.

'I can't stay too long,' she says suddenly.

'You've only just got here!'

'I've got to pick Sadie up from school, and Jake's with Alice. It's not fair to leave him there too long.'

'Half an hour won't hurt, will it?'

We follow the path around the back. The red brick building looms like a stately home, something you might see in a society magazine or upmarket holiday brochure. Ornate chimneys and staggered rooftops, balconies overlooking the grounds. The most exclusive residence in the whole of London and I'd give anything to be somewhere else.

A wooden bench overlooks the flower garden. We reach a sort of unconscious decision to stop and sit down, Justine at one end and me at the other, a mosaic of cigarette butts scattered at our feet. Patients sit around in the warm afternoon sun, watched by the nurses, who blend in subtly, making sure nothing happens to spoil the equilibrium. The whole scene is beguiling, like a picnic area in a concentration camp.

'Nice spot,' Justine says dryly.

'Better out here than it is in there, that's for sure.'

She stares ahead, fixedly, her bag clasped in her lap. Her body language confirms my suspicions. She couldn't get further away if she was sat in the next county.

'How's Alice?' I say, choosing common ground.

'Fine.'

'Does she know I'm in here?'

'Of course. Did you think I'd keep it a secret?'

I don't have an answer. The whole conversation is surreal, sat out here in this leafy glade, tainted by madness.

'Do the kids know?'

'I told them you were working away for a while.'

'What'd you tell them that for?'

'Because it was easier.'

'Than what?'

She looks at me frankly. 'Telling them the truth.'

A bare-chested patient with a shaved head and tattoos lays out on the grass, face up. He looks contented and happy, a holidaymaker enjoying the good weather. Justine puts her head back and sighs.

'I took one look at this place earlier and nearly drove straight back out again.'

'How d'you think I feel?'

She glares at me. 'Oh, I forgot. It's all about you, isn't it.'

Maybe all marriages are the same. One long, tedious row from beginning to end. You forget what it was that attracted you in the first place. I struggle to be amenable, to overcome the fog of sleep and medication and say something meaningful.

'How did you find out I was in here?'

'The police phoned – at six in the morning. What were you doing in someone's shed?'

'Sleeping.'

She stares at me, incredulous.

'It was either that or freeze to death. What would you have done?'

'Gone home, like any normal person!'

The policeman who found me had the same reaction, a kind of baffled irritation that I couldn't come up with a more plausible excuse. But the incident does have a certain comic value. The police radios and the shining torches. The old guy with his white hair sticking up, standing in the garden with his horrified wife.

'I just don't understand what you were thinking,' she says.

'I told you. I was cold. I needed to – '

'I don't mean that. I mean everything else. Throwing away your family. Your career. Bringing that, *stuff* into the house.'

She crosses her legs, irritably. A flicker of desire stirs, harking back to the days when we were still speaking. There was another side to her then, a sensual, alluring side I'd almost forgotten.

'Did you read the Moorcroft article?' she says.

'Some of it.'

'What was it – professional suicide? Your final attempt to bring everyone else down with you?'

'No.'

'That's what it sounded like to me.' She gazes out over the grounds, bemused. 'Oh, well. The damage is done now. You won't have to worry, will you, hidden away in this place.'

I can't believe her lack of sensitivity. The insinuation that I landed up in here by choice, handing control of my life to a bunch of doctors and psychiatrists. Judging by the look on her face, I'd have to be in a straightjacket to elicit any real sympathy.

'I've still got options,' I say resentfully.

'Like what?'

'Solo projects. Working with other people.'

She laughs abruptly. 'You seriously think people are going to want to work with you after this?'

'It's a blip, that's all.'

'What! … You ruin your career and your marriage in one hit and it's a blip? You're unbelievable!'

A male nurse escorts a young female patient along the path. He's smiling and outwardly jovial, content to be in the sun. She walks listlessly beside him, heavily medicated, her anaemic face framed by lank, shapeless hair. They pass by like a premonition.

Justine shudders. 'God, I hate this place.'

'You should try living here. It's like the Island of Dr Moreau sometimes.'

The red-brick building sits beneath the powder blue sky. Two figures stand at one of the balconies, looking over. I think of all the patients in the canteen. For some of them this is home, a place of safety.

'I really miss the kids,' I say.

'You can't come back if that's what you're thinking.'

'I'm gonna sort myself out. Stop drinking.'

'You've said all that before.'

'I mean it this time.'

The male nurse and the anaemic-looking girl sit on a bench further down. Pigeons strut at their feet, their tiny heads stabbing the grass incessantly. The nurse turns to the girl and smiles, engaging her in conversation. They could be lovers, meeting in the grounds of a posh hotel. The lush garden and raised patio add to the deception. All we need now is a waiter to appear with a tray of gin and tonics and the illusion would be complete.

'What's the food like in here?' Justine says.

'Dire.'

'What did you expect – Egon Ronay?'

Even her sarcasm gives me hope. That part of me that still believes in the future. The two of us together as a normal couple, doing normal things.

'What if I promise to clean up my act?'

'Joe – '

'I'll fix the house up. Start taking the kids to school.'

'Really? And how long will that last?'

'I'm serious. Just gimme a chance. I'll make it up to you. I really will.'

'You need to speak to someone.'

'Who?'

'I don't know. The doctors. Psychiatrists.'

'What can they do?'

'They might be able to help you. I certainly can't.'

We share one of those odd moments that pass for tenderness. Her look of pity wavers, a slight tremor at her mouth as if she's about to cry. Instinctively, I move closer, edging my fingers towards her on the back of the bench.

'What's the matter?'

She sits back, staring ahead. 'I feel so fucking angry.'

'With what – me?'

'Everything. You. This place. The way things have turned out.'

I think of the Big Man with his box of Maltesers, railing against the system from a high-backed chair. That could be me in a few years – escorted back to my single room by unfeeling nurses. Justine's bitterness adds to the burden. The inference that whatever it is she's going through, I've been the cause of it.

She wipes her eyes, in control again. 'I tried to understand. I really did. Every time I thought we were getting somewhere something else came along to spoil it.'

The anaemic-looking girl bends to examine something on the grass. I think of the menu I filled in earlier.

'You've no idea what's it's been like for me. Sitting at home, waiting for a phone call. Not knowing where you are or where you've been. Wondering if you're still alive even.'

'Sorry.'

'No you're not. You're not sorry at all. It's just a word that rolls off your tongue whenever it's convenient.'

Her anger fades. The force that's been tearing us apart for so long is put on hold. Only the scenery remains. The flowers and the weeping willows. The heavily-medicated inmates wandering aimlessly among the pigeons.

'I ran into Bill Mac the other day,' she says.

'Does he know I'm in here as well?'

'Yes, he does. Would you rather I'd lied to him too?' She stares at me belligerently. 'Stop being so paranoid. Everyone knows where you are anyway.'

'So what did he say?'

'Not much. He blames the lifestyle. The way you were living.'

Bill Mac – the genial little Scot who helped us out when we first started. Getting gigs and making phone calls for the band. Lugging equipment in a transit van. I'm almost ashamed of the way we treated him. Selling out to Goldstein for the top dollar fix. Losing his easy-going, paternal touch for the megalomania of Hugh Hanley.

The anaemic-looking girl and the nurse stroll back towards the hospital. I'm reminded where I am. A million miles away from civilisation, from my previous employment.

'I should make a move,' Justine says, glancing at her watch. I'm filled with a sudden anxiety.

'Can't you stay a bit longer?'

'I've got to pick Sadie up, I told you.'

'Five minutes won't hurt, will it – please?'

She sinks back, dropping her bag, heavily, beside her. The anxiety leaves me, replaced by a dull resentment at the way things are. I'm a prisoner, weighed down by rules and regulations, wasting away in this ancient mausoleum.

'Mum sends her love.' she says distractedly.

'Did she say anything else?'

'Like what?'

'About me being in here.'

'She hopes you'll get the help you need. It upsets her to think of you in a place like this when you've got so much going for you.'

'Miriam said that?'

'No, I just made it up.' She glares at me. 'Of course she said it. Do you think she liked it – finding you in the state you were in?'

I've always thought of Miriam as uptight and standoffish, lamenting the fact she wasn't born into royalty. I can't imagine what she must make of all this, having a son-in-law in a mental hospital. And yet her concern reaches out to me in some nebulous way, forcing me to reconsider.

'Do you need anything?' Justine says.

'A taxi out of this place might help.'

I light a cigarette, one of the few pleasures left available to me. Justine watches, reserved and aloof.

'I take it Shaz has been in?'

'She came in yesterday. Bought me a bar of Fruit 'n' Nut and a prayer book.'

'A what?'

'Some religious crap she got from the church. She even tried to convince the vicar to come in and see me. What's that all about? She knows I'm an atheist, for fuck's sake.'

Guilt sets in.

'I'll make it up to her when I get out of here.'

'What for?'

'Abusing her hospitality. Upsetting the kids when I was staying there.'

'Oh – so it's alright for you to upset your own family?'

'I didn't mean that. I'm just saying …'

She shakes her head wearily.

'You know the hardest thing of all for me to deal with in all this? Knowing that after everything we talked about, all the trips to doctors and counsellors and everyone else who's tried to help you over the years, you just wouldn't listen.'

I draw on the cigarette, pondering the accusation. She sighs heavily.

'This is ridiculous. I swore I wasn't going to get angry when I came up here to see you. And here we go again.'

'At least we're talking.'

'Talking? Please! It's a wonder I haven't ended up in here myself by now, all the stress you've put me under.'

The weeping willows look impressive. Tiny white buds bowing to the earth in a shimmering cascade. In a strange way it feels like progress. This awkward conversation we're having out here in the grounds. These tentative moves to bring us closer together.

'Remember when we went to Prague?' she says. 'That lovely restaurant by the river? You kept telling me you were going to change back then.'

I picture the floodlit castle across the water. The candles and the wine.

'All those big ideas you had about working with other people. Moving us all to L.A. so you could work with Scott Levine. And the funniest thing was I believed you.'

She takes a deep breath and looks out over the grounds. I can't feel much for my abandoned career other than a mild dissatisfaction. Maybe I'm institutionalised already. A basket case waiting to happen.

'Hugh wanted to come up and see you,' she says.

I gawp at her, astonished.

'In here?'

'Don't worry, I persuaded him not to. I told him you weren't receptive to visitors at the moment.'

I try to picture Hugh Hanley strolling around the grounds, chomping on a cigar. Maybe he'd see it as a public relations exercise, a way of improving his image. People might think he'd developed a caring streak all of a sudden, a desperate need to seek forgiveness for the diabolical way he treated me when I was in the band.

'Fuck him. I hope he has a car crash and dies.'

She stares at me, aghast. 'That's a terrible thing to say.'

'What's he ever done for me? Apart from stitch me up with lawyers and contracts I can't get out of? I should have stayed with Bill Mac. At least he treated me like a human being.'

She stands.

'I really have to go now.'

I look up, crippled with sorrow, regret. 'Can I ask you something?'

'What?'

'Do you hate me for what I've done?'

'No, of course I don't hate you. You think it makes me happy to see you in here like this?'

We walk back to the hospital, along the gravel track. A few male patients are kicking a football about under a nurse's watchful eye, the red brick mausoleum impressive in the background. The scene has a peaceful, tranquil quality, marred by the shadow of mental illness.

Justine prepares herself to leave. We stand apart beneath the awning at reception, neither of us knowing quite what to say. So far, she's resisted the tears and any overt displays of emotion to preserve her dignity. Now it's time for her to go she seems less self-assured.

'I'll call the office tomorrow,' she says. 'See how you are.'

A wave of desolation hits me. 'When can I see the kids?'

'I'm not bringing them here.'

'At least let me speak to them.'

She bites her lower lip, unable to look at me.

'Come on, Justine. Gimme a break, will you?'

She looks up defiantly. 'I don't think it would be good for them right now.'

'Why?'

'They're confused enough as it is. Get yourself sorted out first, then you can speak to them.'

A monstrous sense of injustice boils over in me. I erupt, ranting about the strain I'm under, the indignity of being cooped up in a lunatic asylum without the proper medication, denied even the right to see my own children. She stares me out, refusing to back down.

'Don't start blaming me because you can't see the kids. You brought this on yourself, remember?'

'I just want to talk to them. You can't deny me that, surely?'

She folds her arms stiffly and looks away.

'OK. Fine. You can talk to them.'

'Thank you.'

'But I don't want them thinking you're coming home. That isn't going to happen, OK?'

She leaves me standing in the entranceway. No tender hugs.

No kiss on the cheek as a last goodbye. Beneath all that hostility there's a glimmer of something else. Understanding. Sympathy even. But we've been acting this way for so long now it feels normal. Familiarity breeding contempt. Her contempt for me and this island of lost souls I've washed up on.

*

Noise engulfs me as soon as I walk in the door. Paranoia roaming free like an airborne virus. The men in white coats mingle freely with the population, except these days they're dressed in shirts and ties and don't carry giant hypodermics filled with laudanum. There's an air of industry about the place. A busy office block or factory unit, the workers engrossed in mass production of a different kind.

The staff office looms at the end of the corridor. Two nurses are chatting inside. One of them calls out as I pass by.

'How did it go with your wife, Joe?'

'Great.'

She thrusts a strip of paper at me. 'Someone phoned for you earlier. He said you could reach him on this number.'

I have to read the name several times to make sure I haven't imagined it.

'Everything alright?'

I look up, still in a state of shock. 'Er – yeah. Fine.'

I sit in the alcove with the slip of paper. The past comes up in painful technicolor. Fragments. Flashbacks. Sitting with Justine in the grounds, feeling instinctively that we were making inroads, only to have her turn on me and get vindictive about the kids. Shaz coming up with books and chocolate bars and last month's *NME,* lending me money so I could squander it on pills and dope and whatever else I could lay my hands on in this godforsaken place.

And now the latest twist.

The man who's caused me untold grief in the last few years – the man who put the spoke into what's left of my career and ruined everything – has just left me his phone number.

31

The world looks strange from the tinted windows of a BMW. My first contact with the outside in days and I'm overwhelmed. Unfamiliar streets flash by. People out walking, like extras in a movie. I envy their freedom. The simple choices they have to jump on a bus or hail a taxi, nip in a pub and sink a few ales.

Hanley talks non-stop, veering off on wild tangents without warning. New Labour under Tony Blair. Women drivers. You forget what a showman he is. The born raconteur, thriving on the sound of his own voice. Even his personal struggles take on an epic quality. The maisonette he's just bought in Chelsea, after months of legal wrangling. The financial cost of his recent divorce. Everything revolving around money.

He glances over, slightly sinister in his dark glasses and greased-back hair.

'You hungry?'

'Not really.'

'We'll park up somewhere. Have a little chat. I said I'd have you back in a couple of hours. That alright?'

I try not to be impressed. The ease with which he persuaded the staff to let me out for the afternoon. But then he was always like that, good at convincing people to do things that weren't always in their best interests. He had influence. Wherever you went, he knew someone. From the head waiter at the Savoy to the manager of the Groucho Club. Doors always opened when Hugh Hanley was around.

We find a quiet bistro in a side street, a location he seems to know well. He leads me through a dilapidated back door and into a small kitchen, filled with steam and bodies in transit. A chirpy blonde girl waves us through the kitchen and into a small restaurant area out front. An elegant looking woman in her forties looks up and gives a theatrical gasp, waving us over.

'Hugh, darling! How are you?'

They embrace in a profusion of sugar-sweet kisses. Hanley turns to me, almost as an afterthought, and extends an arm. 'Ronnie, this is Joe – one of my boys from the early days.'

Bowing, she offers a limp hand. Her fingers are long and slim in mine, her gaze steady, quizzical.

'You look familiar, Joe. Have we met before?'

I shake my head, conscious of the clothes I'm wearing, my unkempt hair. Hanley steps-in like a minder, steering me away from the spotlight. 'Joe's been off the circuit for a while, Ronnie. Thought I'd bring him here for one of your lunchtime specials.'

We sit at a table with white linen tablecloths and fancy tea-lights, a world away from the cuisine I've been used to recently. It's hard not to feel intimidated. I don't move in these circles anymore. I can barely hold a conversation.

'What d'you fancy, Joe?'

'I'm not hungry.'

'You've got to eat something. How 'bout a pizza?'

He unzips his jacket and settles back. The first time I've seen him up close for months and he looks restless and ill at ease, trying to put on an act to impress me. Why bother when I know what he's like? Screaming abuse at ticket receipt collectors, and ripping telephone sockets out of the wall. Walking out of band meetings when he can't get his own way. A sound engineer in L.A. called him a 'Monster on Wheels', a title we used for a song on the third album. And yet he's always been good at the charm front. Smoothing things over and making people forget what he's done.

Ronnie comes over with notepad and pen. Hanley orders a coke, and looks at me expectantly. I order coke, too, aware of the glinting optics behind the bar, the sense that everyone's watching me.

'Ready to order now?' she says.

Hanley orders steak, medium rare, with a side salad, declining the French fries on account of his savage indigestion. I order the special pizza to shut him up. Ronnie sweeps away to the kitchen with a gracious smile and a promise to indulge in all the gossip later.

Nice little place she's got here,' he says, gazing out over the restaurant. 'Good wine selection too. Not that we'll be heading down that route, obviously.'

I sit in embarrassed silence, not sure what I'm supposed to do or say. He leans forward, elbows on the table, and stares at me intensely.

'Weren't all my fault, you know.'

'What wasn't?'

'The band. Everything that happened.'

I'm stunned. After all the heinous, double-crossing stunts he's pulled. Withholding information about my mum being in hospital so the tour could continue. Booking us to play a folk festival in Munich because he owed the promoter a favour. Countless occasions when his ruthlessness and power-driving have threatened to destroy everything we'd achieved.

'Why didn't you come to me?' he says.

'About what?'

'The way you were feeling. The grievances you had. I could have done something about it. Helped you out.'

He has that look. Unhinged, bordering on the psychotic.From past experience, I know it's best to act dumb and say nothing.

He turns the gold ring on his finger, shaking his head. 'I know we've had our disagreements over the years. But there's ways of doing things, you know? You could've picked the phone up at any time. You could have asked to see me. I'd have listened.'

The waitress brings the drinks over. Two cokes with ice and a slice. He waits until she's gone and lifts his glass in a vague toast.

'Good health.'

We drink to whatever sociability's still left between us, a gesture devoid of warmth or understanding. He settles back, thoughtful again.

'That interview caused me a lot of embarrassment, you know that?'

'What interview?'

'Come on, Joe. The one you did for *NME*.' He opens a pack of breadsticks and feeds one into his mouth. A glint of black humour shines in his eyes. 'Did you think I wouldn't see it?'

'No?'

'So what was it then? A revenge tactic because I dropped you from the tour?'

'No, I just – '

'Be honest, Joe. I just want to know why you felt the need to air all your grievances in public like that. Did I really treat you that badly?'

'It was bullshit. Moorcroft made most of it up.'

He nods slowly. 'You didn't say any of it then? All that stuff about being sidelined? Deserted when we signed DreemZ?'

I don't have an answer. He stares at me, perplexed.

'What about the advance I got you when you signed to CBS? The publishing deal I set up for you? Doesn't any of that mean anything?'

He snaps another breadstick, shaking his head.

'I just didn't expect you to turn on me like that. After all I've done for you over the years. All the breaks I gotcha.'

I'm aware of the other diners, the bland music. He grins suddenly, a business tactics to confuse rivals.

'Look – I didn't come here to ball you out, Joe. I just want a nice, friendly little chat to see how the land lies, OK?'

He settles back, hands folded over his sizeable paunch. The old pals act, softening me up for more of the same.

'So what's it like up at the funhouse? Plenty of good-looking nurses to tuck you in at night?'

'Not quite.'

'They say it's a thin line, don't they – madness and sanity?'

'Apparently.'

'So what happened – the split with Justine push you over the edge?'

'I fell asleep in someone's shed.'

'You did what?'

'I got hammered in a nightclub and got lost walking home.'

'Christ. I've heard of slumming it, but that's ridiculous!'

He feeds another breadstick into the sawmill and ponders the issue.

'I'm not knocking you, Joe. I've done a lot of crazy shit myself. Run cars off the road pissed. Punched people out in nightclubs. I'm just trying to understand what happened. You know. From your point of view.'

His nicotine voice merges with the music, the scenery. The sound of cutlery scraping plates drifts over from the other side. Irrational fear takes hold of me. The wingtips of paranoia. I'm convinced everyone knows who I am. The whole thing's been set up by Hanley to humiliate and confuse me. Ronnie must be in on it too. And the chirpy, blonde waitress who brought the drinks over. I saw the way she looked at me. The thin sneer on her lips as she sauntered away.

'You're not saying much, Joe. Everything alright?'

'Yeah sure.'

'You look a bit – lost, that's all.'

His trace of concern almost convinces me. The genial host, looking out for my well-being. Maybe he's genuine. The reformed Hugh Hanley, thoughtful and considerate. Not the violent egomaniac I used to know, screaming out of pub car parks in his reconditioned Jag.

'Got you on any medication, have they?'

I reel off the brand names like a connoisseur. Librium. Carbamazapine. He frowns uneasily.

'All Greek to me, mate. I'm a great believer in willpower, personally, but that's another story.'

He shifts uneasily.

'You and Justine OK?'

'Not exactly.'

'No, I didn't think so. What happened?'

'We drifted apart.'

'Anyone else involved?'

'Not that I know of.'

He takes a slug of coke and reflects.

'I was gutted when I heard where you were. Really I was. No one expected it to come to this.'

'Shit happens.'

He shakes his head wryly. 'Remember New Mexico in '87? Snakes, scorpions and forty-degree heat?'

'Vaguely.'

'I was thinking of renaming it the "Joe Byron Walkabout Tour". What a way to earn a living!'

New Mexico was no different than any other tour as far as I can remember. Sure, I drank too much tequila and upset a few A&R people. And I did go missing for a few hours in Santa Fe. But nothing too outrageous in the scheme of things.

'I was under a lot of stress at the time. Sadie had just been born. I was homesick, missing my family.'

'Sure you were. But look at it from my point of view, Goldstein was bankrolling that tour. The financial mess Bill Mac left took years to undo. The last thing I needed was chasing you all over the country.'

Strains of the old Hugh Hanley. The mesmerising gaze and the fixed jaw. The force of his willpower against mine, or anyone else who tries to oppose him. I get the sense he's building up to something, feeling his way in.

He takes a slug of coke and sits back, switching, once again, to his more agreeable persona. 'Forget about all that now,' he says dismissively. 'It's history. Finished. What's important is you. Getting you well again.'

The blonde waitress puts my pizza down – a culinary work of art, dotted with olives and mushrooms. I stare at it vacantly. Hanley orders two more cokes and, when the waitress is gone, attacks his steak with abandon. My misadventures in New Mexico are forgotten as his first love takes over.

'So, what's your plans?' he says, a trickle of steak juice running down his chin. The question catches me off guard.

'Plans?'

'Well. You know.' He pauses, eyeing me carefully. 'There's been talk of you going solo. Working with some girl from

Croydon. Is that right?'

I feign ignorance, wondering how he found out about Naomi. 'I'm not really in a position to do anything at the moment, stuck in that place.'

'No, course not. But I think it's best we talk about it, don't you? get it all out in the open.'

I see the avarice shining in his eyes, the chance to catch me at a low point and take full advantage. My resentment of him grows accordingly, overshadowed by fears for my health, the thought of going back to the hospital.

'Can I ask you something?' I say.

'Sure. Go right ahead.'

'Whose idea was it to bring in Dekko Wainwright to replace me?'

He shrugs, wiping his mouth with a serviette. 'Needs must, I suppose. Dekko was available. You weren't.'

'And that's it?'

'Well, look at it from my point of view. We had to make a decision with the tour due to begin. What else could we do?'

I'm not convinced. The whole thing reeks of a conspiracy. A takeover bid by James T to ease me out of the picture.

'So what happens now the tour's finished?'

'I don't know, son. You tell me.'

Thoughts of the ward intrude. Colin, my subversive roommate, smoking by the dormitory window. The Big Man, mouthing-off at staff because he missed his mum's visit. Hanley belches discreetly into his serviette, and notes my plate with a frown.

'What's up – pizza no good?'

'I said I wasn't hungry.'

'Another coke?'

'No thanks.

'How 'bout a Scotch and soda?' He laughs at his own joke. 'Only kidding. That's about the last thing you need at the moment, that's for sure.'

He's quiet for a long time, weighing me up with the same, brooding intensity.

'You know how I started out in this game?'

'Running a dance hall in Birmingham, wasn't it?'

'That's right. Before that I worked the night shift in a bakery for three years. Know what I learnt from that?'

'What?'

'That most people are content with fuck-all.' He watches my reaction. 'Most people like a drink too, and I'm no exception. But, you have to know when to draw the line, don't you.'

He studies me across the table, the lines in his forehead deepening.

'Know what your two greatest enemies in this world are?'

'What?'

'Time and the tax-man. I ever tell you that before?'

'Several times.'

'Well it's true. Between 'em they'll carve up your assets like nobody's business. But there's other things too. Blind spots. Areas of weakness. You might not know what they are but other people sure will.'

He spreads his hands in appeal.

'I did all I could to help you, Joe. Rearranged tour dates when you were ill. Changed the schedule to make allowances for your family. Weren't my fault it went the way it did.'

His piety sickens me. The self-made man with a caring streak, conveniently forgetting his own flaws. His much publicised drug use in the eighties. The flight attendants and hotel staff he's abused all over the world.

'You know I'd organised a meeting with you and Justine?' he says.

'I was aware of it, yeah.'

'Well that ain't gonna happen now.'

'Why not?'

'Because I've been overruled.'

'Who by?'

'The Board of Trustees at Goldstein.'

Sickness comes over me in waves. I feel like jumping up from the table and running into the street.

'Talk to me, Joe.'

I sip my coke, weighing up the implications.

'So that's it, then. I'm being ousted. Is that what you're trying to tell me?'

He shrugs. 'Out of my hands, son. I did what I could, believe me.'

We sit out an immeasurably long silence, music and conversation from the other diners filling in. He looks pained, undecided.

'Know what I'd do in your position?'

'What?'

'I'd take all the help I could get. Seriously I would. What other option have you got, eh? Look at the mess you're in. Look how you've ended up.'

Ronnie joins us in a breeze of perfume and slender femininity. Her arrival has an immediate calming effect, reducing my fear to an acceptable degree. She chats with Hanley about people they know, unintentionally excluding me from the conversation. I catch a line from the song that's playing – Neil Finn reminding me the dream isn't over – but it sure feels that way to me.

'Lovely to meet you, Joe,' Ronnie says, smiling demurely. 'Drop by anytime, won't you. Any friend of Hugh's is always welcome.'

When she's gone, Hanley drains his coke, and zips up his jacket.

'Come on then, son. Let's get you back. I told the nurse we'd only be a couple of hours.'

We don't speak much during the drive back. I smoke his cigarettes and look out at the streets, knowing I'll soon be back on the ward. I wish I'd had the balls to say what I thought to his face. Instead, I let him bamboozle and intimidate me when my resistance was low.

We shake hands outside the hospital reception. His grip is firm and lingers too long. 'You hang in there, Joe. Sort yourself out, you hear me?'

He sifts through a black leather wallet and hands me a card.

'I don't do this often, but if you need help, give me a call. That's my private number, OK?'

'Thanks.'

'I mean it. Anytime.'

I stare at the card, embarrassed.

'And don't get too comfortable in this place, eh? Book your holidays in Spain next time!'

With a friendly slap on the arm and a lopsided grin, he saunters off to the car park. I put his card in my shirt pocket and head for reception, feeling like the victim of a heartless confidence trick. Although he didn't say it outright, the statement was there all the same. My ten years with the band is officially over.

Hugh Hanley drives off in his new BMW.

I go back to my lonely room to think about loss.

32

The mobile dispensary trundles into view. Enough pills on board to feed a coach load of junkies for six months, and still I can't get my hands on anything stronger than Librium. Cadging sleeping pills from gullible patients doesn't work anymore. The staff have got wise to my little games. Now they've taken to crushing up my night time sedatives with a pestle and mortar so I can't take them back to my room and hoard them for later. There's a constant buzzing in my head, like a generator someone forgot to switch off. I can't risk mentioning it to the doctor in case he sees it as a sign of regression and keeps me in even longer.

Time on the ward does terrible things to your head. I've taken to wandering the corridors with headphones on, trying to drown out the sound of my own demise. Lunch with Hugh Hanley doesn't seem real, an event I dreamed up to cope with the horrors of this place. The hunted animal feeling persists. An insidious, viral sickness that shuts off all hope and contaminates everything. No matter how many mind games you play, no matter how much medication they dose you up on, you can't escape it. It's there permanently, a harbinger of death that never lets you out of its sight.

I talked to Jake last night. Justine snatched the phone away, saying my time was up. She's lost it completely. No concern for how I'm feeling, only her wounded pride at all the things I've done. The drinking and the staying out all night. The recklessness with money and the loss of my job. Why do I still believe there's a slim chance we'll get back together? Maybe that's part of the delusion, the downside of sitting it out in this joint with nothing to do.

*

Roz appears, red-faced, hands on hips. Her mouth moves, but no sound comes out. I stare up at her, inanely, and ease the headphones back, cutting Pat Metheny's guitar solo off in mid-flight.

'Thank you,' she says abruptly.

'What have I done now?'

'You haven't done anything. The doctor's ready to see you.'

Along the corridor we go – first door on the left. The same procedure as before, except I'm more familiar with the routine this time. They're all sat here waiting for me, like garden gnomes. The same odd collection of hatchet-faced women and the student taking notes. I feel like doing something outrageous. Stick my fingers up my nose, or scream at the top of my voice. Let them see the full extent of my sudden flight from reality.

Doctor Reece offers his soft, manicured hand, and smiles pleasantly.

'So – how are you today, Joe?'

'Fine, thanks.'

'Settle in on the ward OK?'

'Kind of.'

'Any problems with the medication?'

'Not really.'

'No side effects? Headaches, blurred vision?'

The questioning goes on in a similar vein, innocent enough at first, but clearly intended to assess my mental state. I feel confident with my performance, certain he'll see I'm *compos mentis* and discharge me without delay.

Roz gives a brief report, detailing my insomnia and a run-in I had with the duty nurse over medication. She acts differently around the doctor. None of the feisty sarcasm or witty one-liners she uses with me. Clearly he's the boss and she's the underling, deferring to his seniority willingly. Maybe they're having an affair, and all this formality is a front to stop people finding out.

Whatever the reality, I'm not in a position to argue. They both have the power to veto my bid for freedom and keep me in even longer.

The doctor turns to me, frowning. 'Why did you ask for more medication?'

'Because I couldn't sleep.'

'Any particular reason for that?'

'Too much noise on the ward. I couldn't relax.'

'And what do you do when you feel like this?'

'He writes songs,' Roz says, without a trace of irony. Doctor Reece raises an eyebrow, as if this might contravene some guideline on mental health.

'Songs?'

'Just words on scraps of paper,' I say quickly. 'Helps keep my mind occupied in the early hours when there's nothing else to do.'

He nods bemusedly.

'Tell me about your referral to C.O.D.A.T., Joe?'

'Doctor Kahn made the appointment for me. I went there a couple of times before I ended up in here.'

'And how did you find it?'

I tell him what he wants to hear. The sessions were helpful and the counsellor was nice. We drank coffee and ate chocolate chip cookies. Talked about abstinence, a concept I embraced wholeheartedly.

The doctor listens carefully, watching me with interest. When I've finished, there's a satisfactory lull, a sign they're all pleased with the answers I've given. He considers the evidence, thoughtfully, before coming to a conclusion.

'I've been thinking a lot about your case, Joe. I strongly feel there's only one way for us to go forward from here.'

'What's that?'

'I'd like you to go into treatment.'

Silence.

His words have a delayed impact, a sudden hammer blow that strikes when I'm least expecting it. He smiles faintly, stroking his chin.

'How do you feel about that?'

'I don't want to go.'

'Why not?'

'I went once before and it didn't work.'

'That was two years ago, I believe.'

'Nothing's changed since then. I still feel the same way.'

No one moves. Roz stares at the wall, cross-legged, casual in jeans and trainers. The rest of the committee sit quietly, waiting for the doctor to speak. There's nowhere for me to go. The whole thing's been worked out beforehand at some sinister meeting. All that's expected of me is to comply. To go along with their treacherous plan without any resistance.

'Think about it,' the doctor says. 'It's probably the best option you've got at the moment. Under the circumstances.'

'So you're keeping me in hospital?'

'No, not at all. I don't think keeping you in any longer would serve any useful purpose.'

I stare at his dimpled chin and say nothing.

'But I would make one proviso if you are discharged.'

'What's that?'

'You attend C.O.D.A.T. on a regular basis until your referral comes up. That is, of course, provided you're willing to go along with the treatment plan.'

A devious thought arises. Treatment could be weeks, months away. By then I'll have found a loophole, some way to wriggle out of it permanently.

'OK, I'll do it.'

'Excellent.' The doctor slaps his thighs and leans forward. 'Do you feel ready to leave?'

'Yes, I do.'

'And you're staying with your sister at the moment, is that right?'

'That's right.'

'I'll contact Joe's sister,' Roz says. 'Let her know he's being discharged.'

He stands, seemingly as pleased with the outcome as I am. 'Right. That's it then. We'll have your medication made up and you can go.'

Sunlight pierces the awful black cloud that's followed me round for so long. For the first time in days, I'm going to be free, released from this place of endless suffering. The doctor appears as a kindly benefactor, not the sinister figure I imagined him to be. Even the room looks brighter, and the people in it all here to help me in some way.

We shake hands formally. Doctor Reece steps back and frowns. 'Think about what I said, Joe. After all, we don't want to see you back in here again, do we?'

I move to the door, overcome with relief. Roz flashes me a scornful look but I'm way beyond reproach. Now I can breathe easier. The role playing is over. I don't have to abase myself anymore and pander to their stupid rules and regulations. The good doctor has certified me fit and able to rejoin society and that's what I intend to do as soon as humanly possible.

Roz catches up with me along the corridor. 'Well done, Joe. You got what you wanted, didn't you.'

'Kind of, yeah. One more day in this place and I *would* have gone nuts.'

She smiles thinly. 'You heard what the doctor said. You need to think seriously about treatment, or you will end up back in here.'

At the office, she turns to me, composed and professional once more. I get the feeling she disapproves somehow, as if I've cheated her and the system.

'Well, that's it. As soon as your medication's made up you can go.'

'Does that mean I'll never see you again?'

She laughs dryly. 'Well, I kind of hope so, for both our sakes. With you around, I'd never get any work done.'

'I could always come back and visit you sometime.'

'I don't think so, Joe. Sorry.'

I sit by the window in a patch of warm sunlight. The freshly-scented lounge looks almost inviting, empty of the usual mob, who must be out in the grounds, or attending their Art classes. I can't believe I'm leaving. I could run along the corridors, shouting the news, and risk another three days locked-up for psychotic behaviour. Instead, I sit quietly waiting for my medication, feeling smugly that I've outwitted them all.

*

The queue for lunch begins to form, and I'm eternally grateful I'm not in it. There's no drawn out speeches or tearful goodbyes to make. No deep and lasting friendships to sever. My biggest regret is leaving Roz – her tantalising hips and coy smile keeping me going through the long days and nights of utter tedium. Her aloof personality must have appealed to the deviant in me. In different circumstances we might have got together – the nursemaid and the lunatic, finding unrequited love in the corridors of madness.

The taxi driver whistles tunelessly to the radio. He's a cheerful old duffer, with absolutely no concept of the nightmare I've just been through. Sitting in the back with my trusty holdall, I gaze out at my former lodgings. Now I'm leaving, the hospital wing doesn't look quite so intimidating. Even the man unloading the bread van adds a touch of homeliness to the place. The few patients milling around reception look sad and dejected rather than psychotic and dangerous. I look upon them all with a distant affection, knowing I'll never be back. I'm leaving the relative safety of the ward for a place of uncertainty. No more clean sheets and three meals a day. No more boisterous repartee with Roz, or Colin's anarchic plots to undermine the system. I'm on my own again with no one to help me.

'Where to, mate?'

'Holland Park Avenue, please.'

We enter the stream of traffic heading uptown. Soon, I'm back in the epicentre, where deals are struck and new futures unveiled. Tall, glass fronted buildings appear, disgorging hordes of people before my eyes. They fill the streets, the Underground, heading blindly for their next destination, desperate to get wherever they're going in the shortest possible time. The cocoon of the taxi cab keeps me shielded, immune from their ongoing struggle.

Freedom is a strange thing. Part illusion, part reality. I drink it down like a cocktail, revelling in so much newly discovered opportunity. But the past puts chains around you that can't easily be slipped. You have to wrestle with it, bargain with it, stumble your way around the maze until you find a way out.

'Change of address,' I say on impulse. The driver eyes me in the mirror.

'Where to, guv?'

'Kensington Park Road.'

Doubt plays on my mind like a mantra. All the things I should do. All the things I shouldn't. Knowing the answers doesn't make it any easier.

Approaching the lights, it all comes back, as if I've been away months rather than days. The off-license on the corner.The clothes boutique with the bald female mannequin in the window. Familiar windswept streets and faceless pedestrians slip by, but no one sees me. They celebrate my homecoming by pretending I don't exist.

One persistent thought nags at me.

I should call Shaz. At least, tell her I've landed.

The thought fades. Wilfulness takes over. A sense of excitement building, but for all the wrong reasons. I'm back, fresh from a detox, heading straight for the frontline.

33

Alone in a bar in Bayswater. Time passes in a void of strangers' chatter and the bland chart hits pumped from a video screen on the back wall. The few punters keep to themselves. Early morning drinkers, fugitives from the real world, there's a barrier between us that can't be breached. Who needs them anyway? Who needs anyone when all your needs are right there in front of you in the glass in your hand?

The swing doors crash open and the manageress comes striding in – a dead ringer for Jackie Collins in black leather trousers and a leopard-skin top. She smiles, woodenly, breaking her busy schedule to serve an ingrate like me.

'Yes, please?' she says breathlessly.

'San Miguel and a double grouse, please.'

She clamps a glass to the optic, her shapely ass framed in stiff, black leather. I picture the two of us romping in the great outdoors, pounding each others bones in a variety of choice locations.

'Anything else?'

'Change for the phone, please.'

She hands me the change from a ten-pound note, the dark valley of her cleavage only inches away. Vague, lecherous thoughts assail me, detached from any real inclination to follow them through. I'm insular, removed. Locked in a world of my own that doesn't include people.

'Would you like one yourself?' I say pleasantly enough. She ponders the question.

'Bit early for me, love. I'll have one for later though, if you don't mind?'

She vanishes through the swing doors, her exit a kind of warning, a portent of all my troubles to come. But I'm safe here for the moment, in this charmless den with its mirrors and neon lights, its fake, electronic music. There's a special brand of emptiness here that can only be filled with one thing.

Carla has limited sympathy for my plight, and complains bitterly that I've woken her up.

'Where are you?' she says, yawning.

'Bayswater.'

'What're you doing there?'

'Hiding from the bodysnatchers. Fancy joining me for a livener?'

She declines, unable to appreciate my comeback from the abyss. As always, *her* problems are far more important than anyone else's. The heating still doesn't work. The letting agent keeps ignoring her calls. I've been listening to her grievances for years now and nothing ever changes. She's like everyone else out there, bored, angry and vindictive, trying to get back at the world whichever way she can.

We discuss St Luke's and the ramifications of my recent departure. She has this strange idea that my stay there was some kind of holiday, that I must have enjoyed it somehow. Even mellowed by the booze and the background music, I'm moved to challenge her right away.

'You've got no idea what it was like in there. No idea at all. And what happened to the visit I was supposed to get?'

She hesitates, caught out. 'I was busy. Anyway, I never promised anything, did I?'

'You could have made the effort though. You knew I was up there, climbing the walls.'

She's really not in the mood to hear about my sordid little drama, but I tell her anyway. She listens for a while and interrupts tetchily. 'Why don't you *do* something? Jump on a plane and go back to L.A. Do some session work. Hang out with Billy Idol!'

I mention Hugh Hanley's surprise visit. The special tour of the countryside he gave me in his brand new BMW. She can't believe someone of his stature would be seen in a place like that, associating openly with mental defectives.

'What the hell did *he* want?'

'Oh, this and that. He just wanted to buy me lunch 'cause he hadn't seen me for a while. You know how much he's always adored me.'

The pips go.

I feed more coins into the slot, soulless pop music playing behind me. I feel grainy and unwashed, like a horse thief after three days in the saddle. I should feel worse. Everything I care about has been taken away, stripped and removed like the contents of a house. But somehow I'm still here, defiant and rebellious, determined to enjoy what's left of my hard won freedom.

'I take it you heard about Danny,' she says.

'What about him?'

'Him and two of his mates robbed a jewellers and crashed a stolen car. He's in intensive care.'

'I'm shocked from my daze.

'What! ... When was this?'

'Last week. Avril from the tattoo parlour told me. It made the local news apparently.'

I picture Danny head-butting the dwarf. The brooding violence in him, constantly needing an outlet. I feel a strange responsibility for him. a deep regret, as if it's my fault he's ended up this way.

'Have you been in to see him?'

She laughs abruptly. 'Me? What would I want to see *him* for? Far as I'm concerned he can stay there. At least he can't come knocking on my door.'

The Jackie Collins look-alike has gone. A flustered young girl flaps around in her place, all red-faced and apologetic. I order another double grouse and think about Danny. All the times I spent avoiding him, or wishing something bad would happen to him so I wouldn't have to pay him back his drug money. In my maudlin state, I can romanticise the adventures we had around the town, imagine him to be something he isn't. But his current predicament leaves a hollow. Puts a taint on the morning's drinking.

The girl puts my drink down, smiling sweetly. For a moment I'm transfixed, her soft, yielding flesh competing with the contents of the glass.

'Anything else?' she says.

'What's your name?'

'Mandy.'

'That's a nice name.'

'Thank you.'

'Ever heard of Scott Levine, Mandy?'

'No. Does he drink in here?'

Funny how these impulses take root, inspired by the vaguest thread. Something Carla said about going back to L.A. I haven't seen Scott for three years. I don't have his address or his phone number. But I know he has a house in Hyde Park because I stayed there one night after the Brit Awards. Maybe I'll run into him on Bayswater Road and we can discuss my future. *'Hi, Scott. Great to see you, man. Sorry I haven't been in touch lately, I've been busy hanging out on the nut farm.'*

A man walks up to the bar and drums his fingers, impatiently, on the counter. The flustered barmaid parks herself meekly in front of him, awaiting his decision. He orders a pint of Murphy's in a gruff northern voice, watching her with malign intent.

When she's gone, he lifts his pint and says a terse 'Good Health!' to no one in particular. We stare up at the video screen, a few feet apart. Four scrawny adolescents dance in sync to an electronic backing track, the kind of drivel you hear in supermarkets while you're perusing the lamb cutlets.

He shakes his head dismissively. 'Fuckin' garbage they put out these days.'

I raise my glass in a grave salute. 'Come back Elvis, all is forgiven.'

He glares at me, his pint inches from his lips.

'What's wrong with Elvis?'

'Nothing.'

'You just made a crack about him.'

'No I didn't.'

244

'Yes you fuckin' did.'

He watches me, lazily, an angry slab of mutton with a grievance against everything. I take a slug of whisky, washed down with lager from the neck of the bottle, and picture Danny, lying in a hospital bed.

'Ever heard of Vlad the Impaler?' he says.

'Who?'

'When people pissed him off he had 'em impaled on stakes. Must have hurt that, don't you reckon?'

'Must have done, yeah. Did he come from Memphis, too?'

The manageress comes barging through the swing doors and strides over to the till. She empties a bag of money into the tray, shuts it with a flourish and leaves smartly. He watches her go, one hand clamped around his pint.

'She'd have some!' he says bluntly. I nod in agreement.

'She would indeed.'

'Who asked you!'

Some people are born ugly. This one's a clone from my dad's era. The bring back National Service brigade who want everyone to get a hair-cut and stop listening to subversive music. He might even be dangerous. One of these psychotic ex-army types who's just come back from a stint in the Aden.

'Come on then,' he says. 'What's wrong with Elvis?'

Two men come in and stroll up to the bar. I work out the distance between me and the door. How long it would take to get past the leery northerner and into the street.

'I asked you a question, pal.'

The barmaid serves the two men. Images of semi-naked women flash up on the screen. Easing cautiously off the barstool, I head for the gents. The northerner's cold, reptilian gaze follows my every move.

The distance between us grows, each step towards the exit increasing my confidence. I reach the door and a knot of devilment stirs within me. The need for a little harmless revenge. I turn and face the bar, like an actor in a stage play.

'There's nothing wrong with Elvis at all. It's cunts like you give me the pip!'

I'm gone before he has the chance to retaliate, laughter and adrenalin going with me. A burst of warped excitement in an otherwise uneventful day.

*

Dimly-lit pubs are the ideal refuge for people like me. This one offers anonymity and a chance to blend-in. Rough, working class men stand knee deep at the bar, festooned with tattoos and gold chains, their loud, abrasive voices ringing out from one end to the other. The noise is atrocious, like some overcrowded Victorian gin mill, with everyone talking at once. I'm alone among the heathens, crushed by failure and disillusion, hanging on to this, my precious independence, before they snatch even that away.

The woman at the end of the bar sits watching me intently. Wine glass in one hand, cigarette in the other, she rocks gently to some private inner rhythm. Difficult to put an age to her – late-thirties, early-forties perhaps. She has a detached, faintly hostile look, pain that's hardened over time into confrontation.

I wander over, casually, and ease onto the barstool next to her. A blue hat and stripy scarf sits on the counter by her drink. I smile to myself at the ease with which it's happened, the certainty that we have the same need.

'Mind if I join you?'

She stares blankly back. Years of excess have eroded her looks, and yet something powerfully attractive still remains.

'I'm looking for someone,' I say airily. 'A record producer called Scott Levine. Not that he'd drink in a place like this. They never do. Always in Palm Springs or Malibu getting a tan.'

She signals the landlady for a drink. There's something about her I can't resist. The way she sits, the way she holds her cigarette. All this mysterious weighing me up from some distant horizon.

The landlady replaces her glass and hurries away. Noise from the bar fills in around us. The rowdy party in the corner laughing at some outrageous joke. The elderly couple by the window looking on, sidelined by the darts-players and the heaving mob. I'm intrigued by her rudeness, her complete lack of social graces.

'What's your name?'

She stares at me obstinately.

'OK, we won't do names. I'm Joe, by the way.'

She takes a sip of her drink, dark, humourless eyes meeting mine. I'm itching to ask the big question, but there's always an element of uncertainty. I could have got it wrong and mistaken her solitary vigilance for something else. But I doubt it. It's the same all over the world. You walk in a room and there they are waiting for the bag man. You can tell at a glance.

A thick-set man with long, dirty-blonde hair walks in. Without a word, she leaves her perch and goes over to him. An intense conversation follows, the man making lots of wild hand gestures and repeatedly shaking his head. Right away I understand what's happening, the code they're using giving them away.

She comes back and sits down irritably.

'Who's your friend?'

'None of your business.'

'Is he your boyfriend?'

'I'll call him over, shall I, you can ask him yourself?'

I'm alone and surrounded by dangerous people. Furtive looking men and women huddled around the dark wood furnishings, smoking and drinking in the murky lamplight. Anything could happen. The most appalling acts of violence quickly absorbed and covered up as if they'd never happened. But this strange, troubled woman knows where it's at. She has the look, the connections.

I take a chance. 'Can I score round here?'

Her lips part in a scowl. 'What?'

'I just thought – '

'You thought wrong. Go away and leave me alone.'

She drains her wine and stands, putting on the blue, sailor's hat and stripy scarf. The disguise softens her appearance, makes her look less severe.

'Where're you going?' I say, with a note of anxiety.

'Out.'

'Can I come with you?'

She shrugs, as if the arrangement is preordained, something she expected to happen anyway.

I follow her outside, the glare of daylight hurting my eyes, and try to keep up with her route march through the afternoon shoppers.

'Where are we going?' I say, catching up.

'Nowhere.'

'Is that a place?'

Her eyes flash a warning. 'I didn't ask you to come with me, did I?'

She stops outside a newsagents and adjusts her hat, pulling the rim down over her eyes.

'I need cigarettes.'

'I'll wait out here for you.'

'Come in with me.'

'What for?'

'Because I want you to.'

I flick through the magazine section while I'm waiting. Ozzy Osbourne's lunatic grin appears on the cover of *Kerrang*. Living proof that you *can* survive decades of chemical abuse and still come out the other side.

She appears beside me. 'Ready?'

We cross the road and head up a side street. With a glance behind her, she opens her coat and unfolds a glossy magazine. I laugh, genuinely shocked.

'How did you do that?'

'What?'

'The magazine? I was standing right next to you!'

She keeps walking, ignoring me. I'm slightly put out that she's used me as a decoy, but it's all part of the seduction routine, her way of proving she's in control.

'D'you do that sort of thing all the time?'

'What?'

'Steal magazines from newsagents.'

'Only when I feel like it.'

'You could have got caught.'

'I didn't though, did I.'

We head down an alleyway between the shops. My fascination grows, a ripple of sexual excitement now that we're away from the numbers. In all the time we've been together she's shown no interest in me whatsoever. And yet there's an undercurrent, an assumption that I'll follow her wherever she's going.

'Now we're partners in crime, do I get to know your name?'

'Christine.'

'Nice to meet you Christine, I'm Joe.'

'I know who you are, you told me already.'

Overcome by a wild impulse, I push her against the wall and kiss her hard on the mouth. Her eyes widen in shock. I'm consumed by the scent of her. The coldness of her thin lips. The sour wine taste on her breath.

She pulls away angrily. 'What d'you think you're doing!'

'Sorry, I was just –'

'Don't touch me!'

'Look, I was just –'

'Don't touch me again! OK?'

A woman comes trundling down the alley pushing a shopping trolley. We stand back and wait for her to pass.

Christine turns to me with a look of artfulness. 'How much money have you got on you?'

'Why?'

'You said you wanted to score.'

The woman and the shopping trolley turn the corner. Christine waits expectantly.

'I'll need to find a cashpoint.'

'OK, I'll come with you.'

She smiles coyly, a new understanding between us. Now we're playing the same game. Me and Christine – this captivating woman I've just met. She has it all. That curious mix of vulnerability and danger, the hint of repressed sexuality to lure me in. All we need now is her dealer and the afternoon will be complete.

34

I let myself in quietly through the front door. The toilet flushes upstairs. Charlie appears on the landing and looks down at me with sleep-filled eyes. I put a finger to my lips, imploring him to be quiet. He wanders, trancelike, back to his room.

I'm about to climb the stairs when Shaz calls out. She emerges from the kitchen, looking surprised, her bare legs poking comically beneath an oversized shirt.

'Joe – where have you been?'

'I stayed with friends in Bayswater.'

'Why didn't you phone and let me know? I've been worried sick about you.'

'Sorry, I got a bit, sidetracked.'

She comes closer. 'God, you look awful. What've you been doing?'

'I just need a few hours sleep. I'll be fine. Honest.'

Her pinched and anxious face reflects the trauma she sees in mine. Remorse kicks-in. The shame of adding to her burden when she's got enough to put up with already. But you can't help sickness, the waves of nausea that dampen any sympathy I might have for anyone else.

'I'm going up to bed, Shaz. I need to get my head down.'

'Joe – we need to talk.'

'Can't it wait?'

'I need to talk to you now, please.'

The kitchen table's been laid for breakfast. Posh blue cereal bowls and floral place-mats. A jar of Seville Marmalade and an empty toast rack. We take our seats for the compulsory debrief.

'Do you want some coffee?' she says.

'No thanks.'

She folds her arms, watching me.

'So what happened? You came out of hospital and just, disappeared.'

My voice is cracked and weary, like it belongs to someone else. I tell her what I can. The reasons for me staying out and not phoning. The restlessness and the insomnia. The disruption to my life caused by the break-up of my marriage and recent hospitalisation. She listens quietly, choosing the right moment to cut in.

'Joe – when you first came here, I told you there were certain things I didn't want you to do.'

'Yeah, and I respect that, Shaz, I really do.'

'But, that's just it. You don't. You come and go as you please. You go off drinking and staying out all night. Look at the state you're in.'

Sunspots flash in my head. Lurid images play over and over. The last forty-eight hours on the frontline, wasted on heroin and crack-cocaine.

'Sorry.' The word lacks sincerity. So disconnected from reality as to carry no meaning at all.

'Why can't you see what you're doing to yourself? I just don't understand. I've been frantic, wondering where you were. I even rang the hospital to see if you were back in there.'

The weight of it all hangs over me, worsening my physical condition.

'Did you take the ten-pound note that was under the vase in the dining room?'

'What?'

'Please tell me if you did.'

I stare at her in utter disbelief. 'How can you accuse me of something like that? Stealing money from my own sister?'

Her eyes glisten with tears.

'Joe – I can't do this anymore.'

'Do what?'

'Sit around like this, waiting for you to show up. You need

help.'

The difference a day makes. Yesterday flying high, today crashed and burned.

'You want me to go?'

She sighs heavily. 'Don't you have any awareness at all? Don't you think I've got enough to put up with?'

Charlie hovers in the doorway, frowning anxiously.

'Mum? ...'

She ushers him gently out, her voice muted out in the hallway. I'm reminded of all the things I've never been. The mess I've made of my home life. Alienating myself from my wife, my children.

She takes her seat. This time there's an edge to her voice that wasn't there before. An unmistakable note of anger. 'When I phoned the hospital, I spoke to one of the nurses. She said you'd agreed to see a counsellor.'

'Oh come on, Shaz. I just said that to keep them happy.'

'You've no intention of going at all then?'

'That's right.'

'So what are you going to do instead?'

Sleazy images fill my mind. Some woman cooking up a shot in the small kitchen of a threadbare house. The lighter flame circling beneath the spoon. There's a place you go that's beyond grief, beyond pain, where even time doesn't exist. But you have to come back. That's the hardest part. Coming back to face what you left behind.

'When was the last time you had something to eat?'

'I'm not hungry.'

'Get some sleep then. I'll make you something when you wake up.'

The sense of unreality lingers. Comedown's best feature – like having your brains fed through a mincer while you're forced to watch.

I stand unsteadily.

'Joe?'

'What?'

'Will you at least think about seeing this counsellor?'

'Whatever.'

'Thank you,' she sits back, drained. 'I can't tell you how relieved that makes me feel.'

I lie on the bed in Charlie's room. Sleep is impossible. The cinema screen flickers on in my head with me in the starring role. Joe E Byron dug into a foxhole on Omaha Beach. Rockets, flares and heavy-duty machine-gun bullets zipping all around. Trapped amongst the burning vehicles and lumps of twisted metal, soaked in sweat. Violent orchestral music pounds the frontal lobes in my head. The symphony of life and death. The tearing-apart of everything worthwhile that could ever happen. And at the centre of it all, my poor, tormented self, cast down into an endless black hole.

35

The room looks different. The posters are the same. The bookshelf sits in the corner like it was before. But something's not right. Maybe it's the glaze over my eyes, the fact I don't want to be here at all. I should feel comfortable with the routine, knowing what's in store. Instead, I feel wasted, an alien life form seeking immunity from the world outside.

She greets me warmly and shakes my hand, a quick intake of breath at my appearance that she hides as best she can. We take our seats, a few feet apart, ready for the session to begin.

'So how are you, Joe?'

'Surviving.'

'I understand you've been in hospital.'

'Er – yeah. I was in under observation. They found out there was nothing wrong with me and let me go.'

She watches me, curiously, a slight frown on her chubby, powdered face. I sniff self-consciously and sit up, affecting a calmness I don't feel.

'So tell me what happened?' she says.

How can you admit to a relative stranger that you were carted off to a lunatic asylum for breaking into someone's shed? My memories of the ward are still vivid. The narrow dormitory with its lime-green windows. The medicine cabinet filled with sedatives under lock and key. The whole place nothing but a warehouse, a retirement home for the mentally deficient.

She asks about Justine. I'm cagey with the details, wondering how much she already knows – the spectacle of Miriam and the tin foil on the coffee table still fresh in my mind. She listens with a suitably blank expression, encouraging me to go on.

'It all started when they went away camping.'

'Is that when you started drinking again?'

My first instinct is to lie outright but it seems pointless. She can see I'm not quite right. My hands are shaking. My head feels like it's stuffed with cotton wool. Confession seems the only option.

'I met someone,' I say casually. 'This woman. She's wants me to move in with her.'

Silence.

'Is that a good idea, moving in with someone you've just met?'

All I can manage is a tired shrug. She firms her lips in concentration, thinking deeply.

'Have you spoken to your wife since you came out of hospital?'

'Couple of times on the phone.'

'And how has that been?'

'Difficult.'

Here in the blue room things have changed irrevocably.The light-heartedness is gone. That humorous banter we had with each other as she tried, unsuccessfully, to sell me the programme. The silences are longer, the searching look on her face reflecting the seriousness of my condition. I'm baffled by it too. Why did I feel the need to down half a bottle of vodka before I came here? Why am I so emotionally on edge, poised on the brink of collapse, every cell in my body crying out for relief?

'What did the doctors say?'

'They want me to go into treatment. I'm waiting for a referral. Part of the deal was I come back and see you.'

'And how do you feel about that?'

I shrug, listlessly, and stare at the window.

'Perhaps it's what you need right now, Joe.'

Her expression is soft, beguiling, lowering my resistance. I remember the role I'm supposed to be playing and harden my resolve.

'I'm not going into treatment. I've been through all that

before. It doesn't work.'

'But you're thinking of moving in with someone you hardly know.'

Why not? I feel like saying. No one else wants me. Even my own family have put me out on the street.

She shifts in the chair, thoughtful.

'Have you heard the term co-dependency?'

'Kind of.'

'It's an over-reliance on other people. You often find it when there's been long term issues with drugs and alcohol. It's about learning different ways to break the cycle.'

'What – become a monk, you mean?'

She smiles faintly. 'I'm saying you should think hard before you make any major decisions concerning your future. It's very easy to get caught up in other people's problems. Very, distracting.'

The drone of traffic on the main road reminds me there's a life out there. The sordid world of addiction, with all its attendant miseries and transient highs. Everything aches. My facial muscles, my neck. Even my brain, turned inside out by all these dire permutations. And at the back of it all, Christine, fast turning into a full-blown obsession.

'What's happening with your job?' she says.

'Not much at the moment.'

'How are you managing financially, if you don't mind me asking?'

'I've got an understanding bank manager. He keeps sending me new credit cards when the old ones run out.'

My sarcasm leaves a hollow, the feeling you get when you can't even entertain yourself anymore. Val sits quietly, absorbing everything, never once letting me know what she's thinking.

'I had a visit from my manager while I was in hospital.'

'Really? How did that go?'

'Great. He bought me lunch then told me I was out of the band.'

She listens carefully, hands splayed on her sizeable thighs.

'I wouldn't have minded so much if it had come from

someone else. But not from him. He's full of bullshit. The only person he's interested in is himself.'

Sweat breaks out on my forehead, a fresh wave of nausea to hide.

'Are you alright?' she says.

'Fine. Just a bit hot, that's all.'

'Would you like me to open the window?'

'No, I'm OK, thanks.'

I sit up, drained by the effort it takes to appear normal. She watches me, closely, with the same blend of pity and consternation.

'Your sister sounded very nice. She said you were staying with her at the moment.'

'Not for much longer. She wants me to move out.'

'Have you told her you're thinking of moving in with this woman you've met?'

'No.'

'Is that because of what she might say?'

'Not really. I just don't want to burden her with the details.'

'Can I ask why?'

'Well, she's been through enough herself lately. She lost her husband to cancer a couple of years ago. Plus she's got two young kids to bring up.'

'So by not telling her you're sparing her the worry, is that it?'

'Something like that.'

I get the feeling she's baiting me, putting me on the spot. Troubling thoughts lurk on the periphery. My relationship with Christine, centred around drugs. The knowledge of what I did in that squalid front room with people I'd never met before.

The words come out unprompted.

'I can't stop.'

'Sorry?'

'It's like I'm in the grip of something. I don't know what it is.'

She sits forward, looking at me intensely. 'Joe – one of the many uplifting aspects of my job is to see people turn their lives around, regardless of their personal beliefs. It is possible, if you want it to happen.'

'Is it?'

'Yes, it is.'

My head begins to pound. The dull ache in my kidneys sets off a warning that I'm in danger of imminent collapse. She looks at me with fresh concern.

'Are you OK – you look a bit pale?'

'I'm fine.'

'Are you sure I can't get you a drink of water?'

'No, honestly, I'm fine. I'll be alright when I get outside.'

She glances at her watch. 'Well, there's still some time left, if you're happy to go on.'

What else can I do? If I don't comply, they'll send me back to Allington to vegetate on the nut ward. I'll lose everything. My hard-won freedom. My new life with Christine.

I reflect on what she said about people. The prospect of change. But she's wrong. People don't change. They just keep making the same mistakes over and over.

'A friend of mine went through the windscreen of a stolen car the other day.'

She frowns. 'Oh dear.'

'Well, he's not a friend. More of an acquaintance, really.'

'And how did that make you feel?'

'Like it was my fault'

'Why?'

'It's complicated. I don't want to go into the details.'

She nods respectfully and talks about a woman she knew who was involved in a motorway pile-up and needed counselling to get over it. I sit it out, begrudgingly, willing the session to end. Where do these people get their calmness from. Their ridiculous equanimity. All I want to do is get out of here and meet up with Christine. Blot it all out Get wasted.

'Sometimes it isn't so much what happens to us in life but how we deal with it. Some things you can't ignore. You have to take responsibility.'

'I hate that word.'

'Why?'

'Adults use it to brainwash children. You grow up feeling

guilty because you can't live up to their expectations.'

'Did your parents have high expectations of you?'

'My dad played saxophone in jazz bands. He was an elitist. He could only relate to perfection.'

'That must have been hard on you.'

'Not really. I just did the opposite of everything he wanted me to do. He bought me a classical guitar for my birthday one year. I smashed it to bits in my room and hid the pieces under my bed.'

'Why did you do that?'

'I don't know. Anger. Boredom.'

She gives a faint nod of understanding, but I'm not convinced. We're straying further and further from the main agenda, and I'm getting sicker by the minute.

'Have you seen much of your children?' she says.

'Not since I left home.'

'But you've spoken to them?'

'A few times.'

Clammy sweat coats my skin. An impish nerve tugs at the corner of my mouth, threatening to expose my performance for the charade it is. And all the time she's watching me, the pressure's building inside, threatening to burst the walls of the dam and drag me under.

'Is everything alright, Joe?'

A huge, black hole opens up inside me. I think of Sadie and Jake, the fact I've haven't seen them in such a long time. I feel I should give in and weep but my heart is a stone.

'I'm fine, thanks … Is it nearly time?'

My one brief moment of weakness seems to endear me to her in a way that no amount of talking could have achieved. She grasps the significance right away. I must be vulnerable and open to the programme. Ready to sign up for the anger management and the abstinence classes without delay.

'Would you like to make an appointment for next week?'

'Yeah, sure. Whatever.'

'Thursday OK?'

'Thursday's fine.'

She straightens her jacket and stands, giving me an odd, pensive look.

'If you ever want to speak to me and I'm not here, leave a contact number and I'll call you back as soon as I can.'

'Thanks.'

She smiles. 'Well, good luck with the referral. I know you're not keen on going, but I'm sure it'll be for the best.'

We part almost as friends, brought closer by my impromptu breakdown. The whole thing has left me drained, pulled in a direction I didn't want to go. Her compassion and understanding made me feel safe, almost human again. In touch with a part of me hidden away for so long.

But I can't stop. That's the frightening thing. I'm driven by something powerful and destructive. Something beyond my control.

36

Over the next few weeks, I survive on a diet of Mars Bars, crisps and the occasional takeaway. Christine's flat in Bayswater becomes my temporary home, a place to crash after long sessions in the pub waiting for her illusive dealer. We lose ourselves in this strange, nocturnal existence, the hours stretching out before us like a desert, filled with illicit distractions and lists of things to do. Valium and Diconal – bought from her contact in the pub when she can't get gear. A binge on crack that cleans out what's left of my building society account and keeps us up all night, leaving us burnt-out and shattered the next morning. And underpinning this, the relentless, never-ending search for heroin that seems to hold it all together. Whatever levels of restraint I might have had at one point are gone, lost in this dangerous compulsion to feed my hunger, this willingness to trade my very soul.

Christine's need eclipses everything – even mine. But she hides it well, buried deep beneath layers of self-justification and wounded pride. What right have I got to trade off her sickness? Pestering her with my constant demands. Adding to her daily burden.

She tells me she's only thirty-one, a year younger than I am. And yet she looks much older, an observation I keep to myself. I think of Carla, her looks intact, having survived the rigours of her own addiction. Christine has a similar insularity, an inner strength that comes from years of foraging and making ends meet, telling people what they want to hear so she can abuse their hospitality and deal with the consequences later. Our conversations are bizarre and superficial, reflecting a woeful lack of understanding neither of us can resolve. She doesn't like to be questioned or told what to do, the implication I might have some influence in her chaotic life too much for her to bear. There's no give and take. She does what she wants to do.

'I'm going out.'

'Where?'

'See a friend.'

'Who?'

'Just a friend.'

'When will you be back?'

'I don't know. Stop grilling me. I can't move without you getting in my face.'

My mental state worsens. I let my beard grow and neglect to wash my hair. I no longer recognise myself when I look in the mirror. My eyes have a wild and startled look like disaster victims you see on TV. All vestiges of my previous life are gone. I've lost touch with my family. My friends won't speak to me. I'm living to drown out the noise in my head, the unseen enemy that draws ever closer. The deeper you go, the worse it gets, like chasing a glimmer of sunlight in a dark wood. Nothing seems to work anymore. Whatever I do, whatever I take, I'm left jaded, dissatisfied. Then there's the fallout, the consequences. Strangers reminding me of the terrible things I'm supposed to have said.

I call Justine one evening. We spend the next few minutes debating my existence, and how utterly loathsome I've become. Rivals in a complex game no one can win, except she has all the advantages. The kids are better off without me, she says, spared the indignity of my onerous ways.

'So when can I see them?'

'When you stop acting like a degenerate and get some help.'

'I *am* getting help! I'm seeing people. Counsellors and shit. Isn't that enough?'

She tells me people have been calling the house, asking about me. Hugh Hanley and James T. The rest of the band. Even a music journalist from Sweden, wanting confirmation of a rumour that I'd died.

The dark wood looms closer. I'm in the grip of something monstrous and all-encompassing, luring me to a place I don't want to go. Insight and awareness vanishes, lost in the next drink, the next fix, whatever I can find to blot out reality.

Christine's turbulent life comes out in fragments. She tells me things sometimes when she's strung out on gear. Her last boyfriend was hit by a car as he was walking back from a New Year's Eve party and left paralysed from the waist down. The one before that died of a heroin overdose, six months after inheriting eighty-grand from an uncle in Australia he never knew he had. She has other stories too, mostly about her dysfunctional family and the trouble she has dealing with them. The details are always sketchy and inconclusive. If I question her too much she gets angry, accusing me of prying into her personal life and making her feel inadequate. We argue constantly. I'm invading her space, she says, draining her resources. She screams at me to leave then begs me to stay, in a whining, childish tone that makes me relent and give in. The whole thing's farcical. Pointless. Exhilarating, too, if I'm honest.

Things start happening that are beyond my control. Lapses in time. Whole interludes I can't remember. I wander into the pub one afternoon, on the pretext of meeting Christine, and the landlord greets me with a raised hand.

'Sorry – not serving you.'

'Why, what have I done?'

'You're barred. I don't have to give a reason.'

I'm confused and angry. A few days ago we watched Chelsea beat Man United on the drop-down screen on the back wall. He even stood me a free pint in celebration. Why the sudden turnaround? These things are baffling, damaging to your integrity and self esteem. You start to question *why* they're happening and what you've done to deserve it. All these hostile reactions from people you thought you knew.

Christine's junkie friend, Tam, finds my outrage amusing, having been barred himself by the same landlord. Now I'm up there with the criminal elite, the seasoned pub brawlers and knock-off merchants who see this kind of thing as an occupational hazard. But the niggling doubts persist. Why am I losing these chunks of time? What's happening to me?

*

One Friday night we go to a party above a clothes shop on the main road – looking for Christine's dealer. She leaves me stranded in the kitchen with a can of Tennent's Super and a joint while she goes off and mingles. Strange people drift in and out. A brutal Techno beat pounds through the floor. I feel like I'm invisible. No one can see me because I'm not really there. But the cosmic debts are mounting fast. All the nights without sleep, the chemical excess. The rollercoaster ride I've been on for the last ten years. Everything has to be paid for.

Christine wanders in with some Neanderthal guy I've never seen before. They look furtive, up to no good, a thought that feeds my growing insecurity. I should have seen it coming. The inevitability that she'd leave me and find someone else. The certainty that, at some stage, I'd be left to my own devices.

An impish-looking blonde girl in her twenties sits next to me and lights a cigarette. She smiles coyly, staring at me with apparent fascination.

'Joe the musician, right?'

'That's right.'

'You're with Christine?'

'I was earlier. Why?'

She nods, amusedly, to herself. Minutes go by. Bodies drift in and out like ghosts in a railway station. Then, without a word, she leans over and kisses me, probing expertly with the tip of her tongue. She pulls back, a strange carnal look in her eye.

'Enjoy!' she says mysteriously and leaves the room.

The pill dissolves in my mouth, washed down with a swig of lager. I've no idea what it is and I don't really care. Like sitting in a plane on a runway. Nothing much you can do but fasten your seatbelt and wait for take-off.

37

I come to in the middle of the road, freezing, shoeless. Twin headlights flash up ahead. The sudden blast of a car horn. I stagger to the side of the road and try to get my bearings. A group of people are sat outside a Pizza parlour. A man eating a burger looks up, watching me with a mystified grin.

A police car pulls into the kerb, blue lights flashing. Two policemen and a policewoman get out and walk towards me.

'OK – stay where you are!'

I'm in a nightmare. The last thing I remember is being at the party with Christine. The girl with blonde hair slipping me a pill.

The first policeman comes over, intimidating in a black flak jacket and peaked cap. He looks like a paramilitary, someone used to dealing with people like me.

'What's your name, son?'

'Joe Byron.'

'Do you mind telling me where you've been?'

I point vaguely in the direction of Queensway. 'I was at a party round someone's flat.'

'What happened to your shoes?'

I shrug lamely. The second policeman joins us, assessing me with a look of grim satisfaction.

'How did you get the blood on your shirt?'

I look down at the stained lapel, as baffled as he is. For a moment we're all spectators, grouped around the strange phenomenon that happens to be me.

'Where d'you live, son?'

'Nowhere.'

'You're homeless, is that what you're saying?'

'Yeah. Well, sort of. I've been staying with my girlfriend.'

'You're homeless but you've been staying with your girlfriend.'

'That's right.'

'Where does she live?'

I hesitate. The group outside the Pizza parlour look-on like ghouls at a roadside crash.

'I can't remember.'

'You can't remember where your girlfriend lives?'

'No.'

'Have you taken anything tonight?' The policewoman says.

'No, I haven't.'

'Nothing at all?'

'Only lager.'

They confer among themselves, leaving me standing in the tiger-stripe socks I borrowed from Christine. The thought of being separated from her bothers me more than the prospect of any trouble I might be in.

'OK, Joe,' the first policeman says. 'Step over to the car for a minute, please.'

'What for?'

'We've reason to believe you've committed an offence.'

'I haven't done anything! I told you. I was at a party and I crashed out. Someone must have taken my shoes!'

I walk to the car in my socks, dazed and humiliated. The group by the takeaway watch intently. The man eating a burger calls out some inane comment and the others laugh. One of the girls shakes her head in scornful disbelief.

A police walkie-talkie coughs into life, the rasping voice like a foreign language. The first policeman talks into it, describing a male suspect, early-thirties, found wandering with no shoes on and blood on his shirt. I know they're talking about me, but it makes no sense. The policewoman looks on piteously, attractive in a plain sort of way, a wisp of dark hair protruding from the rim of her hat. Her look reminds me what I've become, something feral and dangerous, undeserving of sympathy.

'Sit in the back of the car, please,' the first policeman says.

The dark interior smells of worn leather and cold officialdom, the transportation of countless felons to places of custody. The first policeman gets in the passenger side, leaving the door open. He asks me again, where I've been and who I was with. I give hazy, unrehearsed answers that don't seem to bother him either way.

Finally, he looks at me severely and says the words I've heard on only one other occasion in the whole of my life.

'I'm arresting you for Disorderly Conduct. You do not have to say anything, but anything you do say may be …'

Bursts of static from the police radio ground me in the moment. Viewed from the car, the neon lights from the pizza parlour glow intensely. But I'm safe. The fear I felt initially has left me. In its place a sense of inevitability, reassurance even. I've been heading towards this point all my life and now it's over. There's nowhere else for me to go.

38

I'm in a room with strange people. The circle of chairs means there's no escape, no corner to hide in. The girl with the nose stud hugs her knees, worn boot heels hooked over the lip of her chair. She has a brooding, melancholic face, just waiting to take offence at some passing triviality. The man with the boxer's nose and receding hair jokes incessantly with the petite, mixed-race girl sat opposite him. They look intimate together, undeterred by the atmosphere. The others sit around in varying states of boredom and lethargy waiting for something to happen.

'Good morning everyone!'

A tanned and attractive brunette strolls in, her arrival changing the dynamic in the room. The group sit up and mumble a jaded reply, resentful of the interruption. Only the kid with cropped hair and tattoos seems unimpressed, rocking on his chair, grinning inanely.

The brunette stands at the whiteboard, facing the group.

'OK! Everyone fit and raring to go?'

The man with the boxer's nose makes a sarcastic comment and laughter ripples through the circle. The girl with the nose stud hugs her knees tightly and stares at the floor.

'We have a new member joining us today. I'll like you all to welcome Joe.'

'Hi, Joe!'

The response lacks sincerity. Whatever it was meant to achieve, I don't feel any more welcome than I did when I first walked in the door.

'I'm sure you'll all help Joe settle in, won't you.' The circle murmurs its agreement. Smiling, she turns to me. 'I'm Debbie, Facilitator for the Group. If you have any questions feel free to ask. Have you been assigned a key worker yet?'

'Julian.'

'Right. Any problems, speak to Julian after the session.'

She attacks the whiteboard with a cloth, the terms *Peer Review* and *Evaluation of Goals* vanishing beneath her manic efforts. I try to work her out. She's dressed casually in jeans and a fawn jacket, friendly but clearly in control. The only fake thing about her is her deep tan, years of dedicated sun worship applied from a bottle.

The Group's forced welcome fades away and we move on. I'm not ready for the spotlight just yet, the sudden attention that comes from being the latest inductee. Like the others, I'm stuck here in this treacherous circle with no means of escape. The victim of a conspiracy cooked up by doctors and psychiatrists intent on taking my freedom away and burying me in the programme.

*

After the break, we hear from a nervous geek called Malcolm. He has a glazed, myopic look – steel-rimmed specs and a thin, spotty face. I can't imagine him doing anything more excessive than staying up past his bedtime, but he must have done something bad to have ended up in here.

'Why don't you tell the Group about your progress so far,' Debbie says eagerly.

Malcolm sniffs self-consciously and sits up, trying to shift his natural inertia. The Group's empathy is mixed with fear, sensing the profound humiliation he's about to undergo.

He takes us through the details of his prior existence, mumbling and stuttering and chewing his nails. No mention of any chemical excess or criminal escapades, only the sad recollections of someone who's never quite fitted in. Debbie probes expertly to gain a reaction, asking questions about his family and his brother, whose part in all this is yet to be revealed.

The girl with the nose stud becomes more and more agitated as the interrogation goes on. 'Come on Malcolm – tell us about your brother! What did he do that was so terrible you can't talk about it!'

'Alright, that's enough,' Debbie says quickly. 'Anything else you'd like to share with the Group, Malcolm?'

Malcolm squirms in his chair, struggling with some profound, inner chasm. Yes, he admits, there is something else. He has this ex-girlfriend. If it wasn't for her he wouldn't have lost his flat and been assaulted by the landlord. He hates her for the trouble she's caused him. For running off and sleeping with his best mate while he was in hospital.

The girl with the nose stud erupts. 'You can't blame your girlfriend for everything, Malcolm! You have to accept *some* responsibility! That's what all this is about, remember?'

A murmur of agreement goes round the circle. Debbie steps forward and raises a hand tactfully. 'Alright. Let's hear what Malcolm has to say first, shall we?'

My interest wanders. The woman next to me hasn't moved the whole time. She sits slouched in her chair, head down, mousy blonde hair obscuring her face. The kid with the tattoos keeps grinning as if he's here for the fun of it. The portly, middle-aged gent next to him looks like a retired accountant, about as comfortable as a pensioner at a Prodigy concert. His shiny red cheeks and bulbous nose give him away. A lifetime of hitting the bottle and hiding the empties, hoping his wife won't find out.

'Joe – would you like to tell us a bit about yourself?'

The Group's antenna swings my way. I sit in awkward silence, bowed by the sudden pressure. The girl with the nose stud leans forward, keenly, chin cupped in her hands.

'Yes, Joe. Tell us. Why *are* you here?'

I think deeply before answering.

'I'm here because a psychiatrist sent me.'

The man with the boxer's nose sniggers privately. The rest look on in mute condescension. I wish I was somewhere else. A long way away from here.

I make a mug of coffee in the narrow kitchen along the hall. The grey laminate work surface is spotlessly clean and free of clutter. The man with the boxer's nose stands washing up at the sink, humming tunelessly as he delves among the soap suds. Each week, one of us is assigned a task on the rota. Someone gets the kitchen area, someone else the chill-out room. If you're really unlucky you get to clean the toilets and the chance to moan about it later in Group. The rota is compulsory. Refusal to comply means automatic expulsion and a train ticket back to where you came from. For most people that means relapse, sometimes even death.

The girl with the nose stud breezes in and stands beside me at the worktop. She grabs a mug from the wooden rack and tosses a tea-bag in, her sudden, jerky movements setting my nerves on edge.

'Fitting in alright, Joe?' she says abruptly.

'Sort of.'

She forces a smile. 'Don't worry, you'll soon get used to it.'

Her worn, pitying look is tinged with animosity. Defeated, I look away. How is anyone supposed to get better in an atmosphere like this, with so many fucked-up people around? The whole set-up's designed to bring you down.

She makes her tea and strides out. The man with the boxer's nose looks up from the sink.

'This your first time, Joe?'

'In the Lighthouse, yeah.'

'Been in treatment before?'

'I did two weeks in a place in Kent a couple of years ago. Got kicked out for smoking a joint.'

He grins, wryly, and tells me his own history. In and out of prison and detox units for the past ten years, two marriages and a career destroyed along the way. He grabs a tea towel and dries his hands.

'I'm Tom, by the way.'

We shake hands firmly. His flat nose and granite features

give him a subtle menace, but there's an undeniable warmth there too, a simple humanness I haven't found in any of the others so far.

'How long have you been here?' I say.

'This is my tenth week. Another two and I'll graduate – with honours, hopefully.' He laughs wryly. 'Last chance saloon for me, this is. Next stop's the graveyard. Too fucking old for this game, that's for sure.'

I drink my tea from a cancer research mug, alone with Tom in the cramped kitchen. I feel like the new kid on his first day at school. Keep your mouth shut and avoid the bullies. Leap up when the bell goes and disappear to your lonely room.

Two of the girls file in to make drinks. The tall blonde in the denim shirt and the mixed-race girl, who's smaller, almost delicate beside her. They chat among themselves, moaning about the no-smoking policy indoors. Their voices are lively and upbeat, far removed from the subdued atmosphere in the Group Room. For a minute I'm somewhere else. Stood at the bar in a nightclub. Smoking a joint with Carla. Anaesthetised from all this.

What can I say to these people? The social instinct died in me long ago. I feel like one of those buildings bombed in the war. All that's left standing is the façade. The slightest push and I might topple over, buried in a cloud of dust.

*

Julian calls me in to see him in his shoebox office along the main corridor. The pot plant in the corner reminds me of the C.O.D.A.T. building, and Val Moody's subtle charms. The creaking staircase and the scented room. The drug posters and chocolate-chip cookies. I take a seat and try to look composed. Julian sits behind his desk, thoughtful and amenable.

'How're you finding it here, Joe?'

'OK.'

'Any problems with the Group?'

'Not that I can think of.'

He smiles, perfectly at ease with himself, with everything.

'Debbie says you had trouble sleeping last night.'

'That's right. Any chance of a little something for tonight?'

He frowns disapprovingly.

'Just a thought,' I say quickly.

'Have you tried any of the meditation tapes?'

'My head's too busy at the moment. I can't think straight.'

He nods faintly, unfazed by the silence. I wriggle in the chair, compelled to speak.

'Can I make a phone call?'

'Who to?

'My wife.'

'You spoke to your wife last night, didn't you?'

'For five minutes. I want to speak to my kids, my sister. Tell them how I am.'

'You know the policy on phone calls, Joe. You get to make two a week. That was explained when you came in.'

'It's ridiculous, though. What harm's it gonna do?'

'Sorry. That's the rules.' His smile broadens. 'Look upon it as an exercise. You're learning new skills while you're here. Patience is one of them. How's your appetite?'

'So-so.'

'Got your name down on the rota yet?'

'Debbie's put me down for washing-up.'

'Great. Routine's what you need. Doing things you don't really want to do for the good of the group.' He pauses. 'You're a musician, aren't you?'

'I was in another life.'

'What do you play?'

'Guitar.'

'Right. Maybe we could arrange an impromptu concert with some of the others. How would you feel about that?'

'I don't think so.'

He nods respectfully, a kind of veiled humour in his gaze that suggests he might have been joking. Maybe that's the game here. They find out what you do for a living then use it to humiliate you in some way.

His expression changes, serious again.

'We've spoken to the police in Bayswater. They've agreed to drop the charges against you.'

'That's great.'

'Provided you stay on here.'

'I wasn't planning on going anywhere else.'

He strokes his neat goatee and stares at me intensely.

'Joe – I'm going to be straight with you, OK? What happened to you happens to a lot of people out there, every day of the year. It's nothing unusual in the scheme of things. The difference is, you ended up in here. Do you know why that is?'

'No.'

'Because you're one of the lucky ones.'

I wait for the grin, the sign that we can share the joke. His deadpan look never changes.

'While you're in here, I'd advise you to listen. You might not like what you hear, or even agree with it, but it might just save your life one day.'

I nod tactfully, squirming inside. He smiles agreeably.

'OK, Joe. That's the lecture's over for now. You can go back and join the group. Let me know if you have any problems settling in.'

Funny how time changes everything. It seems like months since I was arrested in Bayswater and taken back to the hospital, even though it's only been a couple of weeks. I still think about Christine, but not on the same scale. The obsession has gone, taken away like it never happened. I'm embarrassed at the thought of how stupid I was, chasing something that wasn't there. Stuck in that strange place between madness and sanity, risking my life to be part of her shadowy world.

Sometimes I think of abandoning the treatment and walking out. Then the movie starts up in my head, replaying scenes I never want to go through again. Coming to in the middle of the road with no shoes on. Black flack jackets and police radios closing in. No longer a human being, but something burned-out and unrecognisable.

*

The tattooed kid Ricky graduates Friday. We plan the celebrations as if he's going off on a backpacking tour of New Zealand instead of a dry-house in Stevenage. His silly grins and high-fives don't impress anyone, especially the counsellors, who stand back watching. For Ricky, being on the streets again could be a death sentence. Crack and heroin are still out there, waiting to lure him back to his old ways. His only chance is to stick close to the programme, abandon himself to a life of recovery.

I drift off into fantasy land, dreaming of castles with shark-infested moats, beautiful girls lounging by the pool and servants bringing me lines of cocaine. I don't care much for Ricky. In the three days I've known him, he's done nothing but make stupid jokes and brag about his success with women, rocking back and forth on his chair like some sleazy kingpin. But he's done the time and gone the distance. He gets a grudging respect from all of us because of that.

My thinking is still deeply flawed. The counsellors explain the extent of my delusions, writing up their theories on the whiteboard for all to see. I've spent a lifetime blaming other people for the trouble I've caused. Years of excessive partying and thinking about myself have warped my mind to a severe degree. Most people would have given up willingly by now, if only to spare their family the shame and the indignation. Not me. I'm in a different class. I'm of the type who would crawl through a sewer to get a drink or a drug and not think twice about the consequences.

The slogans are endless. We can learn them by rote to impress the counsellors. *I have a disease, the disease wants to kill me. It's the first drink/drug that does the damage.* These are the truths we learn here at the Lighthouse. We should be grateful, they tell us. Most addicts and alcoholics die out there without any recovery at all, barricaded inside a filthy bed-sit or locked away in some grim institution. I'm forced to see my role here in a different light. The alternative is too awful to contemplate.

Julian gives a sombre presentation. Of the eight of us in this room, four will go back out and die. Three will stay clean for a short time, then relapse. In the long term, only one of us will make it.

'Statistics aren't always right,' the man with the bulbous nose says.

Julian smiles bleakly. 'These are. Take it from me.'

The crude mixture of psychology and spiritual teachings brings out the rebel in me. I want to criticize and heckle but, instead, I'm forced to listen. Where else is there to go? According to Debbie, my entire existence up until now has been chaotic, riddled with selfishness, resentment and the monster of ego. I think of all the self-help books I used to read, full of the same stuff. The guru always turns out to be one more sleek opportunist, riding round in a Rolls Royce Convertible, reeling in the dollar.

Debbie announces the *Peer Evaluation* session marked on my timetable. The group shuffle papers and a studious air descends. As I'm fairly new, I can sit in as an observer and make notes. The object is for each member to assess the progress of their peers, being as honest as possible. The terminology baffles me, but I can read the body language, the nuances, and fill in the gaps. The process is supposed to benefit everyone, even the counsellors who observe quietly from the sidelines, always ready to remind us why we're here. We have a disease. The disease is no respecter of class, creed or colour and destroys with impunity. These are the facts, in case we ever forget.

*

I phone Justine one night. She sounds upbeat, looking forward to a shopping trip with her mum. The future for us, for my marriage, is still uncertain. She makes no promises. No plans for me to move back in after treatment's finished. No indication she even wants me to succeed. The only way either of us can deal with it is by talking about something else.

The kids miss me. I talk to Jake first and then Sadie, the minutes of one of my two weekly phone calls ticking away.

They're the lifeline, a fragile link to the past that keeps me going. Talking to them is like walking backwards through a dream. I don't know what to say. I'm empty, devoid of feeling, stuck here in this emotional bubble pretending to be human. And yet, underpinning this, is a faint glimmer of hope. The thought that one day we'll be together again.

Justine ushers them away and comes back on the line. 'Well, that's it,' she says evenly. 'I'd better say goodbye.'

'Thanks.'

'For what?'

'Letting me talk to the kids. I really miss them. And you.'

'Joe, I really don't – '

'It's OK. I understand. You don't have to say anything. I'll call again later in the week … Look after yourself.'

I sit on the bed in my room and stare at the wall. Something shifts deep inside of me. All these long-held beliefs about myself and who I am. The illusion of well being that's gone. I've had to come to terms with the real me, the side that lies and deceives for its own ends, the side that demands instant gratification.

My timetable: Friday – evaluate Goals with Julian. Saturday and Sunday – Group sessions and free time. I've filled mine with trivia. Menial tasks I've no real intention of doing. Written work that can be put off until the last minute.

This is my life.

A single sheet of A4 with bullet points and scribbled reminders.

The idiot's guide to staying alive.

The idea is to graduate and get out of here. Then it's down to me. And that's the hardest part. Knowing what's out there waiting. Wondering if I'll have the strength to walk away.

I'm hungry.

That's a good sign, they say. It means you're getting better, at least physically. Soon, I'll shuffle along to the canteen and sit with the others. My *Peers*. The oddballs and the misfits, rescued from the sinking ship, just like me. All of us here to be broken down and built back up again.

But I'm here.

I suppose there are worse places to be.

About the Author

Adam Dickson is a novelist and screenwriter. His first novel, *The Butterfly Collector*, was published in 2012. His second novel, *Drowning by Numbers*, was published in 2014. He has also written three non-fiction books in the sports genre, and a book on bipolar disorder.

His screenplays include adaptations of both novels, and a pilot for TV. His period thriller, *Heart of a Murderer*, is based on a real-life murder case and is currently in pre-production. Filming is scheduled in Bournemouth and London in spring 2018.

www.adamdickson.co.uk